# BIBLE PUZZLE 2-IN-1

# BIBLE PUZZLE 2-IN-1

CROSSWORDS & WORD SEARCHES

BARBOUR
PUBLISHING

ISBN 978-1-63609-077-1

*101 Bible Crosswords, Volume 4* © 2005 by Barbour Publishing, Inc.
*101 Bible Word Searches, Volume 4* © 2006 by Barbour Publishing, Inc.

Crosswords were made using licensed Crossword Weaver software (www.crosswordweaver.com), by N. Teri Grottke, David K. Shortess, John Hudson Tiner, and Tonya Vilhauer. Word search puzzles were created by David Austin, N. Teri Grottke, Paul Kent, and John Hudson Tiner.

Published by Barbour Publishing, Inc., 1810 Barbour Drive, Uhrichsville, Ohio 44683, www.barbourbooks.com

*Our mission is to inspire the world with the life-changing message of the Bible.*

Printed in the United States of America.

# WELCOME TO
# BIBLE PUZZLE 2-IN-1!

*Bible Puzzle 2-in-1* is a treasure trove of more than 200 puzzles—101 crosswords and 101 word searches—for anyone who loves God's Word *and* word games!

This book will challenge crossword fans' knowledge of the people, places, events, and ideas of the Old and New Testaments—as well as word search lovers' skill at finding cleverly hidden biblical terms. All word search clues are drawn from the beloved King James Version of scripture. Crosswords are based on the King James, with occasional use of newer translations and other fields of study for variety, and begin on page 8.

The word searches start on page 212, and here's a quick word of explanation for those puzzles based on Bible passages: You'll be seeking the words printed in **bold**. If they're **bold and underlined**, look for that phrase as a unit in the puzzle grid.

Of course, answers are provided, with the crossword keys beginning on page 414, and the word searches on page 431.

Just one final word: Enjoy!

# CROSSWORDS

# PUZZLE 1

CEASAR

## ACROSS

1 Heber's son (1 Chronicles 4:18)
6 "Lest at any time we should let them _____" (Hebrew 2:1)
10 "O daughter of _____" (Lamentations 4:21)
14 Moses' father (Exodus 6:20)
15 Detest
16 Smelling orifice  NOSE
17 "That thou _____ him" (1 Kings 8:25)
19 "Punish the men that are settled on their _____" (Zephaniah 1:12)
20 Your thigh is connected to this
21 "_____ shall see God" (Matthew 5:8)
22 Idols
24 "There is but a _____ between me and death" (1 Samuel 20:3)
25 "_____, Hizkijah, Azzur" (Nehemiah 10:17)
26 "Let him _____ evil" (1 Peter 3:11)
29 "For thou _____ certain strange things to our ears" (Acts 17:20)
33 Jahath's son (1 Chronicles 4:2)
34 Shoham's brother (1 Chronicles 24:27)
35 Always
36 A son of Shem (Genesis 10:22)
37 The son of Eliadah (1 Kings 11:23)
38 Mud  Mire
39 "Ye shall in no _____ enter" (Matthew 5:20)
40 First garden
41 "The head slippeth from the _____" (Deuteronomy 19:5)
42 "The children of Eden which were in _____" (2 Kings 19:12)
44 We have five of these  finger
45 "_____ the death of the cross" (Philippians 2:8)
46 "She _____ in her body that she was healed of that plague" (Mark 5:29)

47 Roman emperor
50 Snare
51 "_____ that ye refuse not" (Hebrews 12:25)
54 "Nevertheless _____ heart" (1 Kings 15:14)
55 "And the chief priests and scribes stood and _____ accused him" (Luke 23:10)
58 Young human female
59 Belonging to Eli
60 Elevate
61 "Knowledge is _____ unto him that understandeth" (Proverbs 14:6)
62 "That dippeth with me in the _____" (Mark 14:20)
63 Tear repeatedly

## DOWN

1 A giant (2 Samuel 21:18)
2 Ahab's father (1 Kings 16:28)
3 Harvest product
4 A son of Noah
5 Left out
6 Fleecy ruminant
7 "The elect _____" (2 John 1:1)
8 Possessive pronoun
9 "What is thy _____" (Esther 9:12)
10 "Shall there _____ and deliverance arise" (Esther 4:14)
11 "When _____ the Edomite was there" (1 Samuel 22:22)
12 "As he saith also in _____" (Romans 9:25)
13 Chaos
18 Show (arch.)
23 "For do I now persuade _____, or God?" (Galatians 1:10)
24 "As one of the vain fellows _____ uncovereth himself" (2 Samuel 6:20)
25 "River _____: behold" (Deuteronomy 2:24)
26 Selected ones
27 Eber's father (Genesis 10:24)

8

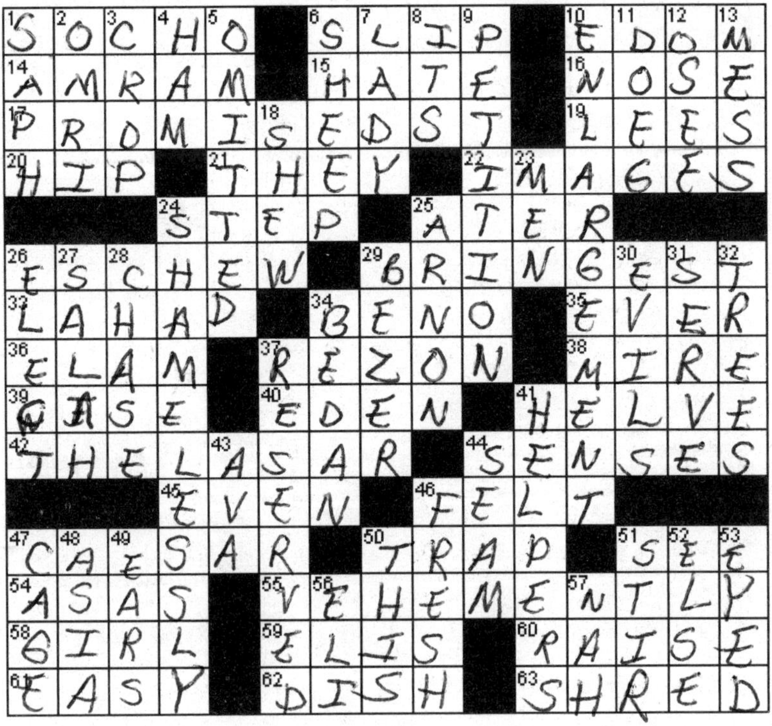

*by N. Teri Grottke*

28 Pursue
29 "Namely, ______ in the wilderness" (Deuteronomy 4:43)
30 "For innumerable ______ have compassed me" (Psalm 40:12)
31 Wait on
32 "______ whose fruit" (Jude 1:12)
34 "Sent Jerubbaal, and ______" (1 Samuel 12:11)
37 "______ in heaven for you" (1 Peter 1:4)
41 "Greet Priscilla and Aquila my ______ in Christ Jesus" (Romans 16:3)
43 Area near Babylon (2 Kings 17:24)
44 Jesus' coat didn't have one
46 "So can no fountain both yield salt water and ______" (James 3:12)
47 Prison
48 Largest continent
49 Hearing organs
50 "What. . .hath been done to Mordecai for ______?" (Esther 6:3)
51 Mix
52 Otherwise
53 Looked at
56 Hophni's father (1 Samuel 4:4)
57 After Micah (abbr.)

# PUZZLE 2 — A RIGHTEOUS HUSBAND

## ACROSS
1 Mary's husband (Matthew 1:16)
5 Gym class (abbr.)
7 The Son of God: "The holy _____"
  (Luke 1:35 NIV)
8 "The winds and the waves _____
  him" (Matthew 8:27 NIV)
10 "Every _____ his parents went
   to Jerusalem for the Feast of the
   Passover" (Luke 2:41 NIV)
12 Paul desired to change his _____
   with the Galatians (Galatians 4:20)
13 What the Magi saw in the east
   (Matthew 2:1–2 NIV)
15 "Glory to God. . .and _____ earth
   peace" (Luke 2:14)
17 God caused the star to _____
   "over the place where the child was"
   (Matthew 2:9 NIV)
19 Greater London police, New
   Scotland _____ (abbr.)
21 The Ocean State (abbr.)
23 Matching coat and trousers
25 Source from which valuable matter
   is extracted
27 "Like the blind we _____ along"
   (Isaiah 59:10 NIV)
29 Ordered; "Job has not _____ his
   words against me" (Job 32:14 NIV)
31 Airman (abbr.)
32 Elizabeth's cousin (Luke 1:36, 38)

## DOWN
1 "The angel said. . . , 'I bring you
  good news of great _____'"
  (Luke 2:10 NIV)
2 Jesus warned against causing little
  _____ to sin (Matthew 18:6)
3 "Pharisees. . .love the most
  important _____ in the
  synagogues" (Luke 11:43 NIV)
4 A south wind precedes _____
  weather (Luke 12:55)
5 A coin (Mark 12:42 NIV)
6 "The _____ is the lamp of the
  body" (Matthew 6:22 NIV)
9 Used to startle or frighten
11 The Philistines made "five gold
   _____" as part of a guilt offering
   (1 Samuel 6:4 NIV)
14 "A strong wind was blowing and the
   waters grew _____"
   (John 6:18 NIV)
16 "We are to God the _____ of
   Christ" (2 Corinthians 2:15 NIV)
18 "_____ king of Jarmuth"
   (Joshua 10:3 NIV)
20 Industrious
22 Formerly Persia
24 Rearrange the letters of the second
   highest voice part in a 4-part chorus
26 Final destination of an ambulance
   (abbr.)
28 "One beka _____ person, that is,
   half a shekel" (Exodus 38:26 NIV)
30 "Why am I _____ favored"
   (Luke 1:43 NIV)

| 1 J | 2 O | 3 S | E | P | 4 H | ■ | 5 P | 6 E |
|---|---|---|---|---|---|---|---|---|
| 7 O | N | E | ■ | ■ | 8 O | 9 B | E | Y |
| 10 Y | E | A | 11 R | ■ | 12 T | O | N | E |
| ■ | 13 S | T | A | 14 R | ■ | 15 S | O | N |
| 16 | ■ | 17 S | T | 18 A | Y | 19 Y | 20 | |
| 21 | 22 | ■ | 23 S | U | I | 24 T | ■ | |
| 25 | | 26 | ■ | 27 | | 28 | | |
| 29 | | | 30 | | | | | |
| 31 | | ■ | | ■ | 32 M | A | R | Y |

*by John Hudson Tiner*

# PUZZLE 3

## ACROSS

1 The son of Asaph, the recorder (Isaiah 36:22)
5 Too
9 "The _____ tree" (Joel 1:12)
14 Father (Galatians 4:6)
15 Opposite of *front*
16 "_____ up a child" (Proverbs 22:6)
17 "All the hills shall _____" (Amos 9:13)
18 Uncovered
19 Weary
20 A quality that makes one able to be tricked
23 Detest
24 Tiny insect
25 Female sheep
28 Enticed
31 A son of Noah
34 Jesus is the prince of this
36 King of Assyria (2 Kings 15:19)
37 Opposite of *despair*
38 "Pitched beside the well of _____" (Judges 7:1)
39 Likely
40 "For as _____ was three days" (Matthew 12:40)
41 Always
42 "And _____ lay at his feet until the morning" (Ruth 3:14)
43 "_____, and Accad, and Calneh" (Genesis 10:10)
44 Color of blood
45 "O thou _____ among women?" (Song of Solomon 6:1)
48 Exclamation of affirmation
49 Transgression
50 "The women. . .brought that which they had _____" (Exodus 35:25)
52 "If the _____ came to thee" (Obadiah 1:5)
59 Bellybutton
60 Charge
61 "Collar of my _____" (Job 30:18)
63 Make a correction

## DOWN

64 "Of _____, the family of Arodites" (Numbers 26:17)
65 Jesus' grandfather (Luke 3:23)
66 "He that ministered to my _____" (Philippians 2:25)
67 To refuse to take responsibility
68 "As he saith also in _____" (Romans 9:25)

## DOWN

1 Like jelly
2 Ruth's son (Ruth 4:13–17)
3 Strong and _____
4 Break out of a shell
5 Paarai was one (2 Samuel 23:35)
6 "To open before him the two _____ gates" (Isaiah 45:1)
7 "Through faith also _____ herself received strength to conceive seed" (Hebrews 11:11)
8 "The heads of _____ and Zeeb" (Judges 7:25)
9 Pay attention to
10 "Put my finger into the _____ of the nails" (John 20:25)
11 Cut back
12 Untruths
13 Opposite of *begins*
21 Comforted
22 Eliasaph's father (Numbers 3:24)
25 A son of Midian (Genesis 25:4)
26 "They that _____ networks" (Isaiah 19:9)
27 "_____ nor sown" (Deuteronomy 21:4)
29 In the _____ Room
30 Slice
31 Bee product
32 "Kings of armies did flee _____" (Psalm 68:12)
33 "Their dwelling was from _____. . . unto Sephar" (Genesis 10:30)
35 The first First and Second of the NT (abbr.)
37 "Ye shall point out for you mount _____" (Numbers 34:7)

*by N. Teri Grottke*

39 Son of Abdiel (1 Chronicles 5:15)
40 Ishmael's son (1 Chronicles 1:31)
42 "They _____ his praise"
(Psalm 106:12)
45 "Who have reaped down your
_____" (James 5:4)
46 Paseah's father (1 Chronicles 4:12)
47 "For he shall make even a _____
riddance of all them"
(Zephaniah 1:18)
49 "The night is far _____, the day is
at hand" (Romans 13:12)
51 A pharaoh of Egypt
(2 Chronicles 35:20)
52 Chew a bone
53 "In _____ was there a voice"
(Matthews 2:18)
54 City in Egypt (Hosea 10:8)

55 "_____ the Canaanite"
(Numbers 21:1)
56 Type of weed
57 Two or more deer
58 "_____ of his patrimony"
(Deuteronomy 18:8)
62 Bind

# PUZZLE 4 — GOD'S GREATEST GIFT

*This is how God showed his love among us: he sent his one
and only Son into the world that we might live through him.*

1 JOHN 4:9 NIV

## ACROSS

1 "To die in the _____ "
(1 Corinthians 4:9 NIV)
6 "Even as _____ obeyed Abraham"
(1 Peter 3:6)
10 Highland topper, for short
13 Anklebone
14 "For he had _____" (Acts 18:18)
(2 words)
15 "And they returned _____ again"
(Acts 21:6)
16 Start of a **VERSE** of gratitude to the
Lord (2 Corinthians 9:15) (4 words)
19 "That they may _____ whole month"
(Numbers 11:21) (2 words)
20 "Enlarge the place of thy _____"
(Isaiah 54:2)
21 "Let us _____" (Exodus 14:12)
22 "Honest" politician of old
23 Part 2 of the **VERSE**
24 "How _____ art thou?" (Genesis 47:8)
25 It may show you the way to go
26 "And of such as _____ cattle"
(Genesis 4:20)
28 Part 3 of the **VERSE**
31 "Eat nothing containing _____"
(Exodus 13:3 NIV)
34 "Sheba and _____ shall offer gifts"
(Psalm 72:10)
35 "And Peter said, _____ am not"
(Luke 22:58) (2 words)
36 Part 4 and end of the **VERSE**
(2 words)
39 Does yard work
40 Actress Hayworth
41 Ancient Greek city
42 Enzyme ending
43 "And Jesus went _____ him"
(Mark 5:24)
44 "And the _____ saw the angel of the
LORD" (Numbers 22:23)
45 "Like a crane _____ swallow"
(Isaiah 38:14) (2 words)
46 Agent (abbr.)
47 Day-care denizen

50 "To sharpen every man his _____"
(1 Samuel 13:20)
53 Scarlet's home
55 "And said, _____ it, O LORD"
(Jeremiah 11:5) (2 words)
56 Start of the **GIFT** in 2 Corinthians
9:15 (John 3:16) (3 words)
59 "The daughter of _____ the Hittite"
(Genesis 26:34)
60 "The high hills _____ refuge for the
wild goats" (Psalm 104:18) (2 words)
61 "And in three days I will _____ it up"
(John 2:19)
62 End of the **GIFT**
63 "I will _____ you with filth"
(Nahum 3:6 NIV)
64 "_____ the friends by name"
(3 John 1:14)

## DOWN

1 Where the queen often is around 4:00
p.m. (2 words)
2 The faithful harlot (Joshua 2:1–24)
3 Buoy up
4 "The son of _____ young man"
(Exodus 33:11) (2 words)
5 "Ye know not what ye _____"
(Mark 10:38)
6 Cavalry sword
7 "From the plain of _____" (Amos 1:5)
8 "Shoot your arrows and _____ them"
(Psalm 144:6 NIV)
9 Grain spikelet
10 "_____ by day and night"
(Exodus 13:21) (2 words)
11 Josiah's father (2 Chronicles 33:25)
12 "In the first year of Darius the _____"
(Daniel 11:1)
15 "_____ not thy peace" (Psalm 109:1)
17 Greek portico
18 "The _____ of the bricks"
(Exodus 5:8)
23 "Children, their _____ is the sword"
(Job 27:14 NIV)
24 Famous DC office

*by David K. Shortess*

25 "The cruel venom of _____"
(Deuteronomy 32:33)
26 "The _____ in the desert"
(Jeremiah 17:6)
27 "_____, Father" (Galatians 4:6)
28 Secretary of State under Pres. Reagan
29 The scoop, for short
30 "The great prostitute, who _____ on
many waters" (Revelation 17:1 NIV)
31 City on the Colorado
32 Son of Seth (Genesis 5:6)
33 "_____ forgive our debtors"
(Matthew 6:12) (2 words)
34 Short, light drama
35 Department heads (abbr.)
37 La Scala highlight
38 "In the land of Nod, on the _____ of
Eden" (Genesis 4:16)
43 Architect of London's Saint Paul's
Cathedral
44 Captured king of the Amalekites
(1 Samuel 15:8)

45 "In any tree, _____ the ground"
(Deuteronomy 22:6) (2 words)
46 "And _____ their wit's end"
(Psalm 107:27) (2 words)
47 "We've come _____ you up"
(Judges 15:12 NIV) (2 words)
48 More than chubby
49 Belief
50 "_____ the right one for me"
(Judges 14:3 NIV)
51 Hawaiian port
52 "On them, _____ us at the
beginning" (Acts 11:15) (2 words)
53 Hiram's kingdom (2 Samuel 5:11)
54 Seth was his stead (Genesis 4:25)
55 "And I will give him the morning
_____" (Revelation 2:28)
57 "Gourds his _____ full"
(2 Kings 4:39)
58 Kin to *com* and *edu*

# PUZZLE 5

## ACROSS

1 "We cannot speak unto thee _____ or good" (Genesis 24:50)
4 Eve was made from Adam's
7 Chop (arch.)
10 "Tower of _____" (Genesis 35:21)
12 Haniel's father (1 Chronicles 7:39)
14 "_____ of Judah" (2 Samuel 6:2)
16 Son of Zerah (1 Chronicles 2:6)
17 King Hoshea's father (2 Kings 15:30)
18 Asher didn't drive out the inhabitants of this town (Judges 1:31)
19 "Shimei, and _____, and the mighty men" (1 Kings 1:8)
20 "Hamath, Berothah, _____, which is between the border" (Ezekiel 47:16)
22 Appendage
25 "_____ king of Hamath" (2 Samuel 8:9)
26 Right hand (abbr.)
29 "As a thread of _____ is broken" (Judges 16:9)
31 Commerce
36 Be in debt to (arch.)
38 Highly respected
41 "Rinnah, Ben-hanan, and _____" (1 Chronicles 4:20)
42 Untruth
43 "Shilshah, and Ithran, and _____" (1 Chronicles 7:37)
45 "And Kattath, and _____, and Shimron" (Joshua 19:15)
47 Below
48 A son of Gad (Genesis 46:16)
49 Luke (abbr., var.)
51 "_____ down here" (Ruth 4:1)
52 Battle where Goliath's brother was slain (2 Samuel 21:19)
55 Peleg's son (Genesis 11:18)
57 "And _____, and Zilthai, and Eliel" (1 Chronicles 8:20)
61 Slice
64 "_____ it, and smote the Philistine in his forehead" (1 Samuel 17:49)
65 Had intimate relations (arch.)
68 Son of Dishan (Genesis 36:28)
70 "As free, and not _____ your liberty" (1 Peter 2:16)
71 "Land from _____ to the wilderness" (Isaiah 16:1)
72 Green citrus
73 Color of blood
74 "To meet the Lord in the _____" (1 Thessalonians 4:17)
75 Became acquainted

## DOWN

1 Sleeping place
2 Twelfth Hebrew month (Esther 9:1)
3 "Even _____ to die" (Romans 5:7)
4 "For ye tithe mint and _____" (Luke 11:42)
5 Sick
6 "By the _____ of God they perish" (Job 4:9)
7 "Helkath, and _____, and Beten" (Joshua 19:25)
8 A son of Shem (Genesis 10:22)
9 Spider's art
11 Revile
13 A son of Jehiel (1 Chronicles 9:37)
14 Barrier
15 "Against Jerusalem, _____" (Ezekiel 26:2)
21 "That shall _____ thee" (Habakkuk 2:7)
23 A son of Helah (1 Chronicles 4:7)
24 Opposite of *stay*
26 Decay
27 Esau and Jacob were these
28 One of the wives of Ashur, the father of Tekoa (1 Chronicles 4:5)
30 Water source
32 Correction
33 So be it
34 Works
35 "Og the king of Bashan, which dwelt at Astaroth in _____" (Deuteronomy 1:4)
37 Elihu's father (1 Samuel 1:1)

16

by N. Teri Grottke

39 "The children of _____"
   (Nehemiah 7:47)
40 "_____ me whether ye sold the
   land for so much?" (Acts 5:8)
44 Are (arch.)
46 "As the trees of _____ aloes"
   (Numbers 24:6)
50 Abram's birthplace
53 Strong trees
54 Moza's son (1 Chronicles 8:37)
56 "Even unto Ithiel and _____"
   (Proverbs 30:1)
57 Otherwise
58 "Have _____ a wound"
   (Obadiah 1:7)
59 Motel
60 Produced by a chicken

62 Thummim's partner
   (Deuteronomy 33:8)
63 Gentle
64 A temple gate (2 Kings 11:6)
66 Hophni's father (1 Samuel 4:4)
67 Fight between countries
69 Rope web

# PUZZLE 6

## ACROSS

1 "_____ hath forsaken me" (2 Timothy 4:10)
5 "The _____ looks of man shall be humbled" (Isaiah 2:11)
8 "Sinners shall be converted _____ thee" (Psalm 51:13)
10 Factory
11 "Came unto Caesarea to salute _____" (Acts 25:13)
13 "The three _____ followed Saul" (1 Samuel 17:14)
16 Budge
17 Abdomen
19 Ardent
21 "Abimelech took an _____ in his hand" (Judges 9:48)
23 Dine
25 "Eber, Peleg, _____" (1 Chronicles 1:25)
26 _____ loving care
29 "Consider the _____ of the field" (Matthew 6:28)
31 "I will settle you after your old _____" (Ezekiel 36:11)
33 "Thou _____ me against him" (Job 2:3)
34 "The _____ shall inherit the earth" (Psalm 37:11)
35 "The land is as the garden of _____" (Joel 2:3)
36 "Which was the son of _____" (Luke 3:35)
39 "Shall we be consumed with _____" (Numbers 17:13)
41 "And fought against _____" (2 Kings 12:17)
45 Cainan's father (Genesis 5:9)
46 "Seven times a day do I praise _____" (Psalm 119:164)
47 "By faith _____ was translated" (Hebrews 11:5)
48 "Also I shook my _____" (Nehemiah 5:13)
50 "Nabal did _____ his sheep" (1 Samuel 25:4)
51 Level
52 "House of Millo, which goeth down to _____" (2 Kings 12:20)
54 "Glean _____ of corn" (Ruth 2:2)
55 Legislature
57 Atonement
59 "Shuthelah: of _____, the family" (Numbers 26:36)
60 "They gave them in full _____ to the king" (1 Samuel 18:27)
61 "All _____, and all men of valour" (Judges 3:29)
62 "Thou _____ make me hope" (Psalm 22:9)

## DOWN

2 Meditate
3 "Go to the _____, thou sluggard" (Proverbs 6:6)
4 Uproot
5 "And the _____ of the valleys" (Song of Solomon 2:1)
6 Antique
7 "The people _____ upon the spoil" (1 Samuel 14:32)
9 "As he saith also in _____" (Romans 9:25)
10 Liquefy
11 "The little _____, that spoil the vines" (Song of Solomon 2:15)
12 "That one _____ happeneth to them all" (Ecclesiastes 2:14)
14 "Their inheritance was unto _____" (Joshua 19:10)
15 Timber
16 Spouse
18 Flog
20 "Whose mouths _____ be stopped" (Titus 1:11)
22 "The same measure that ye _____ withal" (Luke 6:38)
24 Dwell
27 Natives of Damascus
28 "The _____ and flags shall wither" (Isaiah 19:6)
29 House

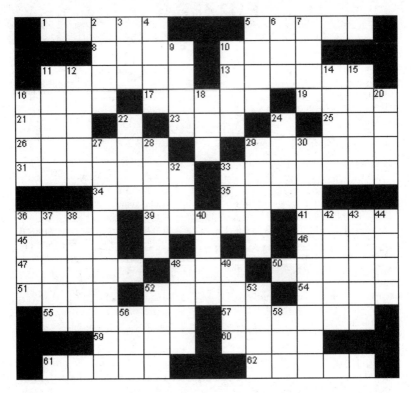

*by Tonya Vilhauer*

30 "Thy days may be _____ in the land" (Deuteronomy 25:15)
32 Firmament
33 "The young _____ from their music" (Lamentations 5:14)
36 "Of Gad the king's _____" (2 Chronicles 29:25)
37 "_____ and Caiaphas being the high priests" (Luke 3:2)
38 Free
40 Nathan's son (2 Samuel 23:36)
42 Leading
43 "Being mindful of thy _____" (2 Timothy 1:4)
44 "Restore all that was _____" (2 Kings 8:6)
48 "Though ye have _____ among the pots" (Psalm 68:13)

49 "Cast him into the _____ of ground" (2 Kings 9:26)
52 Tarry
53 "Alammelech, and _____, and Misheal" (Joshua 19:26)
56 "Thou _____ cursed above all cattle" (Genesis 3:14)
58 "Samuel arose and went to _____" (1 Samuel 3:5)

# PUZZLE 7

## ACROSS

1 Repulsive
5 "By his name _____" (Psalm 68:4)
8 A son of Benjamin (Genesis 46:21)
12 Goods
13 "_____ there yet the treasures" (Micah 6:10)
14 Paradise
15 "He built _____, and restored it to Judah" (2 Chronicles 26:2)
16 "Ye shall point out for you mount _____" (Numbers 34:7)
17 He forsook Paul (2 Timothy 4:10)
19 Joshua's father (Exodus 33:11)
20 Asked (arch.) (Ruth 3:6)
22 A false god of Shechem (Judges 9:46)
23 "Otherwise it is of no strength at all while the _____ liveth" (Hebrews 9:17)
25 Abram's birthplace
26 "God created _____ heaven" (Genesis 1:1)
27 Single
28 Sadoc's father (Matthew 1:14)
30 "Go to the _____" (Proverbs 6:6)
33 Resounded
36 A son of Jehaleleel (1 Chronicles 4:16)
40 "I will make thy _____ brass" (Micah 4:13)
43 This name is taken from the Greek *deuteronomion* (abbr.)
44 Listened
45 "Argob and _____" (2 Kings 15:25)
46 Female sheep
48 Insane
49 What you do with clothes
51 A king of Midian (Numbers 31:8)
54 "_____ that ye refuse not" (Hebrews 12:25)
57 Astatine (sym.)
58 By oneself
63 "Weeping may _____ for a night" (Psalm 30:5)
65 "So they _____ it up" (Micah 7:3)
66 Buzzing stinger
67 "He. . .is _____ than an infidel" (1 Timothy 5:8)
68 Opposite of *good*
69 A Harodite guard of David's (2 Samuel 23:25)
71 Prophet
72 Before (poet.)
73 "The horse and his _____ hath he thrown into the sea" (Exodus 15:1)
74 Snake sound
75 Saul's grandfather (1 Chronicles 8:33)
76 "They shall _____ like torches" (Nahum 2:4)

## DOWN

1 "Ye are of more _____ than many sparrows" (Luke 12:7)
2 Put these in the fire
3 Allow
4 Dishon's son (Genesis 36:26)
5 Jeshishai's father (1 Chronicles 5:14)
6 These cities are forsaken (Isaiah 17:2)
7 "_____ mouth is smoother than oil" (Proverbs 5:3)
8 "Ajalon, and _____, and Shocho" (2 Chronicles 28:18)
9 "Mahli, and _____, and Jeremoth" (1 Chronicles 23:23)
10 Release from the guilt or penalty of sin
11 Shamgar's father (Judges 3:31)
12 "Their sound _____ into all the earth" (Romans 10:18)
18 "And _____ lay at his feet until the morning" (Ruth 3:14)
21 "_____, Hizkijah, Azzur" (Nehemiah 10:17)
22 A son of Nahor (Genesis 22:21–23)
24 Turn over (abbr.)
28 A chill
29 "But the wheat and the _____ were not smitten" (Exodus 9:32)

by N. Teri Grottke

30 "Against Jerusalem, _____"
   (Ezekiel 26:2)
31 "_____ was an hair of"
   (Daniel 3:27)
32 "When _____ king"
   (2 Samuel 8:9)
34 "Arad, and _____"
   (1 Chronicles 8:15)
35 Opposite of *old*
37 A male sheep
38 "Helez the Paltite, _____"
   (2 Samuel 23:26)
39 Increase
41 Not many
42 Sheep clippers
47 "Land from _____ to" (Isaiah 16:1)
50 Partook
52 Venomous snakes
53 Teletypewriter (abbr.)

54 To stitch
55 "Adam, Sheth, _____"
   (1 Chronicles 1:1)
56 "Og the king of Bashan, which
   dwelt at Astaroth in _____"
   (Deuteronomy 1:4)
58 Take an oath (biblical sp.)
59 "Set in _____ the things that are
   wanting" (Titus 1:5)
60 Live with
61 A prince of Midian (Joshua 13:21)
62 365 days
64 Makes use of
68 "Zechariah, _____"
   (1 Chronicles 15:18)
70 Untruth

# PUZZLE 8 — A COMFORTING PROMISE

*"And surely I am with you always,*
*to the very end of the age."*
MATTHEW 28:20 NIV

## ACROSS

1  "Into the _____ of fire" (Revelation 20:14)
5  "Respond to their _____ and heal them" (Isaiah 19:22 NIV)
10  "The LORD _____ great victory for all" (1 Samuel 19:5 NIV) (2 words)
14  Ireland to Yeats
15  Serf
16  "These things saith the _____" (Revelation 3:14)
17  "And what, the son of my _____?" (Proverbs 31:2)
18  "And if a man shall _____ pit" (Exodus 21:33) (2 words)
19  *The Forsyte* _____ (PBS miniseries)
20  Start of a portion of a **VERSE** from Hebrews 13:5 (3 words)
22  "Went before _____, till it came and stood" (Matthew 2:9)
23  Greek market
24  **VERSE**, cont'd from 20 Across
25  Caniff's Canyon
28  Lukewarm
31  **VERSE**, cont'd from 24 Across
32  Pruninghooks' precursors (Micah 4:3)
34  "In purple now lie on _____ heaps" (Lamentations 4:5 NIV)
37  Familiar email server (abbr.)
38  Mimic
39  An unclean animal (Leviticus 11:29 NIV)
40  "And it shall be as the chased _____" (Isaiah 13:14)
41  Word with school or station
42  Thin and tall
44  "They did _____ me" (Psalm 35:15)
45  "Choice fruits, with _____ and nard" (Song of Songs 4:13 NIV)
46  "To sharpen every man his _____" (1 Samuel 13:20)
47  Auras
50  Count of jazz
53  Decorative pitcher

54  **VERSE**, cont'd from 31 Across (2 words)
59  "The rod of Aaron was among their _____" (Numbers 17:6)
60  Shallot kin
61  Epochs
62  Dust bowl victim
63  "They cast four anchors out of the _____" (Acts 27:29)
64  Follows the book of John
65  "And lay them down in their _____" (Psalm 104:22)
66  Like Swiss cheese
67  End of **VERSE**, cont'd from 54 Across

## DOWN

1  Simeon's close younger brother (Genesis 29:33–34)
2  "And _____ of new timber" (Ezra 6:4) (2 words)
3  Fuzzy brown fruit
4  "I will _____ you to your enemies" (Jeremiah 15:14 NIV)
5  LP player, briefly
6  "But he was a _____" (2 Kings 5:1)
7  "Was it a sin for me to lower myself in order to _____ you by preaching" (2 Corinthians 11:7 NIV)
8  "Ho, such _____!" (Ruth 4:1) (2 words)
9  "There shall come a _____ out of Jacob" (Numbers 24:17)
10  "The field is _____" (Joel 1:10)
11  Cow town in Nebraska
12  Judean desert (Judges 1:16 NIV)
13  "And he had _____ written, that no man knew" (Revelation 19:12) (2 words)
21  Not sm. or med. (abbr.)
24  "This is the _____ of the Israelites" (1 Chronicles 27:1 NIV)
25  "He prophesies, his own parents will _____ him" (Zechariah 13:3 NIV)
26  "Surely _____ art my bone and my flesh" (Genesis 29:14)
27  Scaleless fishes

*by David K. Shortess*

29 British rank below a marquis
30 "But when ye _____" (Matthew 6:7)
32 "Goliath, of Gath, whose height was six cubits and a _____" (1 Samuel 17:4)
33 Quaker colonizer
34 "The Jews who lived in that _____" (Acts 16:3 NIV)
35 "Though you _____ like the eagle" (Obadiah 1:4 NIV)
36 "Master, it is good for us to be _____" (Mark 9:5)
38 "By Christ Jesus throughout all _____" (Ephesians 3:21)
43 Mary's angelic messenger (Luke 1:26–27)
44 "I am a God, I sit in _____ of God" (Ezekiel 28:2) (2 words)
45 "Some trust in chariots, and some in _____" (Psalm 20:7)

46 "And I said unto him, _____, thou knowest" (Revelation 7:14)
47 "The leaven of _____" (Mark 8:15)
48 "So I _____" (Genesis 41:21)
49 "They are _____ with joy and gladness" (Psalm 45:15 NIV) (2 words)
51 "For _____ the harvest" (Isaiah 18:5)
52 Cher's erstwhile partner
54 Eat a snack
55 "And pass _____ Zin" (Numbers 34:4) (2 words)
56 Part of a foot
57 *Kiss Me, _____*
58 *They*, in Roma

# PUZZLE 9

**ACROSS**

1 "_____ of blue" (Exodus 39:31)
5 "The children of _____"
 (Nehemiah 7:58)
10 "Cheeks, and the _____"
 (Deuteronomy 18:3)
13 A great distance
14 Thief
15 Galatians, _____, Philippians,
 Colossians (abbr.)
16 Seir was of this nationality
 (Genesis 36:20)
18 "Tappuah, and _____"
 (Joshua 15:34)
19 "Shimei, and _____" (1 Kings 1:8)
20 King of Damascus
 (2 Corinthians 11:32)
21 Third book (abbr.)
22 Opposite of *slow*
23 Places of very little rain
25 Forgive
27 Observe (arch.)
29 "_____, and Idbash"
 (1 Chronicles 4:3)
32 Sack
35 "Down in _____" (Acts 27:27)
37 "For he oft refreshed me, and was
 not ashamed of my _____"
 (2 Timothy 1:16)
38 "_____, and Shema"
 (Joshua 15:26)
40 A son of Bela (1 Chronicles 7:7)
41 Greek form of *Sinai* (Acts 7:30)
42 "And Hazarshual, and _____, and
 Azem" (Joshua 19:3)
44 Biggest part of the hands
47 "All these were _____ of war"
 (Judges 20:17)
48 A Harodite guard of David's
 (2 Samuel 23:25)
49 "To abstain from _____"
 (1 Timothy 4:3)
51 Phaltie's father (2 Samuel 3:15)
54 Joseph's brothers called him this
 (Genesis 37:17–19)
58 Ruth's second husband (Ruth 4:13)

60 "After that the full corn in the
 _____" (Mark 4:28)
62 "Will _____ them as silver"
 (Zechariah 13:9)
63 Utilize
64 Ahab's father (1 Kings 16:28)
65 Chooses
66 Large lake
67 Jumped
69 You (arch.)
70 Zephaniah's son (Zechariah 6:14)
71 Ate in style
72 "The linen _____ at a price"
 (1 Kings 10:28)

**DOWN**

1 Jahath's son (1 Chronicles 4:2)
2 Before (arch.)
3 Concerns
4 Descendants of Eri
5 Female version of Joe
6 Cain's victim
7 Saul's first cousin (1 Samuel 14:50)
8 "Not to _____ thee" (Ruth 1:16)
9 Attached to the shoulder
10 "Go up against the land of _____"
 (Jeremiah 50:21)
11 Larger than monkeys
12 Bit (arch.)
14 This is what the Jews did on the
 Sabbath
17 A son of Micah
 (1 Chronicles 8:35)
22 Community in New York, _____
 Eddy
24 Peel
26 Contemporary of Hosea and Isaiah
 (abbr.)
28 A king of Tyre (1 Chronicles 14:1)
30 Belonging to me
31 "And Ahijah, Hanan, _____"
 (Nehemiah 10:26)
32 "The _____ lying in a manger"
 (Luke 2:16)
33 "Shelesh, and _____"
 (1 Chronicles 7:35)

*by N. Teri Grottke*

34 "He asked whether the man were a
   _____" (Luke 23:6)
36 Was ill
39 "The son of Dekar, in _____"
   (1 Kings 4:9)
43 "Between Bethel and _____"
   (Genesis 13:3)
45 Damaged
46 "The bow of _____" (Job 20:24)
50 "Peace and _____; then sudden
   destruction cometh"
   (1 Thessalonians 5:3)
52 A son of Joseph (Luke 3:26)
53 A brother of Abram (Genesis 11:26)
55 Mephibosheth's son (2 Samuel 9:12)
56 Come in
57 "And _____ between"
   (Genesis 10:12)

58 "An angel of the Lord in a flame of
   fire in a _____" (Acts 7:30)
59 "As he saith also in _____"
   (Romans 9:25)
61 "Harvest is _____" (Joel 3:13)
64 Elderly
68 An altar (Joshua 22:34)

# PUZZLE 10 — SPIES TO THE PROMISED LAND

## ACROSS

1 Agreed with Joshua that the people could take the land (Numbers 13:30 NIV)
5 Joshua, Caleb, and ten others went into Canaan to _____ out the land (Deuteronomy 1:22–23 NIV)
8 A son of Jether (1 Chronicles 7:38 NIV)
9 "Iron is taken from the earth, and copper is smelted from _____" (Job 28:2 NIV)
10 Moses gave Hoshea the _____ Joshua (Numbers 13:16 NIV)
11 First human to die (Genesis 4:8 NIV)
12 Those afraid to enter the Promised Land said, "Wouldn't it _____ better for us to go back to Egypt?" (Numbers 14:3 NIV)
13 Because Caleb followed God wholeheartedly, _____ descendants would inherit the Promised Land (Numbers 14:24 NIV)
14 "See what the land _____ like" (Numbers 13:18 NIV)
15 The LORD said, "Send some _____ to explore Canaan" (Numbers 13:2 NIV)
16 Negative
17 The clock in London is Big _____
18 The frightened spies said that all the people they _____ were of great size (Numbers 13:32)
19 Gorillas and orangutans are examples
21 Book that follows Leviticus (abbr.)
22 The manna stopped the very day that the Israelites _____ the produce of Canaan (Joshua 5:11–12 NIV)
23 "Jesus _____ many who had diseases, sicknesses and evil spirits" (Luke 7:21 NIV)
25 Name of the land God gave the Israelites (Numbers 13:2 NIV)
26 Caleb said, "_____ here I am today, eighty-five years old!" (Joshua 14:10 NIV)

## DOWN

1 Caleb said, "We _____ certainly do it" (Numbers 13:30 NIV)
2 People of the Arabia peninsula
3 "The blind receive sight, the _____ walk" (Matthew 11:5 NIV)
4 Barium (sym.)
5 Loud weeping
6 Before
7 Color between orange and green; slang for being cowardly
11 A southernmost town of the tribe of Judah in the Negev (Joshua 15:32 NIV)
13 Female chicken
14 God made an oath to Abraham, _____, and Jacob (Genesis 50:24 NIV)
15 *My* (Fr.)
16 Numbers 13:4–15 lists the _____ of the men sent to explore the land
17 Joshua "had _____ Moses' aide since youth" (Numbers 11:28 NIV)
18 Jehoiada assigned a third of the men to the _____ Gate (2 Kings 11:6 NIV)
20 Organization for parents and teachers
21 Joshua was the son of _____ (Numbers 13:16 NIV)
23 Circa (abbr.)
24 "What kind of towns _____ they live in?" (Numbers 13:19 NIV)

by *John Hudson Tiner*

# PUZZLE 11

## ACROSS

1 Prison
5 Told
9 A son of Ephraim (Numbers 26:35)
14 Son of Naum (Luke 3:25)
15 Haniel's father (1 Chronicles 7:39)
16 Idol
17 Market
18 "Thou shalt not _____ the harlot" (Hosea 3:3)
19 "A _____ of sedition" (Acts 24:5)
20 Guilty or not guilty
21 "The tongue can no man tame; it is an unruly evil, full of deadly _____" (James 3:8)
23 An altar (Joshua 22:34)
24 "I _____ not" (Luke 17:9)
26 Opposite of *near*
28 Rhymers
30 The second Hebrew month (1 Kings 6:1)
32 Hearing organs
36 Attached to the shoulder
37 The seventeenth order of the priesthood (1 Chronicles 24:15)
39 A chill
40 Look
42 He forsook Paul (2 Timothy 4:10)
44 Little color
45 "The fourth to _____" (1 Chronicles 25:11)
46 A son of Caleb (1 Chronicles 2:18)
48 "Hundred and _____ years old" (Joshua 24:29)
49 Chaos
50 Hophni's father (1 Samuel 4:4)
51 "Nevertheless the men _____ hard" (Jonah 1:13)
53 A dreidel is a type of _____
55 Apples grow on this
56 Beryllium (sym.)
58 "_____ with the villages thereof" (2 Chronicles 28:18)
61 "_____, Hizkijah, Azzur" (Nehemiah 10:17)
65 "And Hazarshual, and _____, and Azem" (Joshua 19:3)
67 What the wind did at the parting of the Red Sea
68 Grapes grow here
69 "Mint and _____" (Matthew 23:23)
70 Comfort
71 Esau's father-in-law (Genesis 26:34)
72 "Ziha and _____ were over the Nethinims" (Nehemiah 11:21)
73 Colored
74 "Give thyself no _____" (Lamentations 2:18)

## DOWN

1 "And compassed the _____ of the saints about" (Revelation 20:9)
2 "Imna, and Shelesh, and _____" (1 Chronicles 7:35)
3 To pierce with horns
4 "Who remembered us in our low _____" (Psalm 136:23)
5 "For he _____ his brethren would have understood" (Acts 7:25)
6 Permit
7 "_____ the Ahohite" (1 Chronicles 11:29)
8 Weeks are made of these
9 Amalek's mother (Genesis 36:12)
10 American Maritime Officers (abbr.)
11 Has ownership
12 Old
13 Saul's grandfather (1 Chronicles 8:33)
22 "And king Ahaz cut _____ the borders of the bases" (2 Kings 16:17)
25 Right hand (3-letter abbr.)
27 Harvest
28 Reward
29 Manna was measured in _____ (Exodus 16:16–18)
30 The son of Salu (Numbers 25:14)
31 Enoch's son (Genesis 4:18)
33 A gem on the third row of the ephod (Exodus 28:19)
34 Reigned

*by N. Teri Grottke*

35 "For thee have I _____"
   (Genesis 7:1)
36 "And _____, and Pharah"
   (Joshua 18:23)
38 "Yea, what _____, yea, what
   revenge!" (2 Corinthians 7:11)
41 Know (arch.)
43 Grieved
47 Greek form of *Noah*
   (Matthew 24:38)
50 One of Paul's churches in Asia
   (abbr.)
52 "I have cut off like a _____ my life"
   (Isaiah 38:12)
54 "And Moses called _____ the son
   of Nun Jehoshua" (Numbers 13:16)
55 "Thought on _____ things"
   (Matthew 1:20)

56 A mighty man of David
   (2 Samuel 23:36)
57 Belonging to Eli
59 Ruth's son (Ruth 4:13–17)
60 Potter's material
62 "Thou also, son of man, take thee a
   _____" (Ezekiel 4:1)
63 Seth's son (Genesis 4:26)
64 Lease
65 Sack
66 Type of snake

# PUZZLE 12 — ONE OF ANOTHER

*To the chief Musician,*
*A Psalm of David the servant of the Lord.*
PREFACE TO PSALM 36

## ACROSS

1 "Each man _____ a sword to his side" (Exodus 32:27 NIV)
6 "The love of many shall wax _____" (Matthew 24:12)
10 Soften up
14 "He is able to _____" (Daniel 4:37)
15 "The ruler of that _____, saw her" (Genesis 34:2 NIV)
16 "Then Jacob _____ up" (Genesis 31:17)
17 Craze
18 "Set me as a _____ upon thine heart" (Song of Solomon 8:6)
19 "These _____ smoke in my nose" (Isaiah 65:5) (2 words)
20 **THESE OF THAT:** Oreb and Zeeb (Judges 8:3) (3 words)
23 "Now _____ was very old" (1 Samuel 2:22)
24 "And _____ the sacrifices of the dead" (Psalm 106:28)
25 "Ye shall in no _____ enter" (Matthew 5:20)
29 Gold purity units
32 Colonel's subordinate (abbr.)
35 "In the house of the _____" (Ezra 6:1)
37 Nobody won the game. It was _____ (2 words)
38 Anger
39 **THIS OF THOSE:** Abram's old home (Genesis 11:31) (4 words)
43 Ike's battleground (abbr.)
44 "And Ahab _____, and went to Jezreel" (1 Kings 18:45)
45 Jean Sebelius's countrymen
46 "Also I shook my _____" (Nehemiah 5:13)
47 Not caring about right or wrong
50 Italian noble family
51 Jeanne d'Arc, e.g. (abbr.)
52 "The _____ of Joppa" (Ezra 3:7)
54 **THESE OF HIM:** The Baptist's followers (Luke 7:18) (3 words)
63 "He went up _____ a mountain" (Matthew 5:1)
64 Seine feeder
65 Fibula's partner
66 "In the land of Nod, on the east of _____" (Genesis 4:16)
67 Soaks flax
68 "Horns of ivory and _____" (Ezekiel 27:15)
69 "The burden of _____" (Isaiah 23:1)
70 Retirement accounts (abbr.)
71 "The paper _____ by the brooks" (Isaiah 19:7)

## DOWN

1 Cornmeal mush
2 Ski lift
3 "Yet they _____: have not spoken to them" (Jeremiah 23:21) (2 words)
4 "_____ water face" (Proverbs 27:19) (2 words)
5 "When I come again in _____" (Judges 8:9)
6 "And _____, out of the ivory palaces" (Psalm 45:8)
7 Nabisco's black and white treat
8 "His _____ also shall not wither" (Psalm 1:3)
9 "Titus unto _____" (2 Timothy 4:10)
10 "And as many as _____ by sea" (Revelation 18:17)
11 "Shaphat the son of _____" (Numbers 13:5)
12 "There was _____ of glass" (Revelation 4:6) (2 words)
13 "But _____ incorruptible" (1 Corinthians 9:25) (2 words)
21 Deer kin

22 "And of the truth _____"
   (3 John 1:12)
25 "Wrath is _____, and anger is
   outrageous" (Proverbs 27:4)
26 It connects to the heart
27 Single-masted sailboat
28 Folklore prankster
30 Black snake
31 He or she finisher (3-letter abbr.)
32 Bearings
33 "Then both the new maketh
   _____" (Luke 5:36) (2 words)
34 Obed's son (Ruth 4:22)
36 Low cloud layers
40 A ship's base (2 words)
41 Tokyo, once
42 "Sick, and ready to _____"
   (Luke 7:2)
48 Estimate value

49 Former Dodger manager Durocher
51 British biscuit
53 "And with your seed _____ you"
   (Genesis 9:9)
54 "And for his _____, there was a
   continual diet" (Jeremiah 52:34)
55 The "500"
56 British money (abbr.)
57 "But his _____ shall not be so"
   (Isaiah 16:6)
58 ¿Como _____ usted?
59 Agree
60 Poignant reed
61 "Naphtali is a _____ let loose"
   (Genesis 49:21)
62 No votes

# PUZZLE 13

## ACROSS

1 "One day is with the Lord as a thousand _____" (2 Peter 3:8)
6 "_____ against the fenced cities" (Zephaniah 1:16)
11 Jehoshaphat's father (2 Chronicles 20:31–32)
14 Phares's son (Luke 3:33)
15 A city on Crete (Acts 27:7–8)
16 Opposite of *women*
17 "In whatsoever ___ _" (Philippians 4:11)
18 Esarhaddon was king here (Ezra 4:2)
19 Became acquainted
20 "All _____, and all men of valour" (Judges 3:29)
22 Snake sound
23 Metal pegs
26 "_____ the devil, and he will flee from you" (James 4:7)
29 "There went out a _____ from Caesar Augustus" (Luke 2:1)
30 Noah was this person (2 Peter 2:5)
31 "_____, and Calneh, in the land of Shinar" (Genesis 10:10)
32 Uncontrolled anger
33 Type of snake
36 "And your feet _____ with the preparation of the gospel of peace" (Ephesians 6:15)
37 Farm buildings
39 "Of Harim, _____" (Nehemiah 12:15)
40 "Ye shall point out for you mount _____" (Numbers 34:7)
41 David wrote Psalms 57 and 142 in one
42 A son of Caleb (1 Chronicles 2:18)
43 "And _____ it with slime" (Exodus 2:3)
45 "Two of them went that same day to a village called _____" (Luke 24:13)
46 What the angel had done to Joseph (Matthew 1:24)
47 "To _____ his brethren the children of Israel" (Acts 7:23)
48 Take care of

49 Say hello
52 _____ salad
53 Jerusalem
55 "The _____ of Ethiopia shall not equal it" (Job 28:19)
60 Before Matthew (abbr.)
61 "Came to_____" (Isaiah 30:4)
62 Cognizant
63 No matter which
64 Bend
65 Inside

## DOWN

1 "_____ verily, their sound" (Romans 10:18)
2 Mordecai's charge (abbr.)
3 Jether's son (1 Chronicles 7:38)
4 Decay
5 "And the LORD _____ a sweet savour" (Genesis 8:21)
6 "_____ for the day" (Joel 1:15)
7 Final
8 "Behold, the _____ was a cedar" (Ezekiel 31:3)
9 Peleg's son (Genesis 11:18)
10 Disfigure
11 Ahiezer's father (Numbers 1:12)
12 "What thou _____, write in a book" (Revelation 1:11)
13 Picnic pests
21 Utilize
22 Strike
23 A pharaoh of Egypt (2 Chronicles 35:20)
24 "_____ he will repay" (Isaiah 59:18)
25 Enoch's son (Genesis 4:18)
27 They are good scrambled
28 "_____ lay at his feet until the morning" (Ruth 3:14)
29 Race
30 Made a mistake
34 Nose of a pig
35 "Baked it in _____" (Numbers 11:8)
37 "The _____ lying in a manger" (Luke 2:16)

by N. Teri Grottke

38 "Praise ye the LORD for the
_____ of Israel" (Judges 5:2)
39 Weapons
41 Cows chew this
42 Jonah's father (Jonah 1:1)
44 Increase
45 Adam's wife
46 Started
48 A son of Ishmael
(Genesis 25:13–15)
50 "They _____ to and fro"
(Psalm 107:27)
51 Otherwise
53 "Against Jerusalem, _____"
(Ezekiel 26:2)
54 "_____ greedily after the error"
(Jude 1:11)
56 Have possession
57 Cooking vessel

58 "_____ there yet the treasures"
(Micah 6:10)
59 "The fenced cities are Ziddim,
_____, and Hammath"
(Joshua 19:35)

# PUZZLE 14

**ACROSS**

1 Aside from
5 Timber
10 "She hath also born. . ._____"
(Genesis 22:20, 22)
12 "Ye have _____ treasure together"
(James 5:3)
14 "The plowman shall overtake the
_____" (Amos 9:13)
15 "Thou lovest. . .lying _____ than to
speak righteousness" (Psalm 52:3)
16 Stumble
17 "They had _____" (John 21:15)
19 "The wheat and the _____ were
not smitten" (Exodus 9:32)
20 "There come two _____ more
hereafter" (Revelation 9:12)
22 Oath
23 "He was desirous to see him of a
_____ season" (Luke 23:8)
24 "The face of the deep is _____"
(Job 38:30)
26 "The _____ of gold" (1 Kings 7:49)
27 Faster than a walk
28 "It was _____ painful for me"
(Psalm 73:16)
29 Turret
32 Three
35 "Duke _____" (Genesis 36:15)
36 "The children of _____"
(Nehemiah 7:47)
37 Chair
39 "His body was _____ with the dew
of heaven" (Daniel 4:33)
40 "And there were seven sons of one
_____" (Acts 19:14)
42 "They. . ._____ the sacrifices of the
dead" (Psalm 106:28)
43 "The king of _____"
(Joshua 12:13)
45 "He reigned _____ years in
Jerusalem" (Jeremiah 52:1)
47 Gad's son (Genesis 46:16)
48 "Wherefore then _____ thou a
snare for my life" (1 Samuel 28:9)
49 Fastener

50 "He _____ him away to his house"
(Mark 8:26)

**DOWN**

1 "The branches _____ are made
white" (Joel 1:7)
2 "A _____ of the word"
(James 1:23)
3 "The sucking child shall play on the
hole of the _____" (Isaiah 11:8)
4 Lack
5 "They. . ._____ dust into the air"
(Acts 22:23)
6 Construe
7 Dine
8 "The border. . .went out to the cities
of mount _____" (Joshua 15:9)
9 "Jesus _____ their faith said, . . .Be
of good cheer" (Matthew 9:2)
10 Team
11 "The ships. . .are _____ of fierce
winds" (James 3:4)
13 "Thou hast drunken the _____"
(Isaiah 51:17)
18 "_____ his son, Jehoshua his son"
(1 Chronicles 7:27)
21 "Of how much _____
punishment. . .shall he be thought
worthy" (Hebrews 10:29)
23 "Thou shalt make _____ of blue"
(Exodus 26:4)
25 "Jehiel. . .and his firstborn son
Abdon, then _____"
(1 Chronicles 9:36)
26 "_____ king of Hamath"
(2 Samuel 8:9)
28 Journey
29 Haul
30 "I am Alpha and _____"
(Revelation 22:13)
31 "Seek him that. . .calleth for the
_____ of the sea" (Amos 5:8)
32 Bind
33 "Seven days shall there be no
_____ found in your houses"
(Exodus 12:19)

by Tonya Vilhauer

34 "In the day that thou _____ thereof
   thou shalt surely die" (Genesis 2:17)
36 "Carry neither purse, nor _____,
   nor shoes" (Luke 10:4)
38 Tabernacle
40 "Send ye the lamb. . .from _____ to
   the wilderness" (Isaiah 16:1)
41 "They shall say in all the highways,
   _____" (Amos 5:16)
44 Cave
46 Vision

# PUZZLE 15

**ACROSS**
1 Petroleum product
4 Salah's son (Genesis 10:24)
8 To stitch
11 A son of Helem (1 Chronicles 7:35)
12 "For if ye do these things, ye shall _____ fall" (2 Peter 1:10)
14 A son of Benjamin (Genesis 46:21)
15 Tear apart
16 Oily fruit
17 "I have stretched out my hands _____ thee" (Psalm 88:9)
18 Caleb's son (1 Chronicles 4:15)
19 Solomon's great-grandson (1 Kings 15:8)
20 Son of Joktan (Genesis 10:26–29)
22 "The _____ with the tongs. . . worketh in the coals" (Isaiah 44:12)
24 Loaded (arch.)
26 Before (arch.)
27 What Lot did in the gate of Sodom
29 Force
32 "Through faith also _____ herself received strength to conceive seed" (Hebrews 11:11)
34 Saul's grandfather (1 Chronicles 8:33)
35 "He. . .sent _____ unto them" (Genesis 43:34)
36 Ontario Basketball Association (abbr.)
37 Instructor
39 Bind
40 "They. . .brought him up to the king of Babylon to _____" (2 Kings 25:6)
42 Not lukewarm or cold but _____
43 When Peter doubted, he began to _____
44 Stories
45 King Saul's father
46 "And it went out to. . .Maaleha-crabbim, and passed along to _____" (Joshua 15:3)
47 "She crieth. . .at the _____ of the city" (Proverbs 8:3)
49 Go get

51 Darling
52 After Jonah (abbr.)
53 Connected to the foot
55 The earth was destroyed by a flood this many times
58 Belshazzar's kingdom was to be given to them (Daniel 5:28)
60 "Then will the LORD be jealous for his land, and _____ his people" (Joel 2:18)
61 Entrance
62 Shamgar's father (Judges 3:31)
63 Shoe bottom
64 Ground moisture
65 Seeing organs
66 No matter which

**DOWN**
1 Sheaves of barley offered in Jewish temple worship on the second day of Passover
2 Too many to count
3 Boy
4 "Adam, Sheth, _____" (1 Chronicles 1:1)
5 Another name for *Zoar* (Genesis 14:2)
6 A king of Midian (Numbers 31:8)
7 Rebel
8 "Joel the _____ of Pethuel" (Joel 1:1)
9 Xerxes's second queen (abbr.)
10 "_____ hath woe?" (Proverbs 23:29)
11 A son of Bela (1 Chronicles 7:7)
13 A prince of Midian (Numbers 31:8)
14 "For _____ are not a terror to good works" (Romans 13:3)
19 Partook
21 A type of venomous snake
23 "_____ the son of Ikkesh" (2 Samuel 23:26)
25 "A _____ in the sounds" (1 Corinthians 14:7)
27 Large lake
28 "Borders of _____ to Ataroth" (Joshua 16:2)

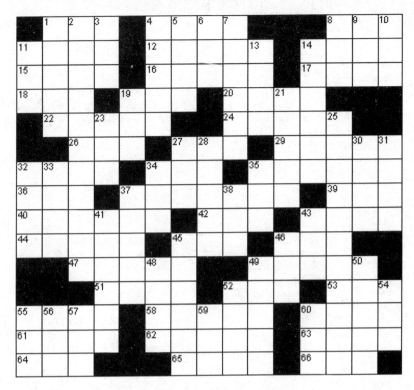

by N. Teri Grottke

30 Blood vessel
31 Well of strife (Genesis 26:20)
32 Classify
33 Asa's father (1 Chronicles 3:10)
34 Rebuilt Jerusalem (abbr.)
35 Became acquainted
37 Flavor
38 Faithful husband (abbr.)
41 "The borrower is servant to the
_____" (Proverbs 22:7)
43 "_____ down here" (Ruth 4:1)
45 The Simon from here carried the
cross
46 Zechariah (abbr.)
48 "In _____ was there a voice"
(Matthew 2:18)
49 _____ Eddy, a community in New
York
50 With heat

52 Measure (arch.)
54 "But the _____ of their God was
upon the elders" (Ezra 5:5)
55 Strange
56 Greek form of Noah (Luke 17:26)
57 Bovine
59 "Even the _____ of the LORD is
near" (Ezekiel 30:3)
60 Public service announcement (abbr.)

# PUZZLE 16 — GOD'S TENDER MERCIES

*For the LORD is good; his mercy is everlasting;*
*and his truth endureth to all generations.*

PSALM 100:5

## ACROSS

1 It walks on pseudopods (var.)
6 "He. . .put them under _____"
(2 Samuel 12:31)
10 "By this time there is a bad _____"
(John 11:39 NIV)
14 Uproar
15 Give off
16 VIP transporter
17 "And he turned _____" (Ruth 4:1)
18 Perform again
19 The Jairite, the Tekoite, and the
Ithrite (2 Samuel 20:26; 23:26, 38)
20 Start of a **QUOTE** from
Lamentations 3:23 describing the
puzzle theme (4 words)
23 "_____ me away, that I may go unto
mine own place" (Genesis 30:25)
24 Compass point halfway between NE
and E
25 "_____ for the day" (Joel 1:15)
29 "And _____ thy kids beside the
shepherds' tents"
(Song of Solomon 1:8)
31 "And as many as _____ by sea,
stood afar off" (Revelation 18:17)
35 Italian noble family
37 "Kill it at the _____ of the
tabernacle" (Leviticus 3:2)
39 _____ *Miserables*
40 **QUOTE**, cont'd from 20 Across
42 **QUOTE**, cont'd from 40 Across
(2 words)
44 "Lead _____ Benjamin"
(Hosea 5:8 NIV) (2 words)
45 So-so grades
47 Threat
48 Chinese cabbage
50 Threat
52 _____ *bien*
53 Passport, driver's license, etc. (abbr.)
55 "Take thee a _____, and lay it
before thee" (Ezekiel 4:1)

57 End of the **QUOTE**, cont'd from
42 Across (2 words)
65 Atoll item
66 Christmas
67 Small ship crane
68 _____ Roberts University
69 "He could not heal you, nor _____
you of your wound" (Hosea 5:13)
70 Sidestep
71 "But he _____ the chains apart and
broke the irons" (Mark 5:4 NIV)
72 Emergency Response Notification
System (abbr.)
73 "_____ our days as of old"
(Lamentations 5:21)

## DOWN

1 "In _____ pasture shall they feed"
(Ezekiel 34:14) (2 words)
2 Iditarod command
3 Lake, city, or canal
4 "Shall I give. . .the fruit of my
_____ for the sin of my soul?"
(Micah 6:7)
5 "Now these are the _____ the
Israelites received" (Joshua 14:1 NIV)
6 Composed
7 Improved
8 "The gates of thy land shall be set
_____ open" (Nahum 3:13)
9 *Uncle Tom's Cabin* author
10 _____ Wendell Holmes Jr.
11 "A _____ vision has been shown to
me" (Isaiah 21:2 NIV)
12 Son of Eliphaz (Genesis 36:11)
13 Optimistic
21 "I. . .will _____ them as silver"
(Zechariah 13:9)
22 Main dinner dish
25 "The children of _____" (Amos 1:13)
26 First name of hotel fame
27 "Behold, the nations are as _____
of a bucket" (Isaiah 40:15) (2 words)

*by David K. Shortess*

28 "Stand in awe, and _____ not" (Psalm 4:4)
30 "A living _____ is better than a dead lion" (Ecclesiastes 9:4)
32 "And the horns of the _____ shall be cut off" (Amos 3:14)
33 Remove rime
34 Marks of satisfaction? Perhaps, "Marks for satisfactory grades"
36 Seventeen-year locust
38 Fake gold
41 "_____ thee down to the floor" (Ruth 3:3)
43 Pismire
46 Ann _____, movie and TV actress of yesteryear
49 Nonsense
51 Remingtons

54 "_____those days were" (Haggai 2:16)
56 "Rebuke not an _____, but entreat him as a father" (1 Timothy 5:1)
57 Between a walk and a run
58 "The Philistines saw that their _____ was dead" (1 Samuel 17:51 NIV)
59 "Both of the first _____" (Leviticus 9:3)
60 Organized trip
61 Cathedral center
62 John in Wales
63 "Thou stoodest on the other _____" (Obadiah 1:11)
64 "When he returned, he cut them up into the pot of _____" (2 Kings 4:39 NIV)

# PUZZLE 17

## ACROSS

1 "Shallum, and Telem, and _____" (Ezra 10:24)
4 One of Shaharaim's wives (1 Chronicles 8:8)
9 "Nevertheless _____ heart was perfect" (1 Kings 15:14)
13 "He _____ down with sleep" (Acts 20:9)
15 Part of the preistly garb (Leviticus 8:7)
16 Son of Shimei (1 Chronicles 23:10)
17 "According to thine _____" (Numbers 18:16)
19 Ahira's father (Numbers 1:15)
20 Rocks
21 Speaking
23 Abijah's brother (2 Chronicles 11:20)
26 Consume food
27 "That which _____ been is named already" (Ecclesiastes 6:10)
30 "_____ down here" (Ruth 4:1)
31 "A voice was heard. . ._____ weeping" (Jeremiah 31:15)
33 A tree (Isaiah 44:14)
34 43,560 sq. ft. x 2
36 An altar (Joshua 22:34)
38 "But the wheat and the _____ were not smitten" (Exodus 9:32)
39 Opposite of *within*
41 Barrier
42 Physical education (abbr.)
43 Eliud's father (Matthew 1:14)
44 Adam's wife
45 Big
48 Before Habakkuk (abbr.)
50 Killed (arch.)
51 Buzzing stinger
52 "He shall _____ with his teeth" (Psalm 112:10)
54 Deep red
58 "The Philistines. . .had taken. . ._____" (2 Chronicles 28:18)
62 Load (arch.)
63 "He saw the wind _____" (Matthew 14:30)
66 Joseph mourned for Jacob at this threshing floor (Genesis 50:10)
67 "A Certain woman. . .had an _____ of blood twelve years" (Mark 5:25)
68 Type of weed that was sown with the wheat in Jesus' parable (Matthew 13:24–30)
69 Will not take responsibility
70 "This only would I _____ of you" (Galatians 3:2)
71 Bind

## DOWN

1 Utilizes
2 Decomposing metal
3 "He had cast _____ the waters" (Exodus 15:25)
4 Wild animals
5 Capable
6 Son of Abdiel (1 Chronicles 5:15)
7 "_____ of Jesse" (Isaiah 11:10)
8 "Of Harim, _____" (Nehemiah 12:15)
9 "The LORD. . .smote them to _____" (Joshua 10:10)
10 "The Hivite, and the Arkite, and the _____" (Genesis 10:17)
11 Ahira's father (Numbers 1:15)
12 "They _____ his praise" (Psalm 106:12)
14 "_____, and Dimonah, and Adadah" (Joshua 15:22)
18 Became acquainted
22 Smallest
24 "He is come to _____" (Isaiah 10:28)
25 "Having _____ ears" (2 Timothy 4:3)
27 "The joy of the _____ ceaseth" (Isaiah 24:8)
28 Jehu's great-grandfather (1 Chronicles 4:35)
29 "God created _____ heaven" (Genesis 1:1)

*by N. Teri Grottke*

31 Peleg's son (Genesis 11:18)
32 "Intreat me not to _____ thee" (Ruth 1:16)
35 Rulers' nationality at Jesus' time
37 "This man. . ._____ away much people after him" (Acts 5:37)
39 Employment pay
40 "Out of whose womb came the _____?" (Job 38:29)
41 False god of Babylon (Isaiah 46)
46 Gideoni's son (Numbers 1:11)
47 Cure
49 Hurry
50 The devil knows his time is this
53 "_____ lay at his feet until the morning" (Ruth 3:14)
54 Clothed
55 Charge

56 Ishmaelite camel driver (1 Chronicles 27:30)
57 Smelling orifice
59 "Collar of my _____" (Job 30:18)
60 Jaroah's son (1 Chronicles 5:14)
61 "As he saith also in _____" (Romans 9:25)
64 After Song of Songs (abbr.)
65 Temple gate (2 Kings 11:6)

# PUZZLE 18

## ACROSS

1 "Lest at any time thou _____ thy foot against a stone" (Matthew 4:6)
5 "Adonijah, Bigvai, _____" (Nehemiah 10:16)
9 "A sore _____ that cannot be healed" (Deuteronomy 28:35)
14 Shammah's father (2 Samuel 23:11)
15 "I am the _____ of Sharon" (Song of Solomon 2:1)
16 "The sons of _____ the Netophathite" (Jeremiah 40:8)
17 "In _____ was there a voice heard" (Matthew 2:18)
18 Suffer
19 Briar
20 Jesus _____ upon the cross
21 King of the Amalekites (1 Samuel 15:8)
22 "The son of _____, in Aruboth" (1 Kings 4:10)
23 Often translated *dill* (Matthew 23:23)
25 "Messengers. . .make the _____ Ethiopians afraid" (Ezekiel 30:9)
27 "The LORD. . .delivered me out of the _____ of the lion" (1 Samuel 17:37)
30 Flog
31 Taxi
34 "_____ the Bethelite" (1 Kings 16:34)
36 "The plain of _____ " (Joshua 13:9)
41 Hushim's father (1 Chronicles 7:12)
43 Caleb's son (1 Chronicles 4:15)
45 "The brook of _____" (Psalm 83:9)
46 A shade of purple
48 "A _____ and a flower" (Exodus 25:33)
50 "The son of _____" (Luke 3:35)
51 "The Egyptians shall _____ to drink" (Exodus 7:18)
53 "They did so at the going up to _____" (2 Kings 9:27)
54 "And the men of _____ made Nergal" (2 Kings 17:30)
55 "His truth _____ to all generations" (Psalm 100:5)
56 "The shipmen _____ that they drew near" (Acts 27:27)
60 Some
61 Limbs
65 "The _____ of the sea" (Esther 10:1)
66 Lifetime
67 Superior
68 "Rejoicing in himself _____" (Galatians 6:4)
69 "Mordecai. . .had taken _____ for his daughter" (Esther 2:15)
70 "Fine linen, and coral, and _____" (Ezekiel 27:16)
71 Boundaries
72 One on which they laded the corn (Genesis 42:26)
73 "Shallum, and _____, and Uri" (Ezra 10:24)

## DOWN

1 "Chalcol, and _____, the sons of Mahol" (1 Kings 4:31)
2 Repeat
3 "Mattathias, which was the son of _____" (Luke 3:26)
4 "They bowed their _____, and worshipped" (Nehemiah 8:6)
5 "And they gave them the city of _____" (Joshua 21:11)
6 "Then answered _____ the Edomite" (1 Samuel 22:9)
7 Rebekah's husband
8 "The men of Cuth made _____" (2 Kings 17:30)
9 "The north side of _____" (Joshua 19:27)
10 "The Nethinims dwelt in _____" (Nehemiah 3:26)
11 "Let all _____ that seek thee rejoice" (Psalm 40:16)
12 "_____ of this life" (Luke 21:34)
13 "He maketh my feet like _____ feet" (2 Samuel 22:34)
24 NT book after Galatians (abbr.)
26 "Take. . .a _____ of three years old" (Genesis 15:9)

*by Tonya Vilhauer*

28 "On the east side of _____"
   (Numbers 34:11)
29 Frail
31 "Whosoever shall _____ on the
   name of the Lord" (Acts 2:21)
32 "And _____ went before the ark"
   (2 Samuel 6:4)
33 Beor's son (Genesis 36:32)
35 Dialects
37 Emission
38 "I gave unto _____ mount Seir"
   (Joshua 24:4)
39 Lock
40 One of Esau's mothers-in-law
   (Genesis 36:2)
42 Rodent
44 "And the _____ go about the
   streets" (Ecclesiastes 12:5)

47 "Carry these ten _____ unto the
   captain" (1 Samuel 17:18)
49 Victim
52 "I am with you always, even unto
   the _____" (Matthew 28:20)
56 Indicator
57 "The son of _____, which was the
   son of Nagge" (Luke 3:25)
58 "And _____, and Thimnathah, and
   Ekron" (Joshua 19:43)
59 "_____, TEKEL, UPHARSIN"
   (Daniel 5:25)
62 Genuine
63 Spouse
64 Bine
66 "_____, she is broken" (Ezekiel 26:2)
67 "Moses. . ._____ him up into the
   mount" (Exodus 24:18)

# PUZZLE 19

## ACROSS

1 Jephthah fled to there (Judges 11)
4 "_____ king of Hamath" (2 Samuel 8:9)
7 43,560 sq. ft. x 2
12 "And in process of _____" (Genesis 4:3)
13 Attached to the shoulder
14 Sofa
15 Jerahmeel's son (1 Chronicles 2:25)
16 Turning away from sin
19 "We. . .shall. . .meet the Lord in the _____" (1 Thessalonians 4:17)
20 Lived (arch.)
21 Tikvath's father (2 Chronicles 34:22)
24 To plant small seed
25 Partook
28 Outfield (abbr.)
29 Seminary (abbr.)
30 Ground moisture
31 "Earth, blood, and fire, and pillars of _____" (Joel 2:30)
33 "Do ye _____ to reprove words" (Job 6:26)
37 Omri bought this hill (1 Kings 16:24)
39 "The mirth of _____ ceaseth" (Isaiah 24:8)
40 Famous
41 "Jozabad, and _____" (2 Chronicles 31:13)
42 Abraham's nephew
43 "God saw that it _____ good" (Genesis 1:21)
45 "_____ reigned nine and twenty years in Jerusalem" (2 Chronicles 29:1)
46 A tree (Isaiah 44:14)
47 Child's favorite seat
48 "Doeth not any of those _____, but even hath eaten upon the mountains" (Ezekiel 18:11)
52 "I brought you to possess the land of the _____" (Amos 2:10)
55 "I _____ alone because of thy hand" (Jeremiah 15:17)
56 "Roebucks, and _____, and fatted fowl" (1 Kings 4:23)
59 Land measurement
60 Giants (Deuteronomy 2:11)
61 "A _____ of dove's dung" (2 Kings 6:25)
62 Peaceful
63 Did (arch.)
64 Before (arch.)
65 "So shall _____ seed be" (Romans 4:18)

## DOWN

1 A son of Jehaleleel (1 Chronicles 4:16)
2 Manna was measured this way
3 "Zechariah, _____" (1 Chronicles 15:18)
4 "They. . .pitched at _____" (Numbers 33:27)
5 "They. . .brought the heads of _____ and Zeeb" (Judges 7:25)
6 "It shall not be lawful to _____ toll, tribute, or custom, upon them" (Ezra 7:24)
7 The only NT history book
8 "Collar of my _____" (Job 30:18)
9 Sprint
10 Book of time (abbr.)
11 "And _____ lay at his feet until the morning" (Ruth 3:14)
12 Zuph's son (1 Chronicles 6:34–35)
17 Joram smote these people (2 Kings 8:21)
18 "No man putteth _____ wine into old bottles" (Mark 2:22)
22 Rulers' nationality at Jesus' time
23 Before (arch.)
25 Maasiai's father (1 Chronicles 9:12)
26 Cloth shelter
27 Female sheep
29 "The mercy _____ were the faces of the cherubims" (Exodus 37:9)
31 "The _____ with the tongs" (Isaiah 44:12)
32 Relatives

*by N. Teri Grottke*

34 Last book of the OT (abbr.)
35 A son of Aaron (Exodus 6:23)
36 Say hello
37 "Land from _____ to the wilderness" (Isaiah 16:1)
38 Son of Naum (Luke 3:25)
44 Each
47 "All the daughters of musick shall be brought _____" (Ecclesiastes 12:4)
48 A city of Lycaonia (Acts 14:6)
49 Milcah's brother (Genesis 11:29)
50 "Wherefore now rise up _____ in the morning" (1 Samuel 29:10)
51 Originate
52 Charity
53 "Priest of the _____ high God" (Hebrews 7:1)
54 Rip

56 Gave food to
57 A family of returned exiles (Ezra 2:57)
58 "Jehoiada. . .bored a hole in the _____ of it" (2 Kings 12:9)
59 College entrance exam

# PUZZLE 20

## ACROSS

1 "The _____ of thy life shall be increased" (Proverbs 9:11)
6 Feline
9 Holler
13 "The battle at _____" (Numbers 21:33)
14 Aram's brother (1 Chronicles 7:34)
15 "The son of _____" (Luke 3:31)
16 Repeat
17 Club
18 "Though I forbear, what am I _____" (Job 16:6)
19 Crimson
20 Coz's son (1 Chronicles 4:8)
22 Tension
23 Indicator
24 Time
25 Appointment
28 "Neither shall ye touch it, lest ye _____" (Genesis 3:3)
29 "Ye _____ a pit for your friend" (Job 6:27)
32 Sharar's son (2 Samuel 23:33)
34 "These made war with _____" (Genesis 14:2)
35 Citron
36 "By me princes rule, and _____" (Proverbs 8:16)
37 Bani's son (Ezra 10:34)
38 "From _____, and from all the mountains" (Joshua 11:21)
39 "Thou. . ._____ not look on iniquity" (Habakkuk 1:13)
40 Affirmative
41 Jonathan's father (1 Chronicles 11:34)
42 "Naaman, _____, and Rosh" (Genesis 46:21)
43 "_____ is confounded" (Jeremiah 50:2)
45 Hushim's father (1 Chronicles 7:12)
46 Close
48 Thirty-six inches
50 "He sat him down in a _____ of the city" (Judges 19:15)
53 Cupola
54 Jitney
57 "The river of _____" (Ezra 8:21)
58 "_____, Elah, and Naam" (1 Chronicles 4:15)
59 "Make a joyful _____ unto the LORD" (Psalm 100:1)
61 "The heathen _____" (Psalm 46:6)
62 Tin
63 "Boaz had _____ and drunk" (Ruth 3:7)
64 "_____ with her suburbs" (1 Chronicles 6:70)
65 "Or if he shall ask an _____" (Luke 11:12)
66 "They that are unlearned and unstable _____" (2 Peter 3:16)

## DOWN

1 Twelve months
2 Rim
3 "South of _____" (Judges 1:16)
4 "_____, and the mighty men" (1 Kings 1:8)
5 The LORD spoke to Moses in Mount _____ (Leviticus 25:1)
6 "_____ on the left" (Joshua 19:27)
7 Ahaziah's father (1 Kings 22:49)
8 _____ for tat
9 Strong desire
10 Besides
11 "A feast of wines on the _____" (Isaiah 25:6)
12 Male youngsters
15 "The same measure that ye _____ withal it shall be measured to you again" (Luke 6:38)
21 "He said, _____; but I will die here" (1 Kings 2:30)
22 "Jashub, and _____, and Ramoth" (Ezra 10:29)
23 Bargains
24 "Cut it into _____" (Exodus 39:3)
25 "Let them praise his name in the _____" (Psalm 149:3)
26 "Abishua, and Naaman, and _____" (1 Chronicles 8:4)

*by Tonya Vilhauer*

27 Ginath's son (1 Kings 16:21)
28 Eliasaph's father (Numbers 1:14)
29 Leah's daughter (Genesis 34:1)
30 Statue
31 Uri's son (1 Kings 4:19)
33 "God _____ Balaam" (Numbers 23:4)
35 Ahumai's brother (1 Chronicles 4:2)
40 "_____ they shall flee away" (Nahum 2:8)
43 Yet
44 Barrage
46 Separate
47 "The _____, even Christ" (Ephesians 4:15)
48 "The _____ man. . .told him, Whence art thou?" (2 Samuel 1:13)

49 "_____ a right spirit within me" (Psalm 51:10)
50 "Through faith also _____ herself received strength" (Hebrews 11:11)
51 Aside from
52 Fury
53 Pull
54 "Surely the serpent will _____ without enchantment" (Ecclesiastes 10:11)
55 "Maintain good works for necessary _____" (Titus 3:14)
56 "He _____ him away to his house" (Mark 8:26)
58 Frozen water
60 Row

# PUZZLE 21

**ACROSS**

1 Son of Abdiel (1 Chronicles 5:15)
4 To stitch
7 "_____, and Magog" (Revelation 20:8)
10 Elevate
12 Should
14 Simon Peter's father (John 1:42)
15 "Imna, and Shelesh, and _____" (1 Chronicles 7:35)
16 "Fathers, provoke not your children to _____" (Colossians 3:21)
17 Ruth's son (Ruth 4:13–17)
18 "We...shall...meet the Lord in the _____" (1 Thessalonians 4:17)
20 "I have _____ unto thy testimonies" (Psalm 119:31)
22 Increase
23 Consume food
24 Home of the Rockies (abbr.)
26 Boy
27 "_____, so would we have it" (Psalm 35:25)
29 Abraham's brother (Genesis 11:27)
31 "To _____ is reserved the blackness of darkness for ever" (Jude 1:13)
33 "Let the _____ return with his brothers" (Genesis 44:33 NIV)
35 "That at the _____ of Jesus every knee should bow" (Philippians 2:10)
36 "Tyrus hath said against Jerusalem, _____" (Ezekiel 26:2)
38 A gem on the third row of the ephod (Exodus 28:19)
40 "The men of Israel answered the _____ of Judah" (2 Samuel 19:43)
41 Weeks are made of these
43 "God saw that it _____ good" (Genesis 1:21)
44 People
47 The first Hebrew month (Esther 3:7)
49 Gym class (abbr.)
50 Before (arch.)

51 A Moabite border city (Numbers 21:15)
52 Oath
54 To make a mistake
55 "Ephraim is joined to _____" (Hosea 4:17)
58 Fuss
59 So be it
62 One who consumes food
64 Lease
68 "They _____ his praise" (Psalm 106:12)
69 "It hath no _____: the bud shall yield no meal" (Hosea 8:7)
70 Foot covering
71 Naaman's brother (Numbers 26:40)
72 A son of Gad (Genesis 46:16)
73 Motel

**DOWN**

1 Jether's son (1 Chronicles 7:38)
2 "And some began to spit on _____" (Mark 14:65)
3 Prophet for King Hezekiah (abbr.)
4 Biggest star in our solar system
5 "As the partridge sitteth on _____" (Jeremiah 17:11)
6 "Do not _____ the edge" (Ecclesiastes 10:10)
7 Battle where Goliath's brother was slain (2 Samuel 21:19)
8 Single
9 A son of Jacob (Genesis 35:26)
11 Tahath's son (1 Chronicles 7:20)
12 Boat paddle
13 Not false
14 Peleg's brother (Genesis 10:25)
19 Zechariah's father (Ezra 5:1)
21 Is able
22 "Giving thanks _____ for all things" (Ephesians 5:20)
24 "_____ up before me" (Jonah 1:2)
25 Jerahmeel's son (1 Chronicles 2:25)
27 To humble

*by N. Teri Grottke*

28 "The king's commandment was urgent, and the furnace exceeding _____" (Daniel 3:22)

30 Jael used this to kill Sisera

32 "They shall give. . .cheeks, and the _____ " (Deuteronomy 18:3)

34 Even

36 "Of Harim, _____" (Nehemiah 12:15)

37 Delilah cut Samson's

39 "Stand in the _____ " (Ezekiel 22:30)

42 "None. . .was cleansed, _____ Naaman the Syrian" (Luke 4:27)

45 Pay attention to

46 Mistakes

48 East of Eden (Genesis 4:16)

53 "There come two _____ more hereafter" (Revelation 9:12)

56 "Even of _____ my people is risen up as an enemy" (Micah 2:8)

57 Night sky illuminator

58 Where the mercy seat was

59 Solomon's great-grandson (1 Kings 15:8)

60 Disfigure

61 "The latter _____" (Ruth 3:10)

63 Phinehas's father (1 Samuel 4:4)

65 A son of Benjamin (Genesis 46:21)

66 Jehoshua's father (1 Chronicles 7:27)

67 "Joshua. . .died, being an hundred and _____ years old" (Joshua 24:29)

# PUZZLE 22 — KING AFTER KING

*Therefore if any man be in Christ, he is a new creature:*
*old things are passed away; behold, all things are become new.*

2 CORINTHIANS 5:17

## ACROSS

1 "Is it _____ for you to flog a Roman"
(Acts 22:25 NIV)
6 "And the third beast had _____ as a
man" (Revelation 4:7) (2 words)
11 "Sir, come down _____ my child die"
(John 4:49)
14 "To _____ for wickedness"
(Daniel 9:24 NIV)
15 Soft drinks
16 "When anyone went to a wine _____
to draw" (Haggai 2:16 NIV)
17 "Go _____ possess the land"
(Deuteronomy 1:8) (2 words)
18 Lock
19 Kin to Ltd. (abbr.)
20 Three successive evil **KINGS** of Israel
(1 Kings 15:25–16:14) (3 words)
23 Over there
24 So long
25 "The proud have _____ snare for me"
(Psalm 140:5) (2 words)
29 "Giving all diligence, _____ your
faith virtue" (2 Peter 1:5) (2 words)
32 "Let thy servant abide instead of the
_____ bondman to my lord"
(Genesis 44:33) (2 words)
36 "An _____ pleasing to the LORD"
(Leviticus 1:13 NIV)
38 "_____ that my words were now
written! _____ that they were printed
in a book" (Job 19:23) (2 words)
40 *Its,* in Paris
41 Two successive evil **KINGS** of Israel
(2 Kings 15:17–26) (2 words)
45 _____ Arbor, Michigan
46 Away from the wind
47 Walk like a crab
48 "The Lord hath _____ of them"
(Matthew 21:3)
50 Where Saul's medium lived
(1 Samuel 28:7)
53 Hardy heroine
54 "The. . .child shall play on the hole of
the _____" (Isaiah 11:8)
56 "I tell you, _____" (Luke 13:3)

58 Three successive, **KINGS** of Israel
(1 Kings 16:16–22:53) (3 words)
67 Snow, English, or split
68 "No _____ shall come on his head"
(Judges 13:5)
69 "He. . .cannot _____ much"
(Leviticus 14:21) (2 words)
70 Work unit
71 Something taboo (2 words)
72 Very angry
73 "We. . . passed to the _____ of
Cyprus" (Acts 27:4 NIV)
74 Spread about
75 "My _____ for me"
(1 Chronicles 22:7) (2 words)

## DOWN

1 "Where the body of Jesus had
_____" (John 20:12)
2 Sicilian volcano
3 "Shamgar. . .slew six hundred men
with an ox _____" (Judges 3:31)
4 "There was one _____, a prophetess"
(Luke 2:36)
5 "Being _____ the hand of them. . .,
I came into Damascus" (Acts 22:11)
(2 words)
6 "Instead, he puts it on _____"
(Luke 8:16 NIV) (2 words)
7 "Not seeing the sun _____ season"
(Acts 13:11) (2 words)
8 Summer drinks
9 Ledger, at times
10 English 101 paper
11 "Ye thought _____ against me"
(Genesis 50:20)
12 American bullfrog genus
13 What acid does on glass
21 Python, for example
22 Snaky fish
25 "So they hanged _____ on the
gallows" (Esther 7:10)
26 Actress Dunne
27 He wrote, "No man is an island"
28 "I _____ poor man"
(1 Samuel 18:23) (2 words)

30 Lacquered the cloth on an airplane's skin
31 "_____ Lord is at hand" (Philippians 4:5)
33 "They are all gone _____" (Psalm 14:3)
34 "Two tenth _____ unto one ram" (Numbers 28:28)
35 "And he sat down among the _____" (Job 2:8)
37 "_____! I am warm" (Isaiah 44:16 NIV)
39 "My heart _____ turned to wax" (Psalm 22:14 NIV)
42 Proboscidean pachyderm
43 "Blessed are ye, when _____ shall revile you" (Matthew 5:11)
44 "And the archers _____ him" (1 Chronicles 10:3)

49 Southeast Asia language group
51 "Set them in two rows, six _____" (Leviticus 24:6) (3 words)
52 Cry at the stadium
55 The woman named in Hebrews 11:11 and her namesakes (var.)
57 Horizontal, multi-element antennas
58 German auto
59 "You, a _____ man" (John 10:33 NIV)
60 "I know. . .thy _____ against me" (Isaiah 37:28)
61 "_____ begat Sadoc" (Matthew 1:14)
62 "A _____ of a man" (Numbers 19:16)
63 Not a one
64 "Make _____ oil" (Exodus 30:25) (2 words)
65 Pooch in *The Thin Man*
66 Cultivates, at times

## ACROSS

1 Captain of David's army
   (1 Chronicles 11:6)
5 First letter of the Greek alphabet
10 Zuph's father
   (1 Chronicles 6:34–35)
14 A child of Gad (Numbers 26:16–18)
15 "Judgment is come. . .upon _____"
   (Jeremiah 48:21)
16 Uncontrolled anger
17 Caused to go to a destination
18 "A tower of _____"
   (Song of Solomon 7:4)
19 Jerahmeel's son (1 Chronicles 2:25)
20 First book of the Gospels
22 "_____ wings of a great eagle"
   (Revelation 12:14)
24 South Africa (abbr.)
25 A deliverer of Israel (Judges 3:15)
26 To beat
27 "For if God _____ not the angels"
   (2 Peter 2:4)
30 A son of Zophah
   (1 Chronicles 7:36–37)
34 "I am meek and _____ in heart"
   (Matthew 11:29)
35 Give for temporary use
36 Indebted
37 "He removeth _____ the speech of
   the trusty" (Job 12:20)
38 "Not _____ your liberty"
   (1 Peter 2:16)
40 Son of Joktan (Genesis 10:26–29)
41 Saul's grandfather
   (1 Chronicles 8:33)
42 "Ahijah, Hanan, _____"
   (Nehemiah 10:26)
43 Talked (arch.)
44 "To the twelve tribes which are
   scattered abroad, _____"
   (James 1:1)
46 "Then went Abimelech to
   _____"(Judges 9:50)
47 Bag
48 Son of Shammai (1 Chronicles 2:45)
49 *I* in French
51 Fuss

52 Going without food
55 Daniel had a vision by this river
57 Cook
59 "Moses drew _____"
   (Exodus 20:21)
61 "The plain of _____" (Daniel 3:1)
62 A caretaker in sickness
63 "I will send a fire on the wall of
   _____" (Amos 1:7)
64 Type of trees
65 In place of
66 "_____. . .begat sons and
   daughters" (Genesis 11:11)

## DOWN

1 More than one Jo
2 A brother of David
   (1 Chronicles 2:15)
3 Temple prophetess in Jesus' time
   (Luke 2:36)
4 "Peter went out, and wept _____"
   (Luke 22:62)
5 "The prince of the tribe of the
   children of Asher" (Numbers 34:27)
6 "Thou hast _____ righteousness"
   (Hebrews 1:9)
7 Till
8 "Ye shall point out for you mount
   _____" (Numbers 34:7)
9 "If we ask _____ according to his
   will, he heareth us" (1 John 5:14)
   (2 words)
10 "Now gather thyself in _____"
   (Micah 5:1)
11 Boat paddle
12 Generations
13 "_____, and Ivah" (Isaiah 37:13)
21 "_____ shall see God"
   (Matthew 5:8)
23 "Thou, being a _____ olive tree,
   wert grafted in among them"
   (Romans 11:17)
26 At a certain time
27 "David. . ._____ it, and smote the
   Philistine" (1 Samuel 17:49)
28 "Force and _____" (Ezra 4:23)
29 Cognizant

*by N. Teri Grottke*

30 David used this to defeat Goliath
31 Moses' brother-in-law
(Numbers 10:29)
32 "Nor _____ my love, until he
please" (Song of Solomon 8:4)
33 Eleasah's father (1 Chronicles 2:39)
38 "The _____ shall come down"
(Isaiah 34:7)
39 This happened to the Egyptians in
the Red Sea
40 "She crieth in the. . ._____ of the
gates" (Proverbs 1:21)
42 Joseph mourned for Jacob on the
threshing floor of _____
(Genesis 50:10)
43 "The archers _____ at King Josiah"
(2 Chronicles 35:23)
45 Greek form of *Isaiah* (Matthew 3:3)
46 Experienced flavor

48 A son of Ishmael
(1 Chronicles 1:30–31)
49 Brother of Jesus
(Matthew 13:55; Jude 1:1)
50 Nehemiah's wall was finished in this
month (Nehemiah 6:15)
52 "_____ ye well" (Acts 15:29)
53 The border went to here from
Remmonmethoar (Joshua 19:13)
54 Look at
56 Attached to the shoulder
58 "The frogs died _____ of the
houses" (Exodus 8:13)
60 A male sheep

# PUZZLE 24

## ACROSS

1 Plenty
5 "_____ and Caiaphas being the high priests" (Luke 3:2)
10 Hushai's son (1 Kings 4:16)
12 "Friend, lend me three _____" (Luke 11:5)
14 "We sailed under Crete, over against _____" (Acts 27:7)
15 "They. . ._____ the Holy One of Israel" (Psalm 78:41)
17 Maim
18 Cay
20 Colonize
21 "_____, and Thimnathah, and Ekron" (Joshua 19:43)
22 Rent
23 "The sorrows of _____ compassed me" (2 Samuel 22:6)
24 Left
27 "So shall the _____ be calm unto you" (Jonah 1:12)
28 "_____ them with brass" (Exodus 27:6)
31 Strive
32 Simon's father (John 1:42)
34 "Hewed stones, _____ with saws" (1 Kings 7:9)
35 "The Syrians of _____" (2 Samuel 10:6)
37 Cave
38 "_____ shall we escape" (Hebrews 2:3)
41 "Behold now _____, which I made with thee" (Job 40:15)
44 "The way of the plain from _____" (Deuteronomy 2:8)
46 "Alammelech, and _____, and Misheal" (Joshua 19:26)
47 "Eber, Peleg, _____" (1 Chronicles 1:25)
49 Zoheth's father (1 Chronicles 4:20)
50 Sup
51 Statute
53 Gait

54 "Nethaneel the fourth, _____ the fifth" (1 Chronicles 2:14)
57 Mail
59 "To _____ the most Holy" (Daniel 9:24)
60 "Paul departed from _____" (Acts 18:1)
61 "Benjamin's _____ was five times" (Genesis 43:34)
62 Storage building

## DOWN

1 "Gird yourselves, and _____" (Joel 1:13)
2 "Children of Lod, Hadid, and _____" (Ezra 2:33)
3 Cistern
4 Linen
5 "_____ power is given unto me" (Matthew 28:18)
6 "Make a joyful _____ unto the LORD" (Psalm 100:1)
7 "His _____ shall be called Wonderful" (Isaiah 9:6)
8 "The name of his city was _____" (Genesis 36:35)
9 "Thou _____ a crown of pure gold on his head" (Psalm 21:3)
10 "David. . .went. . .from _____ of Judah" (2 Samuel 6:2)
11 "_____ with her suburbs" (Joshua 21:18)
13 Vendor
14 "They _____ the Ammonites" (1 Samuel 11:11)
16 Deferment
19 "For _____ is the kingdom of God" (Luke 6:20)
25 "The King. . .brought men. . . from Cuthah, and from _____" (2 Kings 17:24)
26 "The tower of _____" (Ezekiel 29:10)
28 Atarah's son (1 Chronicles 2:26)
29 Male youngster
30 Reverence
32 Careah's son (2 Kings 25:23)

*by Tonya Vilhauer*

33 "The house of _____ the Gittite" (2 Samuel 6:10)
35 "The sons of Becher; _____" (1 Chronicles 7:8)
36 "They. . ._____ the sacrifices of the dead" (Psalm 106:28)
38 Accelerate
39 "Leave their wealth to _____" (Psalm 49:10)
40 "My father chastised you with _____" (2 Chronicles 10:11)
41 Evil
42 "Praise him with stringed instruments and _____" (Psalm 150:4)
43 One of Aram's sons (Genesis 10:23)
45 Tabulated
48 "If he. . ._____ thee ought, put that on mine account" (Philemon 1:18)

52 "They shall say in all the highways, _____" (Amos 5:16)
55 "Neither shall ye touch it, lest ye _____" (Genesis 3:3)
56 "That which groweth of _____ own accord" (Leviticus 25:5)
58 "Restore unto me _____ joy" (Psalm 51:12)

# PUZZLE 25

## ACROSS

1 First place
5 Requested (arch.) (Ruth 3:6)
9 "_____ body also was like the beryl" (Daniel 10:6)
12 "Girded with fine gold of _____" (Daniel 10:5)
14 Generations
15 Arabian city (Job 6:19)
16 "They were much perplexed _____" (Luke 24:4)
18 "The joy of the _____ ceaseth" (Isaiah 24:8)
19 Not false
20 Daughter of Asher (Genesis 46:17)
21 Jacob's God-given name
24 The daughter of Solomon (1 Kings 4:15)
27 Tied
28 "Jedidah, the daughter of Adaiah of _____" (2 Kings 22:1)
29 Decay
30 Color of a horse
31 To make a mistake
32 "He that overcometh shall _____ all things" (Revelation 21:7)
35 "The word of God is. . .a discerner of the thoughts and _____ of the heart" (Hebrews 4:12)
39 "The beauty of old _____ is the grey head" (Proverbs 20:29)
40 "_____ according to the law" (Deuteronomy 17:11)
41 Son of Abdiel (1 Chronicles 5:15)
42 Sickness
44 Foreigner
46 Under
47 Eliphaz's son (Genesis 36:12)
48 "Hali, and _____" (Joshua 19:25)
49 "One. . ._____ about" (Revelation 1:13)
50 Jerahmeel's son (1 Chronicles 2:25)
51 "All the days that he _____ himself unto the LORD" (Numbers 6:6)
57 Bird home
58 "The mountains shall reach unto _____" (Zechariah 14:5)
59 Menan's son (Luke 3:31)
60 Consume food
61 "It. . .shall be eaten: as a _____ tree" (Isaiah 6:13)
62 Circle

## DOWN

1 "_____ upon mount Zion shall be deliverance" (Obadiah 1:17)
2 The heathens of these people worshiped Diana (abbr.)
3 "_____ lay at his feet until the morning" (Ruth 3:14)
4 "_____ came unto Ashdod" (Isaiah 20:1)
5 "They. . .found. . .the _____ lying in a manger" (Luke 2:16)
6 Time past
7 Book of laws (abbr., var.)
8 This queen prevented a Babylonian holocaust (abbr.)
9 Fireplace
10 A son of Zophah (1 Chronicles 7:36)
11 A giant (2 Samuel 21:18)
13 "We went over the brook _____" (Deuteronomy 2:13)
15 "They rushed with one accord into the _____" (Acts 19:29)
17 American University in London (abbr.)
20 Hurt
21 A son of Merari (1 Chronicles 24:27)
22 "A bishop must be. . .not _____ angry" (Titus 1:7)
23 Boaz's wife
24 "She placed the _____ under one of the shrubs" (Genesis 21:15 NKJV)
25 Arsenic (sym.)
26 Light smell
28 Winged rodent
30 Moza's son (1 Chronicles 8:37)
33 Famous

56

*by N. Teri Grottke*

34 "And _____ between Nineveh and Calah" (Genesis 10:12)
35 "Out of whose womb came the _____" (Job 38:29)
36 Crucifixion instrument
37 You (arch.)
38 When Peter doubted, he began to _____
40 A tree (Isaiah 44:14)
42 Despise
43 Astatine (sym.)
44 Moses' father (Exodus 6:20)
45 Later (arch.)
46 Paul and Silas were sent by night here (Acts 17:10)
47 "To meet the Lord in the _____" (1 Thessalonians 4:17)
48 Skeletal component

49 "A root that bareth _____ and wormwood" (Deuteronomy 29:18)
51 "The same day went Jesus out of the house, and _____ by the sea side" (Matthew 13:1)
52 Saw spinning wheels (abbr.)
53 "The name of his city was _____" (1 Chronicles 1:50)
54 Hophni's father (1 Samuel 4:4)
55 "Hundred and _____ years old" (Joshua 24:29)
56 Prophet who called the Israelites to finish rebuilding the temple (abbr.)

# PUZZLE 26 — BIBLICAL BIG BOY

*And there we saw the giants. . .and we were in our own
sight as grasshoppers, and so we were in their sight.*
NUMBERS 13:33

## ACROSS

1 Its capital has been Agana
5 "In _____ also is his tabernacle" (Psalm 76:2)
10 "And he _____ the sin of many" (Isaiah 53:12)
14 Taj Mahal city
15 North Florida city
16 Son of Seth (Genesis 4:26)
17 "_____ in the earth in those days" (Genesis 6:4) (3 words)
20 Help a felon
21 *Dead*, in Paris
22 "Surely in vain the _____ is spread" (Proverbs 1:17)
25 "And they filled them up to the _____" (John 2:7)
27 In abundance
31 "And _____ of oil" (Leviticus 14:21) (2 words)
33 Company head
35 "Able was I _____ saw Elba" (2 words)
36 Slightest
39 Home of the Mets
42 Japanese volcano
43 "There went out a champion. . .named _____, whose height was six cubits and a span" (1 Samuel 17:4) (3 words)
46 Pale
47 Malayan sailboat (var.)
48 Treble clef guys
50 "The _____ are a people not strong" (Proverbs 30:25)
52 Swift boat from Vietnam War (abbr.)
54 Three in Thüringen
55 Put away
58 Kind of hoop
61 1,760 equal 1 mi. (abbr.)
62 "He. . .measured the _____ all around" (Ezekiel 42:15 NIV)
64 "How much _____ shall I answer him" (Job 9:14)
66 "With all Bashan, which was called _____" (Deuteronomy 3:13) (4 words)
73 "Wherein I _____ erred" (Job 6:24)
74 Tapeworm (var.)
75 "_____ certain man was sick" (John 11:1) (2 words)
76 "And Abraham lifted up his _____" (Genesis 22:13)
77 Fishhook leader
78 "The nations are as a _____ of a bucket" (Isaiah 40:15)

## DOWN

1 "And Moses _____ him into the camp" (Numbers 11:30)
2 Cry of disgust
3 "_____ not my days few" (Job 10:20)
4 "Call me not Naomi, call me _____" (Ruth 1:20)
5 "Hear ye therefore the parable of the _____" (Matthew 13:18)
6 Acid found in vinegar
7 Roman household god or spirit
8 Primary school (abbr.)
9 "And I will send a fire on _____" (Ezekiel 39:6)
10 George Harrison was one
11 New England Cape
12 "But the name of the wicked shall _____" (Proverbs 10:7)
13 Ogee shape
18 "As their lives _____ away in their mothers' arms" (Lamentations 2:12 NIV)
19 "Was _____ the son of Ikkesh" (1 Chronicles 27:9)
22 Viet _____
23 Appealing to refined taste
24 Blue Jays' home
26 Furnace survivor (Daniel 3:26)
28 Public speaking
29 Tear up again
30 Old MacDonald's refrain ending
32 Hair goop
34 Expression of discovery
37 A little drink
38 "Now the Valley of Siddim was full of _____ pits" (Genesis 14:10 NIV)
40 Newt

by David K. Shortess

41 "He is of _____; ask him" (John 9:23)
44 "From the _____ of the rocks I see him" (Numbers 23:9)
45 "_____ the Word was made flesh" (John 1:14)
46 "There _____ a man sent from God" (John 1:6)
49 Bro's sib
51 Marshlands
53 "I am not come to destroy, but to _____" (Matthew 5:17)
56 Baseball stat
57 Fender blemishes
59 "It must be settled in a _____ assembly" (Acts 19:39 NIV)
60 "As many _____ love, I rebuke and chasten" (Revelation 3:19) (2 words)
63 "Ye have made it _____ of thieves" (Luke 19:46) (2 words)

65 "I shall multiply my days as the _____" (Job 29:18)
66 "_____ LORD is my light" (Psalm 27:1)
67 "The _____ is withered away" (Isaiah 15:6)
68 "Adam was. . .formed, then _____" (1 Timothy 2:13)
69 "I am _____ that bear witness of myself" (John 8:18)
70 "Fight neither with small _____ great" (1 Kings 22:31)
71 "No man can serve _____ masters" (Matthew 6:24)
72 "The trees. . .are full of _____" (Psalm 104:16)

# PUZZLE 27

## ACROSS
1  Rabbit
5  Perished
9  "Girded with fine gold of_____"
   (Daniel 10:5)
14 "Nevertheless _____ heart was
   perfect" (1 Kings 15:14)
15 "I will _____ all that afflict thee"
   (Zephaniah 3:19)
16 This Hararite was father to Jonathan
   in David's army (1 Chronicles 11:34)
17 "They looked unto him, and were
   _____" (Psalm 34:5)
19 The father of Sychem (Acts 7:16)
20 Flavor
21 Seth's son (Genesis 4:26)
23 The valley of craftsmen
   (Nehemiah 11:35)
24 Manna measurement
26 One who charges interest
29 Samuel's mother
32 Eshcol's brother (Genesis 14:13)
33 "_____ there yet the treasures"
   (Micah 6:10)
34 Simeon was called this (Acts 13:1)
37 Jacob's daughter (Genesis 34:1)
41 Teacher of Judaism
43 Jether's son (1 Chronicles 7:38)
44 Idol
45 "The devil, as a roaring lion, walketh
   _____, seeking whom he may
   devour" (1 Peter 5:8)
46 Boundary
48 Adam was the first
49 "Yea, what _____, yea, what
   revenge" (2 Corinthians 7:11)
51 Jael killed him (Judges 4:18–21)
53 "_____ the devil, and he will flee
   from you" (James 4:7)
56 Son of Shammai
   (1 Chronicles 2:45)
57 Tenth NT book (abbr.)
58 Nagge's son (Luke 3:25)
61 "They. . .came into an harlot's
   house, _____ Rahab" (Joshua 2:1)
65 Allotment

68 "Rejoice not thou, whole _____ "
   (Isaiah 14:29)
70 Opposite of *giver*
71 Micaiah's father (2 Chronicles 18:7)
72 Potter's material
73 Strainer
74 Bird home
75 Edges of garments

## DOWN
1  Stop
2  Largest continent
3  Worn-out clothing
4  Paseah's father (1 Chronicles 4:12)
5  Payment
6  Inside
7  First garden
8  Father of Puah (Judges 10:1)
9  Utilize
10 People's Health Movement (abbr.)
11 Shechem's father (Genesis 33:19)
12 "Three days _____ I fell sick"
   (1 Samuel 30:13)
13 The son of Bechorath
   (1 Samuel 9:1)
18 "Husham of the land of the _____
   reigned in his stead"
   (1 Chronicles 1:45)
22 Biggest star in our solar system
25 A son of Benjamin (Genesis 46:21)
27 "Wrath, strife, _____, heresies"
   (Galatians 5:20)
28 Thummim's partner
29 "Habor, and _____ "
   (1 Chronicles 5:26)
30 "_____, and Dumah" (Joshua 15:52)
31 "The other _____ "
   (Nehemiah 7:33)
32 A son of Shem (Genesis 10:22)
35 "It is the _____ of asps within him"
   (Job 20:14)
36 A son of Gad (Genesis 46:16)
38 "At the _____ of Jesus"
   (Philippians 2:10)
39 Greek form of *Hagar*
   (Galatians 4:24)

by N. Teri Grottke

40 "_____, and Ivah" (Isaiah 37:13)
42 Ezekiel's father
47 OT prophet who served four kings (abbr.)
50 Partook
52 "And he shall _____" (Isaiah 9:20)
53 Takes a break
54 This man was a Netophathite (Jeremiah 40:8)
55 "_____ off the dust under your feet" (Mark 6:11)
56 Grinds flour
59 Turn quickly
60 Crippled
62 "Whosoever shall compel thee to go a _____, go with him twain"

(Matthew 5:41)
63 "Tappuah, and _____" (Joshua 15:34)
64 Weeks are made of these
66 Prophetic end book (abbr.)
67 Before (poet.)
69 Consume

# PUZZLE 28 — ARK BUILDER

**ACROSS**

1  By faith he built an ark to save his family
4  Sick people wanted to touch the _____ of Jesus' cloak (Matthew 14:36 NIV)
8  "At the _____ of the hundred and fifty days the water had gone down" (Genesis 8:3 NIV)
9  "So make yourself an _____ of cypress wood" (Genesis 6:14 NIV)
10  To kill
12  "Every good _____ bears good fruit" (Matthew 7:17 NIV)
13  Herod had been quarreling with the people of _____ and Sidon (Acts 12:20 NIV)
14  Cuts with blows of a heavy cutting instrument
15  A sailor's word for *yes*
16  Skirmish
19  Used to catch fish
23  One of Noah's sons (Genesis 5:32)
24  "These _____ the generations of Noah" (Genesis 6:9)
25  "So the LORD was sorry he had _____ made them" (Genesis 6:6 NLT)
27  Russian ruler, generally
28  Daniel interpreted the writing on the wall, which was "_____, MENE, TEKEL, PARSIN" (Daniel 5:25 NLT)
29  A kind of cultural revolution, one person at a time

**DOWN**

1  "Your _____ is set in a rock" (Numbers 24:21 NIV)
2  After the flood, "_____ Noah was left, and those with him in the ark" (Genesis 7:23 NIV)
3  A month in the Jewish calendar (Ezra 6:15)
5  Moses did not _____ to look on the face of God (Acts 7:32 NIV)
6  "Nimrod. . ._____ to be a mighty warrior" (Genesis 10:8 NIV)
7  Supplements income
11  The flood began in the six hundredth _____ of Noah's life (Genesis 7:11)
12  The dove returned with an olive leaf! "_____ Noah knew that the water had receded from the earth" (Genesis 8:11 NIV)
16  One of Noah's sons (Genesis 5:32)
17  Lay the way
18  Word to end a prayer
20  "My couch will _____ my complaint" (Job 7:13 NKJV)
21  Otherwise known as a streetcar (Brit.)
22  Threadbare (arch.)
26  In regard to (abbr.)
27  Signifying company's ownership (abbr.)

|   1   |   2   |   3   |       |       |   4   |   5   |   6   |   7   |
|   8   |       |       |       |       |       |   9   |       |       |
|  10   |       |       |  11   |       |  12   |       |       |       |
|  13   |       |       |       |       |  14   |       |       |       |
|       |       |       |  15   |       |       |       |       |       |
|  16   |  17   |  18   |       |       |  19   |  20   |  21   |  22   |
|  23   |       |       |       |       |       |  24   |       |       |
|  25   |       |       |  26   |       |  27   |       |       |       |
|  28   |       |       |       |       |  29   |       |       |       |

*by John Hudson Tiner*

# PUZZLE 29

## ACROSS

1 Burial place
5 Too
9 "And he called them the land of
_____ unto this day"
(1 Kings 9:13)
14 Son of Joktan (Genesis 10:26–28)
15 "Every man should _____ rule"
(Esther 1:22)
16 Absalom's captain (2 Samuel 17:25)
17 Another name for *Zoar*
(Genesis 14:2)
18 "The king's _____" (Genesis 14:17)
19 Loaded (arch.)
20 Able to be tricked
23 "Every _____ should bow"
(Philippians 2:10)
24 OT book prior to Jonah (abbr.)
25 Fight between countries
28 Opposite of *newness*
31 He met a friendly fish (abbr., var.)
34 Abraham's heir
36 Utilize
37 Dwelling
38 "In the _____ day"
(Leviticus 23:32)
39 Are (arch.)
40 Pumpkins grow on these
41 Furthest part
42 Opposite of *hers*
43 Idol
44 "_____ that ye refuse not"
(Hebrews 12:25)
45 "Burst into song. . .you _____"
(Psalm 29:2)
48 "He _____ horns" (Habakkuk 3:4)
49 A knight
50 "What. . .hath been done to
Mordecai for _____" (Esther 6:3)
52 "For the _____ of this service"
(2 Corinthians 9:12)
59 "For in him we live, and move, and
have our _____" (Acts 17:28)
60 Jerahmeel's son (1 Chronicles 2:25)
61 Sadoc's father (Matthew 1:14)
63 David would do this before the ark
64 7 days

65 "_____, and Ivah" (Isaiah 37:13)
66 "Nor _____ the thing"
(Psalm 89:34)
67 Peter fished with these
68 So be it

## DOWN

1 Jephthah fled there (Judges 11:3)
2 Ruth's son (Ruth 4:13–17)
3 Not female
4 "The one with the _____ horses
is going toward the north country"
(Zechariah 6:6 NIV)
5 Guni's son (1 Chronicles 5:15)
6 "To open before him the two
_____ gates" (Isaiah 45:1)
7 Heber's father (Luke 3:35)
8 "They. . .brought the heads of
_____ and Zeeb" (Judges 7:25)
9 "And Othniel the son of Kenaz,
_____ younger brother"
(Judges 1:13)
10 "Look from the top of _____"
(Song of Solomon 4:8)
11 Asked (arch.) (Ruth 3)
12 Utilizes
13 Boys
21 Father of Methuselah (Genesis 5:21)
22 "We _____ not" (2 John 1:8)
25 "A feast of _____ on the lees"
(Isaiah 25:6)
26 Digression
27 Realm
29 A caretaker in sickness
30 Underwent beauty treatments in
the palace before attaining a higher
position (abbr.)
31 Undigested whale food
32 The ending
33 "The son of _____" (1 Kings 4:10)
35 Partook
37 "One shall then open _____ the
gate" (Ezekiel 46:12)
39 "To meet the Lord in the _____"
(1 Thessalonians 4:17)
40 "To _____ his brethren the
children of Israel" (Acts 7:23)

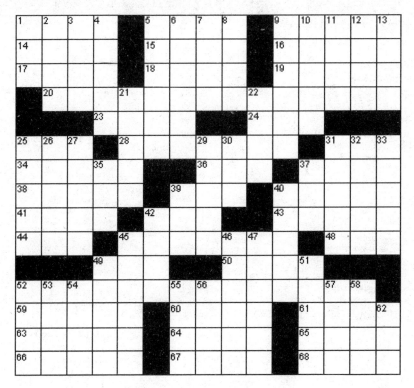

*by N. Teri Grottke*

42 Lotan's son (1 Chronicles 1:39)
45 "Jesus. . .with his _____ wrote on the ground" (John 8:6)
46 Lane
47 "But rather giving of _____" (Ephesians 5:4)
49 "For _____ the fathers fell asleep, all things continue" (2 Peter 3:4)
51 "The children of _____" (Ezra 2:44)
52 Adoniram's father (1 Kings 4:6)
53 "Lookest thou upon them that _____ treacherously" (Habakkuk 1:13)
54 "For ye tithe _____ and rue and all manner of herbs" (Luke 11:42)
55 "The fruit of righteousness is _____ in peace" (James 3:18)
56 Cherries grow on this

57 David's brother (1 Chronicles 2:15)
58 Not any
62 "They have. . ._____ greedily after the error" (Jude 1:11)

# PUZZLE 30

## ACROSS

1 Compassion
5 They shall divide it into seven _____" (Joshua 18:5)
10 "She bare a son, and called his name _____" (Genesis 4:25)
14 "_____, lama sabachthani" (Mark 15:34)
15 "Nadab and _____ died" (1 Chronicles 24:2)
16 "He. . .brought them unto Halah, and Habor, and _____" (1 Chronicles 5:26)
17 Exchange for price
18 "Behold, thou art _____ than Daniel" (Ezekiel 28:3)
19 "Nevertheless _____ heart was perfect" (1 Kings 15:14)
20 Cultivate
21 "They shall be as though they had not _____" (Obadiah 1:16)
22 Hyssop
23 "Thy god, O _____, liveth" (Amos 8:14)
26 Each
28 "He. . .smote them with _____" (1 Samuel 5:6)
31 "The emptiers have. . ._____ their vine branches" (Nahum 2:2)
32 Exchanged
33 Expose
35 "Thou _____ cursed above all cattle" (Genesis 3:14)
36 Bind
37 God _____ blessed me
40 "If an ox _____ a man or a woman" (Exodus 21:28)
42 Drag
43 Jewish confession of faith
45 "Thou shalt not rule over him with _____" (Leviticus 25:43)
47 "Goshen, and _____, and Giloh" (Joshua 15:51)
48 Abyss
49 "He might know how much every man had gained by _____" (Luke 19:15)

51 "Thou art the God that _____ wonders" (Psalm 77:14)
54 At this present place
55 Lodging
56 Lion's cry
60 Point of former attachment of the umbilical cord
63 Soil
64 "Sinners shall be converted _____ thee" (Psalm 51:13)
65 "He _____ them from the judgment seat" (Acts 18:16)
66 Lack
67 Strike

## DOWN

1 Bane
2 "_____ the Ahohite" (1 Chronicles 11:29)
3 Fee
4 "Ye have _____ your members" (Romans 6:19)
5 "The LORD. . .delivered me out of the _____ of the lion" (1 Samuel 17:37)
6 "Observe the month of _____" (Deuteronomy 16:1)
7 Ascend
8 "Seven times a day do I praise _____" (Psalm 119:164)
9 "Another shall. . ._____ himself" (Isaiah 44:5)
10 "He was buried in _____" (Judges 10:2)
11 "It is _____ for heaven and earth to pass" (Luke 16:17)
12 Daze
13 "They were troubled, and _____ away" (Psalm 48:5)
24 "By grace ye _____ saved" (Ephesians 2:5)
25 "Cain. . .dwelt in the land of _____" (Genesis 4:16)
27 "In a _____ it shall be made with oil" (Leviticus 6:21)
28 Mistake

*by Tonya Vilhauer*

29 "The family of _____ was taken" (1 Samuel 10:21)
30 Sod
32 License plate
34 "The son of _____, sons of Reuben" (Numbers 16:1)
36 Peat
37 "Joseph, . . .the son of _____" (Luke 3:23)
38 Josiah's father (Jeremiah 1:2)
39 "Then Israel _____ this song" (Numbers 21:17)
41 "He that eateth of their _____ dieth" (Isaiah 59:5)
42 King of Assyria (2 Kings 15:19)
43 Ahiam's father (2 Samuel 23:33)
44 "The children of _____" (Nehemiah 7:43)

46 "The other disciple did _____ Peter" (John 20:4)
50 "I. . .will _____ the caul of their heart" (Hosea 13:8)
51 Platter
52 "Children of Lod, Hadid, and _____" (Ezra 2:33)
53 Terminate
57 "Thou believest that there is _____ God" (James 2:19)
58 "They. . ._____ the sacrifices of the dead" (Psalm 106:28)
59 Pole
61 "_____, and Rekem, and Zur" (Joshua 13:21)
62 Allow

# PUZZLE 31

**ACROSS**

1 "Two cheeks, and the _____"
(Deuteronomy 18:3)
4 Nineteenth OT book (abbr.)
7 A male sheep
10 A son of Ulla (1 Chronicles 7:39)
12 "He must bring two _____ lambs and
one ewe lamb" (Leviticus 14:10 NIV)
13 A servant of the church at Cenchrea
(Romans 16:1)
15 "The _____ after his kind"
(Leviticus 11:14)
16 A son of Judah (1 Chronicles 2:3)
17 Sisera was captain of this host
(Judges 4:2)
18 "Mahli, and _____"
(1 Chronicles 23:23)
19 Gaddi's father (Numbers 13:11)
20 Not dead
21 Not easily found
22 Ahira's father (Numbers 1:15)
23 Battles are drawn on these
24 "I have come into my garden,
my _____, my bride"
(Song of Solomon 5:1 NIV)
26 Throw
28 Son of Joktan (Genesis 10:28)
30 Should
34 Out of danger
36 "As he saith also in _____"
(Romans 9:25)
39 "For ye tithe mint and _____"
(Luke 11:42)
40 "Of _____, the family of the
Arodites" (Numbers 26:17)
41 Sixteenth letter of the Hebrew
alphabet (heading for Psalm
119:121–128)
42 A king of Tyre (1 Chronicles 14:1)
44 Son of Eliphaz (Genesis 36:11)
45 "_____ the waters"
(Exodus 15:25)
46 "At the _____ of the city"
(Proverbs 8:3)
47 "And I will purge out from among
you the _____" (Ezekiel 20:38)
49 Beach surface

51 Strong trees
54 Roman emperor
58 "A great well that is in _____"
(1 Samuel 19:22)
62 The border went to here from
Remmonmethoar (Joshua 19:13)
64 Elevate
65 Made a mistake
66 Hand-driven boat propellers
67 Dirt prepared for crops
68 Test
69 Guilty or not guilty
70 In other words, no

**DOWN**

1 "They shall go to confusion together
that are _____ of idols"
(Isaiah 45:16)
2 A son of Haman (Esther 9:9)
3 The Spirit of God moved upon the
face of this
4 Zalaph's son (Nehemiah 3:30)
5 A son of Pashur (Ezra 10:22)
6 "Hodijah, Bani, _____"
(Nehemiah 10:13)
7 King of Syria (Isaiah 7:1)
8 Opposite of *below*
9 "Tarshish, _____, Marsena"
(Esther 1:14)
11 "Being absent now I write to them
which _____ have sinned"
(2 Corinthians 13:2)
12 "Jaakan to _____"
(Deuteronomy 10:6)
13 A son of Reuben (Genesis 46:9)
14 "Their border was Helkath, and
_____" (Joshua 19:25)
25 Gaal's father (Judges 9:26)
27 Small deer
29 "The _____ which is lent"
(1 Samuel 2:20)
31 Teeth
32 Injured
33 Rip
34 Identical
35 "_____, and Dumah"
(Joshua 15:52)

*by N. Teri Grottke*

37 "_____ down here" (Ruth 4:1)
38 Seth's son (Genesis 4:26)
42 "_____, and Ivah?" (Isaiah 37:13)
43 Relating to me
44 "Either good _____ bad" (Genesis 31:24)
45 This prophet appears on the Sistine Chapel (abbr.)
48 "All the country wept with a _____ voice" (2 Samuel 15:23)
50 Daughter of Caleb (1 Chronicles 2:49)
52 "A _____ and a flower" (Exodus 25:33)
53 Closure
55 "Come out of _____" (Romans 11:26)
56 China's continent
57 Depend on

58 To place
59 To violate an accepted standard of conduct
60 Weep
61 "_____ will reign for ever and ever" (Revelation 11:15 NIV)
63 "_____ there yet the treasures" (Micah 6:10)

# PUZZLE 32 — BIBLICAL SUCCESSION

*A melange of children, servants, robes, and retinues.*
*What do these have in common? It doesn't take special training to find out.*

**ACROSS**

1 "The seventh _____" (Revelation 8:1)
5 Letters at O'Hare (abbr.)
9 Job side benefits
14 "Eloi, Eloi, _____ sabachthani?" (Mark 15:34)
15 "Their hope will become a dying _____" (Job 11:20 NIV)
16 "Men condemned to die in the _____" (1 Corinthians 4:9 NIV)
17 "And she came to Jerusalem with _____" (1 Kings 10:2) (4 words)
20 _____ cavae (the two major veins)
21 Rani's wrap-around
22 British Inc. (abbr.)
23 Third tones of diatonic scales
25 "So shall thy _____ be" (Genesis 15:5)
28 "He armed his _____" (Abram's impromptu army, in Genesis 14:14) (2 words)
36 Heavy frost
37 Muscle spasm
38 Cancel a mission
39 Dentists organization (abbr.)
40 Billy Graham Center location
43 Film actress West
44 Metric prefix (hundredth)
46 "_____ voice from heaven" (Matthew 3:17) (2 words)
47 Green _____ plum
48 "_____ the way he should go" (Solomon's advice in Proverbs 22:6) (5 words)
52 "I was at _____" (Job 16:12)
53 "_____ not vain repetitions" (Matthew 6:7)
54 Colorado tribe
57 Book after Nehemiah (abbr., var.)
60 Coherent light
64 "And his train _____" (What Isaiah saw in Isaiah 6:1) (3 words)
68 Satellite path

69 Former monetary unit of Italy
70 Gaelic
71 "The chief _____ in the synagogues" (Matthew 23:6)
72 "_____ was a cunning hunter" (Genesis 25:27)
73 "__ __ garments" (Isaiah 63:1)

**DOWN**

1 Eastern European
2 Roof overhang
3 "Even so, _____" (Revelation 1:7)
4 Wyoming city
5 "If he asks for an _____?" (Luke 11:12 NIV)
6 Short for tarpaulins (sailors)
7 "And I saw as it were _____ of glass" (Revelation 15:2) (2 words)
8 Growing thinly
9 Tamp
10 "They do alway _____ in their heart" (Hebrews 3:10)
11 "For my flesh is _____ food" (John 6:55 NIV)
12 "_____ together in love" (Colossians 2:2)
13 "I stood upon the _____ of the sea" (Revelation 13:1)
18 "Glory _____ his holy name" (1 Chronicles 16:10) (2 words)
19 One who knots
24 "Adam...called his name _____" (Genesis 5:3)
26 John in Wales
27 Brylcreem quantity, usually
28 "The _____ of land that Jacob bought" (Joshua 24:32 NIV)
29 "His _____ shall fall backward" (Genesis 49:17)
30 "Look from the top of _____" (Song of Solomon 4:8)
31 "Lest ye _____" (Genesis 3:3)
32 *La* _____ (Milan opera house)
33 "You...sat like a _____ in the desert" (Jeremiah 3:2 NIV)

*by David K. Shortess*

34 _____-comedy play
35 Seventeenth-century Dutch painter
40 "You travel. . .to _____ single convert" (Matthew 23:15 NIV) (2 words)
41 Tic-_____ (says the clock)
42 Hawaiian island
45 "_____ them about thy neck" (Proverbs 6:21)
47 "Their feet. . ._____ like burnished bronze" (Ezekiel 1:7 NIV)
49 "They have _____ deceit" (Romans 3:13)
50 "Bray. . .with a _____" (Proverbs 27:22)
51 "Which had wintered in the _____" (Acts 28:11)
54 Andromedan transports? (abbr.)
55 "Bind the _____ of thine head" (Ezekiel 24:17)

56 Island of exile
58 "_____ I say then" (Galatians 5:16)
59 "To make _____ public example" (Matthew 1:19) (2 words)
61 Lively
62 "Or _____ I die" (Genesis 30:1)
63 "A _____ shaken with the wind" (Matthew 11:7)
65 "He. . ._____ the torches" (Judges 15:4–5 NIV)
66 Parisian ands
67 The nineteenth letter in the Greek alphabet

# PUZZLE 33

## ACROSS

1 To clothe
6 Father of Rachel and Leah (Genesis 29:16)
11 "_____ is like your people Israel" (2 Samuel 7:23 NIV)
14 Place at the edge of the wilderness (Exodus 13:20)
15 Cognizant
16 Hebrew for *embrace* (abbr.)
17 "The one with the _____ horses toward the west" (Zechariah 6:6 NIV)
18 Place in wilderness of Etham where the Israelites camped (Numbers 33:5–8)
19 When the Hebrew women gave birth in relation to midwives (Exodus 1:19)
20 "The parts of _____" (Acts 2:10)
22 "Of _____, the family of A[r]odites" (Numbers 26:17)
23 Distributed cards
26 "He shall be _____ away" (Job 20:8)
29 Walls of shrubs
30 "He. . .burnt up both the _____" (Judges 15:5)
31 Zorobabel's son (Matthew 1:13)
32 "All the hills shall _____" (Amos 9:13)
33 Means "the Lord's servant" in Hebrew (abbr.)
36 Birth till death
37 "Destitute of _____ food" (James 2:15)
39 Act
40 A son of Gad (Genesis 46:16)
41 Sister of a parent
42 A bird that is forbidden to be eaten (Leviticus 11:13–15)
43 Johanan's father (2 Kings 25:23)
45 Jael killed him (Judges 4:18–21)
46 "Thou _____ in the throne judging right" (Psalm 9:4)
47 Amasa's father (2 Samuel 17:25)
48 Detest
49 This place is on the left hand of Damascus (Genesis 14:15)
52 Hophni's father (1 Samuel 4:4)
53 Before (arch.)
55 Chalcol's father (1 Kings 4:31)
60 He was a prophet to the Northern Kingdom but a native of the Southern Kingdom (abbr., var.)
61 "See, here is _____" (Acts 8:36)
62 Chief among the captains of David's mighty men (2 Samuel 23:8)
63 Cooking vessel
64 The son of Zerah (1 Chronicles 6:41)
65 "Now faith is the substance of things _____ for" (Hebrews 11:1)

## DOWN

1 Ground moisture
2 Book of Ruth (abbr., var.)
3 A son of Benjamin (Genesis 46:21)
4 "The king _____ upon his royal throne" (Esther 5:1)
5 "And the LORD _____ a sweet savour" (Genesis 8:21)
6 Baby sheep
7 "I will take _____ the chariots from Ephraim" (Zechariah 9:10 NIV)
8 Elihu's father (Job 32:2)
9 Jether's son (1 Chronicles 7:38)
10 Jerusalem was this man's main concern (abbr.)
11 "_____ the body is, thither will the eagles be gathered together" (Luke 17:37)
12 "Gideon. . .pitched beside the well of _____" (Judges 7:1)
13 Ruth's son (Ruth 4:13–17)
21 Possessive pronoun
22 Question
23 "Name of _____" (Judges 1:11)
24 The building up of one's faith
25 A chill
27 Pure
28 Take action
29 "Lest he _____ thee to the judge" (Luke 12:58)

*by N. Teri Grottke*

30 "The _____ with the tongs"
(Isaiah 44:12)

34 "Shilshah, and Ithran, and _____"
(1 Chronicles 7:37)

35 "Of Harim, _____"
(Nehemiah 12:15)

37 Render therefore to all their _____"
(Romans 13:7)

38 "Get thee to _____, unto thine
own fields" (1 Kings 2:26)

39 Race

41 "_____ there yet the treasures"
(Micah 6:10)

42 "They. . .pitched in _____"
(Numbers 33:18)

44 Partook

45 "The children of _____"
(Nehemiah 7:47)

46 Nahshon's son (1 Chronicles 2:11)

48 "For in so doing thou shalt _____
coals of fire on his head"
(Romans 12:20)

50 Jerahmeel's son (1 Chronicles 2:25)

51 A son of Zophah
(1 Chronicles 7:36)

53 Reverent fear

54 Obese

56 Fuss

57 Your thigh is connected to this

58 Single

59 "_____, Hadid, and Ono"
(Ezra 2:33)

# PUZZLE 34

**ACROSS**

1 Adage
4 Dine
7 "Make thee an _____ of gopher wood" (Genesis 6:14)
10 Blackbird
12 Exceed
14 "_____ with joy receiveth it" (Matthew 13:20)
15 "Strangers of _____" (Acts 2:10)
16 "Solomon's servants: the children of _____" (Ezra 2:55)
17 Menahem's father (2 Kings 15:17)
18 "Jezreel, and Ishma, and _____" (1 Chronicles 4:3)
20 Mart
22 "Cut off from Ahab him that _____" (2 Kings 9:8)
24 "The _____, and the box tree together" (Isaiah 41:19)
25 "_____, lama sabachthani" (Mark 15:34)
26 "My lips shall _____ praise" (Psalm 119:171)
30 Libel
32 "Found him sitting under an _____" (1 Kings 13:14)
34 "Lest at any time thou _____ thy foot against a stone" (Matthew 4:6)
36 "Even with a _____ destruction" (Micah 2:10)
37 Gera's son (Judges 3:15)
40 "The word of God was preached of Paul at _____" (Acts 17:13)
41 "The children of _____ of Hezekiah" (Ezra 2:16)
42 Merodachbaladan's father (Isaiah 39:1)
44 Flurries
46 "The two and twentieth to _____" (1 Chronicles 24:17)
47 Platter
50 "A _____ of three years old" (Genesis 15:9)
51 Cleft

53 "_____ power is given unto me" (Matthew 28:18)
54 "Over the camels also was _____ the Ishmaelite" (1 Chronicles 27:30)
56 "Rejoicing in himself _____" (Galatians 6:4)
58 "They gave them the city of _____" (Joshua 21:11)
60 Facts
61 "God _____ it unto good" (Genesis 50:20)
62 Panorama
63 Storage building
64 "Like _____, who obeyed Abraham" (1 Peter 3:6)
65 Verily

**DOWN**

1 "Carry neither purse, nor _____, nor shoes" (Luke 10:4)
2 "Shuni, and Ezbon, Eri, and _____" (Genesis 46:16)
3 "The LORD. . .closed up all the _____" (Genesis 20:18)
4 Flight (abbr.)
5 "The LORD shall. . .bring to pass his _____" (Isaiah 28:21)
6 Pekoe
7 "Talmai, the children of _____" (Joshua 15:14)
8 "And they _____ upon the camels" (Genesis 24:61)
9 "Being _____ together in love" (Colossians 2:2)
11 Pekan
12 Bethrapha's father (1 Chronicles 4:12)
13 Boundary
14 Correspond
19 "From _____ to the wilderness" (Isaiah 16:1)
21 "Go to the _____, thou sluggard" (Proverbs 6:6)
23 Perdu
24 Handbags

by Tonya Vilhauer

27 "Judah shall yet again take _____" (2 Kings 19:30)
28 Brother of Jamin (1 Chronicles 2:27)
29 "Make their nobles like _____" (Psalm 83:11)
30 "What will ye see in the _____" (Song of Solomon 6:13)
31 Lug
33 "By grace ye _____ saved" (Ephesians 2:5)
35 "He that _____ a matter wisely shall find good" (Proverbs 16:20)
36 "And cut them with _____" (1 Chronicles 20:3)
38 "The children of _____" (Ezra 2:45)
39 Barrage
40 "She. . .crushed _____ foot against the wall" (Numbers 22:25)

43 "I _____ this well" (Genesis 21:30)
45 Lubricant
48 Malchijah's father (Nehemiah 3:11)
49 "His sword _____ in his hand" (Numbers 22:23)
50 "Thrice was I beaten with _____" (2 Corinthians 11:25)
52 "Between blood and blood, between _____" (Deuteronomy 17:8)
53 "There was one _____, a prophetess" (Luke 2:36)
55 Youngster
57 Row
58 "From Cuthah, and from _____" (2 Kings 17:24)
59 "For the _____ that is in the land of Assyria" (Isaiah 7:18)

# PUZZLE 35

## ACROSS

1 Filth
5 Increase
8 One of the Hebrew midwives (Exodus 1:15)
12 King Hoshea's father (2 Kings 15:30)
13 "They shall _____ God" (Matthew 5:8)
14 "For thy name's sake, O LORD, _____ mine iniquity; for it is great" (Psalm 25:11)
16 Employment pay
18 A son of Aaron (Exodus 6:23)
20 Fuss
21 Descendant of Jacob
23 "The _____ of truth shall be established for ever" (Proverbs 12:19)
24 To make a mistake
25 "They. . ._____ greedily after the error" (Jude 1:11)
26 Zibeon's son (1 Chronicles 1:40)
27 "And after him _____, Sallai" (Nehemiah 11:8)
30 "Jeremiah of _____" (Jeremiah 52:1)
32 To carry out directions
33 "Drink of _____ wine" (Song of Solomon 8:2)
35 Bind
36 The archangel (Jude 1:9)
38 "How is the gold become _____" (Lamentations 4:1)
41 Inside
42 These kind of men came from the east to find the King of the Jews
43 "_____ with the villages thereof" (2 Chronicles 28:18)
45 "They. . .were all baptized of him in the river of _____" (Mark 1:5)
47 "He that hath a _____ nose, or any thing superfluous" (Leviticus 21:18)
48 "Destroy _____ kings and people" (Ezra 6:12)
50 Son of Abdiel (1 Chronicles 5:15)
51 Boat paddle
52 "Coasts of Geshuri and _____" (Deuteronomy 3:14)
56 First mother
57 "Chalcol, and _____" (1 Kings 4:31)
58 Works
60 The spy from the tribe of Asher (Numbers 13)
62 A king of Midian (Numbers 31:8)
64 Riverbank (Exodus 2:5)
65 Foot covering
66 "As a lion in his _____" (Psalm 10:9)
67 "I _____ not" (Luke 17:9)

## DOWN

1 Ground moisture
2 "_____ the Ahohite" (1 Chronicles 11:29)
3 Worn-out clothing
4 "That the Son of God might be glorified _____" (John 11:4)
5 Arsenic (sym.)
6 "Lookest thou upon them that _____ treacherously" (Habakkuk 1:13)
7 "Name of _____" (Judges 1:11)
8 "His city was _____" (Genesis 36:39)
9 Abram's birthplace
10 A son of Haman (Esther 9:8–10)
11 Sister of Naham (1 Chronicles 4:19)
14 "They passed through _____" (Acts 15:3)
15 "_____ shall have distresses" (Ezekiel 30:16)
17 "Through faith also _____ herself received strength to conceive seed" (Hebrews 11:11)
19 Someone from Italy
22 A son of Gad (Genesis 46:16)
26 "Joshua was clothed with filthy garments, _____ stood" (Zechariah 3:3)
27 Received
28 King Hezekiah's mother (2 Kings 18:1–2)

*by N. Teri Grottke*

29 "The _____ that is in the land of Assyria" (Isaiah 7:18)
31 God of Babylon (Isaiah 46)
33 Good student
34 Twenty-first letter of the Greek alphabet
36 Prophet whose name means "Who is like the Lord?" (abbr.)
37 A son of Aaron (Exodus 6:23)
38 "God _____ tempt Abraham" (Genesis 22:1)
39 Biblical book of sixty-six chapters (abbr.)
40 Opposite of *women*
41 "_____ ye not" (Romans 11:2)
42 "For thou _____ bitter things against me" (Job 13:26)
43 "Chariots, and _____, and souls of men" (Revelation 18:13)

44 "David. . .came into the forest of _____" (1 Samuel 22:5)
45 "By his name _____" (Psalm 68:4)
46 "Jamin, and _____" (Genesis 46:10)
47 Enemies
49 Loaded (arch.)
53 David hid from Saul here
54 Person who inherits
55 Zechariah's father (Ezra 5:1)
57 Payment owed
59 Famous Betsy could do this
61 "_____, every one that thirsteth" (Isaiah 55:1)
63 Indium (sym.)

# PUZZLE 36 — A COMFORTING PROMISE

*"And surely I am with you always, to the very end of the age."*
MATTHEW 28:20 NIV

## ACROSS

1 "The sky is _____" (Matthew 16:2)
4 "Epicurean and _____ philosophers" (Acts 17:18 NIV)
9 "They _____ him" (Numbers 21:35)
14 "Shimei son of _____—in Benjamin" (1 Kings 4:18 NIV)
15 "But _____ man answers harshly" (Proverbs 18:23 NIV) (2 words)
16 Emanations
17 Start of a **QUOTE** (Psalm 62:5 NIV) (5 words)
20 Member of an American Indian people originally from Utah
21 Clear the board
22 "To abide _____ ever" (1 Kings 8:13) (2 words)
25 "You who _____ about the law" (Romans 2:23 NIV)
26 "And a _____ the breadth thereof" (Exodus 39:9)
30 British snack time
31 Uniform decoration
34 Third son of Jether (1 Chronicles 7:38)
35 "The _____ is a great city" (Genesis 10:12)
37 Robert Louis Stevenson initials
38 A bit crazy
40 **QUOTE**, cont'd from 17 Across (2 words)
42 **QUOTE**, cont'd from 40 Across
43 "He removed his _____" (Ruth 4:8 NIV)
45 Little Women author's monogram
46 Chedorlaomer was its king (Genesis 14:1)
49 "That _____ their tongues" (Jeremiah 23:31)
50 Glacial deposit
53 Seen at JFK
54 Atlantis org.
56 Georgia Office of Homeland Security (abbr.)
57 "Ye that. . .are heavy _____" (Matthew 11:28)
59 Young pigeon
61 Defunct orbiter
62 **QUOTE**, cont'd from 42 Across (4 words)
69 "I shall _____ sorrow" (Revelation 18:7) (2 words)
70 Refuse
71 "Prop" or "prof" ending
72 Ahasuerus's chief aide (Esther 3:1)
73 Hot South American music
74 End of the **QUOTE**, cont'd from 62 Across

## DOWN

1 Official on the field (abbr.)
2 Father of Phinehas (1 Samuel 1:3)
3 Son of Bilhah (Genesis 35:25)
4 *No Exit* playwright
5 "And under every green _____" (1 Kings 14:23)
6 Quebecer's ending, in Quebec
7 Jaundice
8 Choir-related
9 "Say only what the LORD _____?" (Numbers 24:13 NIV)
10 Ruminates
11 Cortez's quest
12 Sigma follower
13 Course for new arrivals (abbr.)
18 Two of a kind
19 Strait joining the Atlantic and Pacific
22 "Of _____ own accord" (Leviticus 25:5)
23 Teachers organization (abbr.)
24 "And there shall be _____" (Matthew 24:7)
25 "Every head shall be _____" (Jeremiah 48:37)
27 "Living in your _____ houses" (Haggai 1:4 NIV)
28 "We. . ._____ come to worship him" (Matthew 2:2)
29 "And he said, _____; but thou didst laugh" (Genesis 18:15)
32 Play introduction

*by David K. Shortess*

33 "Is there any thing _____ hard for me?" (Jeremiah 32:27)

36 "Alway, even unto the _____" (Psalm 119:112)

39 "Even thou wast as _____ of them" (Obadiah 1:11)

41 Herd of whales

42 Friends in Paris

43 "The _____ waxed hot" (Exodus 16:21)

44 "All hold John _____ prophet" (Matthew 21:26) (2 words)

45 "For a _____ kid" (Numbers 15:11) (3 words)

47 "They. . ._____ the sacrifices of the dead" (Psalm 106:28)

48 "And have put on the new _____" (Colossians 3:10)

51 Reciprocates

52 Elijah gave him his mantle (1 Kings 19:19)

55 "And engrave on it _____ seal" (Exodus 28:36 NIV) (3 words)

58 Sandy's two-cent's worth

60 M–R reverse connection

61 "A _____ of meat from the king" (2 Samuel 11:8)

62 Intermedin, initially

63 "_____, though I walk" (Psalm 23:4)

64 "Round about the _____ thereof" (Exodus 28:33)

65 Last OT book (abbr.)

66 Stadium cheer

67 "I put it _____ have washed my feet" (Song of Solomon 5:3) (2 words)

68 Word preceding Psalm 119:97

## ACROSS

1 "Zechariah, _____, and Jaaziel" (1 Chronicles 15:18)
4 "Who layeth the _____ of his chambers" (Psalm 104:3)
9 "_____ lay at his feet until the morning" (Ruth 3:14)
12 "Doth God take care for _____" (1 Corinthians 9:9)
14 Bathsheba's first husband (2 Samuel 11:3)
15 "_____ not unto thine own understanding" (Proverbs 3:5)
17 Dimensions
18 Pagan goddess of the Ephesians
19 Otherwise
20 Mountain where Jesus liked to pray
22 "Prove me now _____" (Malachi 3:10)
24 "They _____ against me" (Hosea 7:14)
25 "Ye shall point out for you mount _____" (Numbers 34:7)
26 "All the _____ of it" (Numbers 9:3)
30 Bird homes
34 Staff
37 "Of Hena, and _____?" (2 Kings 19:13)
39 A judge of Israel (Judges 3:15)
41 Snare
43 A son of Japheth (Genesis 10:2)
45 Weed of grain fields especially of biblical times
46 "Restore all that was _____" (2 Kings 8:6)
47 "_____ not the world" (1 John 2:15)
48 "I saw a _____ heaven" (Revelation 21:1)
49 One of Shaharaim's wives (1 Chronicles 8:8)
52 "And he must _____ go through Samaria" (John 4:4)
55 Jether's son (1 Chronicles 7:38)
57 This many souls were saved in the ark
61 "Azariah, Raamiah, _____" (Nehemiah 7:7)

## DOWN

66 "Mattithiah, and Shema, and _____" (Nehemiah 8:4)
67 Was indebted to
68 "They set the altar upon his _____" (Ezra 3:3)
70 "Helkath, and _____, and Beten" (Joshua 19:25)
71 Farm building
72 Son of Ribai (1 Chronicles 11:31)
73 "Ahijah, Hanan, _____" (Nehemiah 10:26)
74 Exclamation of affirmation
75 Enan's son (Numbers 1:15)
76 "God created _____ heaven" (Genesis 1:1)

## DOWN

1 Baalam's father (2 Peter 2:15)
2 Banish
3 "Jiphtah, and Ashnah, and _____" (Joshua 15:43)
4 Flower beginnings
5 A son of Gad (Genesis 46:16)
6 Zibeon's son (1 Chronicles 1:40)
7 "Fifteen shekels, shall be your _____" (Ezekiel 45:12)
8 "I am the rose of _____" (Song of Solomon 2:1)
9 Killed (arch.)
10 Jesus' grandfather (Luke 3:23)
11 From _____ to west
13 "For if ye do these things, ye shall _____ fall" (2 Peter 1:10)
16 Restored the walls in just fifty-two days (abbr.)
21 Phinehas's father (1 Samuel 4:4)
23 Before (poet.)
27 Letter written by Paul to one person (abbr.)
28 Great wickedness
29 "At Lydda and _____" (Acts 9:35)
31 To place
32 "Now the serpent was more subtil _____ any beast" (Genesis 3:1)
33 Certain
34 Not left hand but _____ (abbr.)

*by N. Teri Grottke*

35 "The heads of _____ and Zeeb" (Judges 7:25)
36 Son of Zerah (1 Chronicles 2:6)
38 Has ownership
40 Ground moisture
42 David wrote these (abbr., var.)
44 "_____ that ye refuse" (Hebrews 12:25)
50 A male sheep
51 "Mount Sinai in _____" (Galatians 4:25)
53 "A lion in his _____" (Psalm 10:9)
54 Returning exiles—the children of _____ (Ezra 2:44)
56 Shamgar's father (Judges 3:31)
58 Goliath was one
59 The king of Assyria took Israel here in their captivity (2 Kings 17:6)

60 Yours (arch.)
61 A city of the priests (1 Samuel 22:19)
62 "Then he was no more, because God took him _____" (Genesis 5:24 NIV)
63 In this place
64 "Of Harim, _____" (Nehemiah 12:15)
65 Rephaiah's father (1 Chronicles 4:42)
66 Largest continent
69 "O Lord, let your _____ be attentive" (Nehemiah 1:11 NIV)

# PUZZLE 38

**ACROSS**

1 "Zur, and Hur, and _____, which were dukes" (Joshua 13:21)
5 "Used curious _____ brought their books" (Acts 19:19)
9 Buns
10 "_____ the chancellor" (Ezra 4:8)
12 "The vine of _____" (Isaiah 16:8)
13 "Shalt not be to him as an _____" (Exodus 22:25)
15 "They _____ in the dry places like a river" (Psalm 105:41)
16 "The pen of the _____ is in vain" (Jeremiah 8:8)
18 "_____ joy of the LORD" (Nehemiah 8:10)
20 "Thou shalt not approach to his wife: she is thine _____" (Leviticus 18:14)
22 "The brook of _____" (Psalm 83:9)
23 "Thy rod and thy staff _____ comfort me" (Psalm 23:4)
24 "Worthy is the Lamb that was _____" (Revelation 5:12)
26 Dine
27 "Esther _____, and stood before the king" (Esther 8:4)
28 "Malchishua, Abinadab, and _____" (1 Chronicles 8:33)
30 Ruler of the half part of Keilah (Nehemiah 3:18)
32 Coxa
33 "Bethel on the west, and _____ on the east" (Genesis 12:8)
34 "The people gat them by _____" (2 Samuel 19:3)
38 "The Beerothites fled to _____" (2 Samuel 4:3)
42 Army
43 Frozen water
45 "The _____ that the king rideth upon" (Esther 6:8)
46 "God had sworn with an _____ to him" (Acts 2:30)
47 Nail heads
49 Mellow
50 Wood

51 "As when one _____ out water" (Proverbs 17:14)
53 "I _____ down under his shadow with great delight" (Song of Solomon 2:3)
54 "Husham of the land of _____" (Genesis 36:34)
56 "The merchants of Sheba and _____" (Ezekiel 27:22)
58 "Whose soever sins ye _____, they are remitted unto them" (John 20:23)
59 Nathan's father (1 Chronicles 2:36)
60 "Straightway the spirit _____ him" (Mark 9:20)
61 Reck

**DOWN**

1 "Will a man _____ God?" (Malachi 3:8)
2 "Under oaks and poplars and _____" (Hosea 4:13)
3 Ebony
4 "_____, whom she bear" (1 Chronicles 7:14)
5 "The son of Hesed, in _____" (1 Kings 4:10)
6 "_____ between Nineveh and Calah" (Genesis 10:12)
7 "_____ saith thy son Joseph" (Genesis 45:9)
8 "At the gate of _____" (2 Kings 11:6)
9 "Amnon, and _____, Benhanan" (1 Chronicles 4:20)
11 Procedure
12 "_____ uncle said unto him" (1 Samuel 10:14)
14 "Joanna, which was the son of _____" (Luke 3:27)
15 Level
17 A prophet son of Amoz (2 Kings 19:20) (abbr.)
19 "Saul _____ David" (1 Samuel 18:9)
21 "Likewise from _____, and from Chun" (1 Chronicles 18:8)

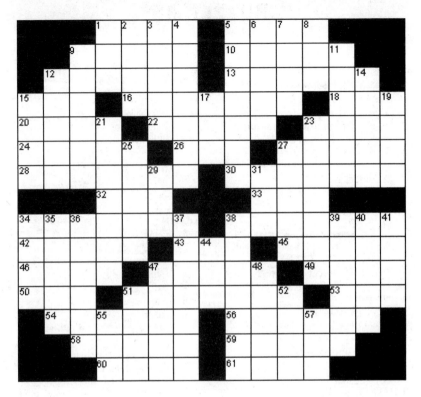

*by Tonya Vilhauer*

23 "Judas Iscariot, which also was the _____" (Luke 6:16)
25 "His _____ of brass" (Daniel 7:19)
27 Father of Shamgar (Judges 3:31)
29 Prone
31 "Naaman, _____, and Rosh" (Genesis 46:21)
34 "The Chaldeans, Pekod, and _____" (Ezekiel 23:23)
35 Sippet
36 "_____ put on her royal apparel" (Esther 5:1)
37 "Send me Uriah the _____" (2 Samuel 11:6)
38 "Sharaim, and Adithaim, and _____" (Joshua 15:36)
39 "Parmashta, and _____, and Aridai" (Esther 9:9)

40 "Michael, and _____, and Joha" (1 Chronicles 8:16)
41 Assemble
44 Saw
47 "Fir trees of _____" (Ezekiel 27:5)
48 "All my _____ shall Tychicus declare unto you" (Colossians 4:7)
51 "Eloi, Eloi, _____ sabachthani?" (Mark 15:34)
52 "If the world _____ you" (John 15:18)
55 "And God _____ Balaam" (Numbers 23:4)
57 Very angry

# PUZZLE 39

## ACROSS

1 The city Lot fled to (Genesis 19:22–23)
5 A great distance
9 "She. . .daubed it with slime and with _____" (Exodus 2:3)
14 Along with
15 "_____ the door after her" (2 Samuel 13:17)
16 Amasa's father (2 Samuel 17:25)
17 Hold back (arch.)
19 Bed covering
20 Area near Babylon (2 Kings 17:24)
21 "We _____ not those things which we have wrought" (2 John 1:8)
22 "Thou. . .hast fenced me with bones and _____" (Job 10:11)
23 "The children of _____" (Ezra 2:52)
25 She left Peter at the door (Acts 12:13–14)
27 Brother of Shammai (1 Chronicles 2:28)
29 Conspicuous
33 "Hammoleketh bare _____" (1 Chronicles 7:18)
36 Son of Micah (1 Chronicles 8:35)
38 Exclamation of affirmation
39 "_____ not unto thine own understanding" (Proverbs 3:5)
40 "_____ wings of a great eagle" (Revelation 12:14)
41 Spiders spin these
42 To perform
43 Saw
45 One of David's priests (1 Kings 1:8)
46 Son of Aaron (Exodus 6:23)
48 Mix
50 Son of Jahdai (1 Chronicles 2:47)
52 High respect (var.)
56 Make unclean
59 Symbol of power
61 Make good _____ of
62 Another name for Jerusalem (Isaiah 29:1)
63 Former inhabitants of Jerusalem
65 Spear
66 "Nevertheless _____ heart was perfect" (1 Kings 15:14)
67 "Give thyself no _____" (Lamentations 2:18)
68 Finished
69 "All the hills shall _____" (Amos 9:13)
70 "Many. . .used curious _____" (Acts 19:19)

## DOWN

1 Sibling of Jeush (2 Chronicles 11:19)
2 Oily fruit
3 "Children of _____" (Ezra 2:50)
4 Staff
5 In an overseas country
6 Enemies
7 "Nor _____ the thing that is gone out of my lips" (Psalm 89:34)
8 Most people use their _____ of the two (2 words) (abbr.)
9 "They came to Antioch in _____" (Acts 13:14)
10 "Kedesh, and Hazor, and _____" (Joshua 15:23)
11 You (arch.)
12 Team
13 Headcovers
18 "_____ and Medad" (Numbers 11:27)
22 "Let fall also _____ of the handfuls" (Ruth 2:16)
24 "Smote _____, and Dan" (1 Kings 15:20)
26 "Joanna the wife of Chuza _____ steward" (Luke 8:3)
28 Clothing
30 Looked at
31 "Men of the other _____" (Nehemiah 7:33)
32 Job
33 "_____ the Ahohite" (1 Chronicles 11:29)
34 Adherents of creed

*by N. Teri Grottke*

35 "That which _____ been is named already" (Ecclesiastes 6:10)
37 Reverent fear
41 To tell about danger
43 "The LORD _____ a sweet savour" (Genesis 8:21)
44 Little color
45 "For _____ sake will I not hold my peace" (Isaiah 62:1)
47 Each
49 "He would _____ out a little from the land" (Luke 5:3)
51 "He thought on _____ things" (Matthew 1:20)
53 "Cast ye the unprofitable servant into _____ darkness" (Matthew 25:30)
54 Utilizes (arch.)
55 Takes a break

56 "Valley of Shaveh, which is the king's _____" (Genesis 14:17)
57 "Shuthelah: of _____" (Numbers 26:36)
58 Opposite of *lose*
60 Son of Joktan (Genesis 10:26–29)
63 Like jelly
64 "_____ the son of Ikkesh" (2 Samuel 23:26)

# PUZZLE 40 — FORTIFIED ON ALL SIDES

## ACROSS

1 "As the deer _____ for streams of water" (Psalm 42:1 NIV)
6 Tolkien creature
9 WW II battle site in France (2 words) (abbr.)
13 Howdy in HI
14 "He shall not go out to _____" (Deuteronomy 24:5)
15 "And _____ went before the ark" (2 Samuel 6:4)
16 **FIRST SIDE:** "And there stood a watchman on the _____" (2 Kings 9:17) (3 words)
19 "And the king sat upon his _____ at other times" (1 Samuel 20:25) (2 words)
20 Military address (abbr.)
21 "They brought the _____" (Mark 12:16 NIV)
23 Units of resistance
25 Home of the Globe and Mail
27 "He is _____ creature" (2 Corinthians 5:17) (2 words)
30 "_____, our eye hath seen it" (Psalm 35:21)
32 "But the _____ charged them" (Mark 7:36) (2 words)
33 "Are you not _____ men" (1 Corinthians 3:4 NIV)
34 "_____ shadow of death" (Job 34:22)
35 "The _____ of man" (Psalm 144:3)
36 "_____ of all creatures" (Genesis 7:15 NIV)
38 "The street of the city _____ pure gold" (Revelation 21:21)
40 "And _____ out heaven with the span" (Isaiah 40:12)
44 "And all that handle the _____" (Ezekiel 27:29)
46 Big snake
48 Designated part
49 "For with my _____ passed over" (Genesis 32:10) (2 words)
52 "There _____ in a window" (Acts 20:9)
53 "Each has its _____" (Song of Solomon 6:6 NIV)
54 "Thou shalt not _____ unto him" (Deuteronomy 13:8)
56 Perform again
58 "His _____ also was like the beryl" (Daniel 10:6)
59 "They neither _____ nor reap" (Luke 12:24)
61 "When the _____ comes" (Matthew 19:28 NCV) (2 words)
65 **SECOND SIDE:** "Israel. . .spread his tent beyond _____" (Genesis 35:21) (4 words)
68 Whet
69 "For if _____ not away" (John 16:7) (2 words)
70 "_____ trying to please men" (Galatians 1:10 NIV) (3 words)
71 British gun
72 "Eat _____ of it raw" (Exodus 12:9)
73 German steel center

## DOWN

1 Servings of butter
2 Burn balm
3 "_____ certain man was sick" (John 11:1) (2 words)
4 **THIRD SIDE:** "From _____ even unto the border of Ethiopia" (Ezekiel 29:10) (4 words)
5 Wife of Abraham (Genesis 17:15)
6 "After their _____ lusts" (2 Peter 3:3)
7 Indian prince
8 "Men _____ in unawares" (Jude 1:4)
9 Old patriotic organization (abbr.)
10 **FOURTH SIDE:** "Fortified cities and against _____" (Zephaniah 1:16 NIV) (3 words)
11 "Neither _____ to another" (Leviticus 19:11) (2 words)
12 Small round bodies set within sedimentary rock
17 "What _____ the better" (Ecclesiastes 6:11) (2 words)
18 Runs fast
22 "In the days of _____" (Luke 17:26)
24 "Who will _____ us any good" (Psalm 4:6)
26 "And yet there is _____" (Luke 14:22)
27 Power booster
28 Teachers organization (abbr.)

*by David K. Shortess*

29 "Of _____, the family of the Erites" (Numbers 26:16)

31 "Cretans and _____—we hear" (Acts 2:11 NIV)

37 "But for you it is _____" (Philippians 3:1)

39 "Though you _____ like the eagle" (Obadiah 1:4 NIV)

41 "They are quenched as _____" (Isaiah 43:17)

42 Samuel's "dad"

43 "A _____ of dragons" (Jeremiah 10:22)

45 Oxydol rival

47 "I _____ pleasant bread" (Daniel 10:3) (2 words)

49 Non-arts degree, sometimes (abbr.)

50 "Let him go free for his _____ sake" (Exodus 21:27)

51 "The anger _____ displeasure" (Deuteronomy 9:19) (2 words)

55 "I became like a Jew, _____ the Jews" (1 Corinthians 9:20 NIV) (2 words)

57 Robinson Crusoe author

60 "Lord, to whom shall _____" (John 6:68) (2 words)

62 Cities in Ohio and Oklahoma

63 "Eat some of my _____" (Genesis 27:31 NIV)

64 The Emerald Isle

66 "Joseph's _____ brethren went" (Genesis 42:3)

67 "A tree that will not _____" (Isaiah 40:20)

# PUZZLE 41

## ACROSS

1 "_____ was of the king's seed in Edom" (1 Kings 11:14)
3 Cooking vessel
6 Attached to the shoulder
9 "The name thereof _____" (Judges 1:26)
10 "Anab, and Eshtemoh, and _____" (Joshua 15:50)
12 "His spirit came _____" (Judges 15:19)
14 A son of Gad (Genesis 46:16)
15 "We came to Myra, a city of _____" (Acts 27:5)
17 Hurry
18 "The melody of thy _____" (Amos 5:23)
20 Elderly
21 "Of the _____ Ruth" (Ruth 1:4)
22 No
23 Humanity
25 Get older
26 Nobelium (sym.)
27 "While their feast _____" (Judges 14:17)
31 One of three postexilic prophets (abbr.)
32 A son of Pashur (Ezra 10:22)
35 Vision-impaired priest (1 Samuel 3:2)
36 After Nahum (abbr.)
37 The father of Ethan (1 Chronicles 6:44)
38 Appendage
39 Single
40 The home of the Hebrews in Egypt
41 "Against Jerusalem, _____" (Ezekiel 26:2)
42 "Who hath _____ you to flee from the wrath to come" (Luke 3:7)
44 Arsenic (sym.)
45 A son of Jacob (Genesis 35:26)
46 Joab's brother (2 Samuel 2:18)
49 A temple gate (2 Kings 11:6)
50 A city in Benjamin (Joshua 18:21–28)
53 To consume

54 "Thou settest a print upon the _____ of my feet" (Job 13:27)
57 Abraham's father (Luke 3:34)
58 "Have I received any _____ to blind mine eyes" (1 Samuel 12:3)
60 Large lake
61 David fought the Syrians here (2 Samuel 10:17)
62 Prophet
63 "He _____ horns" (Habakkuk 3:4)
64 "Shimei, and _____, and the mighty men" (1 Kings 1:8)
65 Commanded militarily
66 "Say in their hearts, _____" (Psalm 35:25)

## DOWN

1 Jaroah's son (1 Chronicles 5:14)
2 "Encamped at _____" (Numbers 33:35)
3 "The sick of the _____" (Mark 2:9)
4 No matter which
5 "Be diligent to come unto me to _____" (Titus 3:12)
6 Type of quartz (pl.)
7 Hasty
8 "Very last _____" (Luke 12:59)
9 Book of ceremonial laws (abbr.)
11 "Whosoever shall compel thee to go a _____, go with him twain" (Matthew 5:41)
12 Aholibah's sister (Ezekiel 23:4)
13 Saul's grandfather (1 Chronicles 8:33)
16 Fuss
19 Eliasaph's father (Numbers 3:24)
24 "The _____ of Jericho" (2 Kings 25:5)
25 "Look from the top of _____" (Song of Solomon 4:8)
26 "The children of _____, six hundred fifty and two" (Ezra 2:60)
28 "Telmelah, _____, Cherub, Addon" (Nehemiah 7:61)
29 A son of Zabad (1 Chronicles 7:21)
30 Bore
33 Burnt residue

*by N. Teri Grottke*

34 Zerubbabel's father (Haggai 1:1)
36 "_____ shall we escape"
    (Hebrews 2:3)
40 A son of Jahdai (1 Chronicles 2:47)
41 A chill
43 Ezbai's son (1 Chronicles 11:37)
47 The author of this NT book is
    unknown (abbr.)
48 Hearing organs
49 "A _____ to take fire"
    (Isaiah 30:14)
50 Right hand (abbr.)
51 "Sons of _____" (1 Chronicles 7:12)
52 "Kill every _____ among the little
    ones" (Numbers 31:17)
55 Rachel's sister
56 Unhappy
59 Buzzing stinger

# PUZZLE 42

## ACROSS

1 "Even with a _____ destruction" (Micah 2:10)
5 A great distance
9 "From _____ to the wilderness" (Isaiah 16:1)
13 Wrongdoing
14 Cush's son (Genesis 10:7)
15 "They shall say in all the highways, _____" (Amos 5:16)
16 To make right
17 "Adonijah, Bigvai, _____" (Nehemiah 10:16)
18 Fewer
19 "Gave the _____" (Nehemiah 8:8)
20 Group
21 Geuel's father (Numbers 13:15)
22 "He sold them into the hand of _____" (1 Samuel 12:9)
24 Level
26 Alchitran
27 Hymns
29 Voyage
30 "The son of _____" (Nehemiah 11:13)
35 Faultless
39 "To the moon, and to the _____" (2 Kings 23:5)
40 Individually
41 Sick
42 "Goeth out to Remmonmethoar to _____" (Joshua 19:13)
43 "Tread down the wicked in _____ place" (Job 40:12)
44 "At the name of Jesus every _____ should bow" (Philippians 2:10)
45 "The son of _____" (Luke 3:28)
46 Book of creation (abbr.)
48 Buss
50 "Esau was a cunning _____" (Genesis 25:27)
53 "They. . ._____ the sacrifices of the dead" (Psalm 106:28)
54 Reverence
57 Confident

58 "With a _____ round about the hole" (Exodus 39:23)
60 Mutineer
62 "He that eateth of their _____ dieth" (Isaiah 59:5)
63 "The burning _____" (Leviticus 26:16)
64 Gad's son (Genesis 46:16)
65 Assemble
66 "Rulers of _____" (Exodus 18:21)
67 "The cattle upon a thousand _____" (Psalm 50:10)

## DOWN

1 "Mattathias, which was the son of _____" (Luke 3:26)
2 "Upon thy people, and into thine _____" (Exodus 8:3)
3 "It shall be both scoured, and _____ in water" (Leviticus 6:28)
4 "Submit yourselves unto the _____" (1 Peter 5:5)
5 "Nevertheless _____ heart was perfect" (1 Kings 15:14)
6 _____ government
7 Shephatiah's father (2 Samuel 3:4)
8 "They _____ in the dry places like a river" (Psalm 105:41)
9 "The son of _____" (Luke 3:35)
10 "The faith of God's _____" (Titus 1:1)
11 "Zeboim, even unto _____" (Genesis 10:19)
12 "The son of _____" (1 Chronicles 6:37)
16 "Thy King cometh, sitting on an _____ colt" (John 12:15)
21 King of Moab (2 Kings 3:4)
23 Swiftly
25 "Are ye unworthy to judge the _____ matters" (1 Corinthians 6:2)
28 "Ye that _____ in judgment" (Judges 5:10)
29 Arcane
31 "There was one _____, a prophetess" (Luke 2:36)

*by Tonya Vilhauer*

32 "In the morning sow thy _____"
   (Ecclesiastes 11:6)
33 "They came to the threshingfloor
   of _____" (Genesis 50:10)
34 Zoheth's father
   (1 Chronicles 4:20)
35 Noddle
36 NT book after Galatians (abbr.)
37 "Wheat and the _____ were not
   smitten" (Exodus 9:32)
38 "Thou _____ them out of thine
   own heart" (Nehemiah 6:8)
39 "Canst thou bind the sweet
   influences of _____" (Job 38:31)
41 "I would not write with paper and
   _____" (2 John 1:12)
47 Jeroboam's father (2 Kings 15:18)
49 "Beriah, and _____ their sister"
   (Genesis 46:17)

50 Gigantic
51 "The Pharisees began to _____
   him vehemently" (Luke 11:53)
52 Fury
54 Cain's brother
55 Healthy
56 Asked for a double portion of
   Elijah's spirit (abbr., var.)
57 "The son of _____, which was the
   son of Noe" (Luke 3:36)
59 Joshua's father (Joshua 2:1)
61 "Of _____, the family of the
   Erites" (Numbers 26:16)

# PUZZLE 43

**ACROSS**

1 Panhandle
4 A Canaanite city (Joshua 11:21)
8 "Dwelling was from _____"
   (Genesis 10:30)
13 Sadoc's father (Matthew 1)
15 Elihu's father (1 Samuel 1:14)
16 Fire product
17 "The glory of the _____ is one"
   (1 Corinthians 15:40)
19 "Only the _____ of Dagon was left
   to him" (1 Samuel 5:4)
20 "Ard, the family of the _____"
   (Numbers 26:40)
21 "_____ sister was Timna"
   (Genesis 36:22)
23 "Sister in law is _____ back"
   (Ruth 1:15)
24 Not dry
25 "God _____ be tempted with evil"
   (James 1:13)
28 "The howling thereof unto _____"
   (Isaiah 15:8)
33 Kish's father (1 Samuel 9:1)
34 "_____ of spices"
   (Song of Solomon 6:2)
35 Prophet father of Maher-shalal-
   hash-baz (abbr.)
36 Real estate
37 A son of Jahdai (1 Chronicles 2:47)
38 A child of Shobal (Genesis 36:23)
39 Archenemy of Haman (three letter
   abbr.)
40 A son of Judah (1 Chronicles 2:3)
41 "Saul leaned upon his _____"
   (2 Samuel 1:6)
42 "But if any man think that he _____
   himself" (1 Corinthians 7:36)
45 "From _____ come wars and
   fightings among you" (James 4:1)
46 Abraham's nephew
47 A city of Hadarezer
   (1 Chronicles 18:8)
48 Hunger
51 "He was of the house and _____ of
   David" (Luke 2:4)
55 Azor's son (Matthew 1:14)

56 Done away with
58 Get up
59 Thorny flower
60 Exhaust
61 "I saw the _____" (Habakkuk 3:7)
62 Female sheep
63 Boat paddle

**DOWN**

1 "Valley of _____" (Psalm 84:6)
2 Jeshua's son (Nehemiah 3:19)
3 Precious metal
4 *Attention* (Dutch)
5 "The _____ of a whip"
   (Nahum 3:2)
6 "Against Jerusalem, _____"
   (Ezekiel 26:2)
7 A male bovine
8 Lord
9 "Who remembered us in our low
   _____" (Psalm 136:23)
10 Ostracize
11 Edges of garments
12 Type of snake
14 "Ye have _____ as kings without
   us" (1 Corinthians 4:8)
18 Small chair
22 Be indebted to (arch.)
25 A faithful spy (Numbers 14:6)
26 To humble
27 "In the _____ day"
   (Leviticus 23:32)
28 A son of Benjamin (Genesis 46:21)
29 First garden
30 Flax cloth
31 Abraham's heir
32 Abram lived in this plain
   (Genesis 13:18)
34 Not straight
37 Rhymers
38 "Thou _____ thine hand"
   (Psalm 104:28)
41 A son of Gad (Genesis 46:16)
43 "_____ thou persuadest me to be a
   Christian" (Acts 26:28)
44 "The _____ of them and of the
   chief priests prevailed" (Luke 23:23)

*by N. Teri Grottke*

45 "And _____ I was speaking"
(Daniel 9:20)
47 "They sailed _____ by Crete"
(Acts 27:13)
48 "_____ ye well" (Acts 15:29)
49 Returned exiles—children of _____
(Ezra 2:15)
50 Rabbit
52 A son of Abinadab (2 Samuel 6:3)
53 A son of Benjamin (Genesis 46:21)
54 "Mahli, and _____"
(1 Chronicles 23:23)
55 "The Egyptians _____ at their own
table" (Genesis 43:32 NLT)
57 Arrow ejector

# PUZZLE 44 — MAN'S WAY OR GOD'S WAY

## ACROSS

1 Git outta here!
6 Relating to style or manner
11 What will be, will be—*Che sarà*, _____
15 Start of a **QUOTE** from Proverbs 14:12 NIV
16 "And behold, _____ horse" (Revelation 6:8) (2 words)
17 "In heaven _____ earth" (Deuteronomy 3:24) (2 words)
18 Capital of Morocco
19 "And _____ foot" (Mark 6:33 NIV) (2 words)
20 "She opened it and saw the _____" (Exodus 2:6 NIV)
21 **QUOTE**, cont'd from 15 Across (5 words)
24 "One beka _____ person, that is" (Exodus 38:26 NIV)
25 "The _____ of hell and of death" (Revelation 1:18)
26 "He that planted the _____" (Psalm 94:9)
27 "And wilt thou _____ it up in three days?" (John 2:20)
28 "That which was _____" (Matthew 18:11)
30 "The fourth part of a _____" (2 Kings 6:25)
33 Tribal Kenyans
36 "The son of _____" (Job 25:6)
37 "Children of _____ men" (Job 30:8)
38 **QUOTE**, cont'd from 21 Across (6 words)
42 July times in NY
43 "Stricken in _____" (Joshua 23:1)
44 "And _____ rod that budded" (Hebrews 9:4)
45 _____ Plaines, Illinois
46 "So Tibni died, and _____ reigned" (1 Kings 16:22)
48 Use a crystal ball
49 *Angle* or *pod* prefix
50 Swiss river
51 Sound of pleasure

54 **QUOTE**, cont'd from 38 Across (5 words)
59 Greek god of war
60 "It is _____ am Alpha and Omega" (Revelation 21:6) (2 words)
61 "Not for your _____ do I this" (Ezekiel 36:32)
62 "Even where Satan's _____ is" (Revelation 2:13)
63 _____ Island, one-time immigrant exam station
64 "One jot _____ tittle" (Matthew 5:18) (2 words)
65 "And _____ for your flocks" (Numbers 32:24 NIV)
66 End of the **QUOTE**, cont'd from 54 Across
67 Slang expression of disgust

## DOWN

1 "Lest I _____ her naked" (Hosea 2:3)
2 "And let the angel of the LORD _____ them" (Psalm 35:5)
3 Steel in concrete
4 "I got _____ deal!" (unfair treatment) (2 words)
5 "And he said unto _____, and eat it up" (Revelation 10:9) (3 words)
6 "Antipas was my faithful _____" (Revelation 2:13)
7 Moonfish
8 "Of the tribe of _____ craftsman" (Exodus 38:23 NIV) (2 words)
9 "There was also _____" (Joshua 17:1) (2 words)
10 Magnifiers
11 "Be ye therefore _____" (1 Peter 4:7)
12 "And _____ on every altar" (Numbers 23:14) (2 words)
13 "And he took one of his _____" (Genesis 2:21)
14 "Is _____ thing too hard for the LORD" (Genesis 18:14)
22 "Eat nothing made with _____" (Exodus 12:20 NIV)
23 "For thou shalt _____ the labour of thine hands" (Psalm 128:2)
27 Stadium cheers

*by David K. Shortess*

28 "And the _____ walk" (Matthew 11:5)
29 "Put it _____ reed" (Matthew 27:48) (2 words)
30 Roman politician who was opposed to Julius Caesar
31 "For _____ the days that were before the flood" (Matthew 24:38) (2 words)
32 Hur, -Gay, and Franklin
33 TV's talking horse (2 words)
34 "Joshua son of Nun, Moses' _____" (Joshua 1:1 NIV)
35 Ranking NCOs (abbr.)
36 "_____ from the east came to Jerusalem" (Matthew 2:1 NIV)
37 "Canaan, there shalt thou _____ me" (Genesis 50:5)
39 "And all that handle the _____, the mariners" (Ezekiel 27:29)
40 Mother-of-pearl
41 "And she conceived, and _____" (Isaiah 8:3) (3 words)
46 "And my people the _____" (Jeremiah 6:27 NIV)

47 "For to be carnally _____ is death" (Romans 8:6)
48 British Columbia First Nation tribe
49 "The LORD _____ the heart" (Proverbs 17:3 NIV)
50 "And _____ up" (Revelation 10:10) (2 words)
51 "Above all that we _____ think" (Ephesians 3:20) (2 words)
52 "When a man dieth in _____" (Numbers 19:14) (2 words)
53 Gardening accessories
54 "Behold, I am a dry _____" (Isaiah 56:3)
55 "And there builded _____ altar unto the LORD" (Genesis 12:7) (2 words)
56 "They will _____ out the bread" (Leviticus 26:26 NIV)
57 Terry Gilliam film, *Lost _____ Mancha*
58 "Some would even _____ to die" (Romans 5:7)
59 "On the hole of the _____" (Isaiah 11:8)

## ACROSS

1 "God hath not given us the spirit of _____" (2 Timothy 1:7)
5 "Punish the men that are settled on their _____" (Zephaniah 1:12)
9 "If she have _____ strangers" (1 Timothy 5:10)
11 Simon Peter (John 1:42)
13 Opposite of *me*
14 "Abiezer the _____" (1 Chronicles 27:12)
16 Have possession
17 Forgive
18 Motel
20 Goat baby
21 "See, here is _____; what doth hinder me to be baptized" (Acts 8:36)
23 "Ye shall in no _____ enter" (Matthew 5:20)
24 "Till I make thine _____ thy footstool" (Luke 20:43)
27 "_____ of Berea" (Acts 20:4)
29 "It will _____ him to powder" (Luke 20:18)
30 "_____ whose fruit" (Jude 1:12)
31 "Forasmuch as _____ excellent spirit" (Daniel 5:12)
32 We
33 Subdued
36 Trap
39 "He shall give thee the _____ of thine heart" (Psalm 37:4)
41 Peresh's brother (1 Chronicles 7:16)
43 Ahira's father (Numbers 1:15)
44 Ammihud's son (1 Chronicles 9:4)
46 Article
47 "_____ was an hair of their head singed" (Daniel 3:27)
48 "The elements shall melt with fervent heat, the _____ also" (2 Peter 3:10)
50 "Out of whose womb came the _____" (Job 38:29)
51 "Shemaiah the _____" (Jeremiah 29:31)
55 Staff

56 Singed
57 Biblical den dweller, for a time
59 Told an untruth
60 "The Lord is at _____" (Philippians 4:5)

## DOWN

1 "His mother. . .gave them to the _____" (Judges 17:4)
2 An altar (Joshua 22:34)
3 Greek form of *Hagar* (Galatians 4:24)
4 Made new again
5 Allow
6 A book of four written by Paul in prison (abbr.)
7 A son of Benjamin (Genesis 46:21)
8 "And I will _____ the soul of the priests" (Jeremiah 31:14)
9 Calling for a calf (arch.)
10 He forsook Paul (2 Timothy 4:10)
11 "_____ for flocks" (2 Chronicles 32:28)
12 We have five of these
13 Wooden collar
15 One of Paul's most trusted missionary friends (abbr.)
19 Saul's grandfather (1 Chronicles 8:33)
22 Decay
23 Roman emperor
25 A son of Parosh (Ezra 10:25)
26 Opposite of *outer*
28 Dried plum
33 "Two _____ shall there be in one board" (Exodus 26:17)
34 Son of Jehaleleel (1 Chronicles 4:16)
35 This book is a series of speeches by Moses (abbr.)
36 "The cedar, the _____ tree, and the myrtle" (Isaiah 41:19)
37 Went to bed
38 Mamre's brother (Genesis 14:13)
39 "As a lion in his _____" (Psalm 10:9)
40 In place of

*by N. Teri Grottke*

41 Zebulun's border was to this city
   (Joshua 19:12)
42 Pay attention to
45 A son of Noah
49 "_____, and Ivah?" (Isaiah 37:13)
52 "Between Bethel and _____"
   (Genesis 13:3)
53 Before (arch.)
54 Commanded militarily
58 Indium (sym.)

# PUZZLE 46

## ACROSS

1 Wrote last book of the NT (Revelation 1:1)
5 "We are being called to account today for _____ act of kindness" (Acts 4:9 NIV)
7 "The fields. . ._____ ripe for harvest" (John 4:35 NIV)
8 Not mixed with anything else; John saw a "city of _____ gold" (Revelation 21:18 NIV)
10 "Come, follow _____, Jesus said" (Mark 1:17 NIV)
11 A small private room for prayer; also an enclosed place for hanging clothes
12 Jacob's brother (Genesis 25:26)
14 Simon and Andrew fished in the _____ of Galilee (Mark 1:16)
15 "Can. . .the leopard change its _____" (Jeremiah 13:23)
18 *Tank* or *truck* (abbr.)
19 The yellowhammer is the state bird here (abbr.)
20 Shuah's grandson (Genesis 38:2–3)
21 "God. . ._____ all things" (Revelation 4:11 NIV)
24 Distance across; length, _____, height
25 Possessive of nonhuman pronoun; "The world and _____ desires pass away" (1 John 2:17 NIV)
27 "I _____ the Alpha and the Omega" (Revelation 1:8 NIV)
28 OT prophet of righteousness

## DOWN

1 Brother of John, son of Zebedee (Matthew 4:21)
2 Minerals that contain metals
3 "Going on from there, _____ saw two other brothers" (Matthew 4:21 NIV)
4 John was an _____, one of 12 disciples Jesus chose (Matthew 10:2)
5 An enclosed space; "Jesus spoke. . . while teaching in the temple _____" (John 8:20 NIV)
6 John used this to catch fish (Matthew 4:21)
9 "A man of knowledge _____ words with restraint" (Proverbs 17:27 NIV)
11 "Can you drink the _____ I drink" (Mark 10:38 NIV)
13 "How can this be? Nicodemus _____" (John 3:9 NIV)
16 "Do not break your _____" (Matthew 5:33 NIV)
17 Jesus had the people sit down on the _____ (John 6:10)
18 To clip
21 Organization started by Beverly LaHaye to bring biblical principles into public policy
22 John "took the little scroll from the angel's hand and _____ it" (Revelation 10:10 NIV)
23 Lacking brightness
26 "They had Peter and John brought before them and began _____ question them" (Acts 4:7)

by John Hudson Tiner

# PUZZLE 47

## ACROSS

1 Prophet sent to King Ahab (abbr., var.)
4 Soft infant food (pl.)
8 Very young person
13 Bird home
15 Asa's father (1 Chronicles 3:10)
16 Gomer's husband (Hosea 1:2–3)
17 This priest rebuilt the temple
18 Transgression
19 Situated down or below
20 Ehud escaped here (Judges 3:26)
22 "_____ that ye refuse not" (Hebrews 12:25)
23 Predicted Assyrian invasion of Judah (abbr.)
24 "Neither _____ they the king's laws" (Esther 3:8)
25 "Mine eyes fail with looking _____" (Isaiah 38:14)
28 Child's favorite seat
29 "Give _____ to His command-ments" (Exodus 15:26 NKJV)
30 Son of Joktan (Genesis 10:26–29)
34 Twenty-first letter of the Greek alphabet
36 "_____, Hadid, and Ono" (Ezra 2:33)
39 Eve was made from Adam's
41 A son of Benjamin (Genesis 46:21)
42 Abraham's nephew
43 Before (arch.)
44 Disfigure
45 "Dip the _____ of his finger in water" (Luke 16:24)
46 Female sheep
47 "She. . ._____ down across from him at a distance of about a bowshot" (Genesis 21:16 NKJV)
48 "And _____ lay at his feet until the morning" (Ruth 3:14)
49 Book presents God's faithfulness and love for His people (abbr.)
50 As well
52 "A _____ of dove's dung" (2 Kings 6:25)
54 "Against Jerusalem, _____" (Ezekiel 26:2)

56 "I am _____ than thou" (Isaiah 65:5)
59 Ripped
61 A family of returned exiles (Ezra 2:57)
64 Writing tool
65 Abraham's firstborn (Genesis 21:3)
68 "And the shekel shall be twenty _____" (Ezekiel 45:12)
70 Songs of praise, forgiveness, thankfulness, and power are a few themes in this book (abbr., var.)
71 Father (Galatians 4:6)
72 "_____, Nekeb, and Jabneel" (Joshua 19:3)
73 "Sons of _____" (1 Chronicles 7:12)
74 "Gilalai, _____, Nethaneel" (Nehemiah 12:36)
75 Penuel's son (1 Chronicles 4:4)
76 A son of Helem (1 Chronicles 7:35)
77 Kept from detection

## DOWN

1 "Day of _____ birth" (Ecclesiastes 7:1)
2 "They slew of them in _____ ten thousand men" (Judges 1:4)
3 "And of Asriel, the family of the _____" (Numbers 26:31)
4 Opposite of *future*
5 A son of Aaron (Exodus 6:23)
6 Bowling target
7 Known as The Rainbow Country (abbr.)
8 "Then were they all of good _____" (Acts 27:36)
9 "This bread of ours we took _____ for our provision" (Joshua 9:12 NKJV)
10 Rephaiah's father (1 Chronicles 4:42)
11 "Punish the men that are settled on their _____" (Zephaniah 1:12)
12 Son of Zerah (1 Chronicles 2:6)
14 A son of Micah (1 Chronicles 8:35)
19 Shemaiah's son (1 Chronicles 3:22)
21 Round, red fruits

*by N. Teri Grottke*

22 "I will send _____ of flies upon thee" (Exodus 8:21)

26 The seventeenth letter of the Hebrew alphabet

27 Accomplish

31 "Passed along by the north of _____" (Joshua 15:6)

32 A son of Jehiel (1 Chronicles 9:37)

33 Parts of the mouth

34 Guilty or not guilty

35 "Awake, ye drunkards, and weep; and _____" (Joel 1:5)

37 "Unto them were committed the _____ of God" (Romans 3:2)

38 "Though thou _____ me, I will not eat of thy bread" (Judges 13:16)

40 "He giveth to all life, and _____, and all things" (Acts 17:25)

51 This state's name comes from the Iroquois, meaning "good river" (abbr.)

53 Beryllium (sym.)

55 Lotan's son (1 Chronicles 1:39)

57 "The queen in gold of _____" (Psalm 45:9)

58 "Christ. . ._____ again" (Acts 17:3)

60 "Hariph, Anathoth, _____" (Nehemiah 10:19)

61 Samuel killed this Amelekite king (1 Samuel 15:32–33)

62 Darius was one (Daniel 11:1)

63 Enoch's son (Genesis 4:18)

66 "Through faith also _____ herself received strength to conceive seed" (Hebrews 11:11)

67 "They. . .have _____ a wound" (Obadiah 1:7)

69 Advanced Medical Optics (abbr.)

70 Talks about Onesimus, the slave, in this book (abbr., var.)

73 Conquered by Joshua (Joshua 8:1–3)

# PUZZLE 48 — LOVE NEVER FAILS

*And now abide faith, hope, love, these three;*
*but the greatest of these is love.*
1 CORINTHIANS 13:13 NKJV

## ACROSS

1 Ruffled shirt front
6 "Put it upon a _____"
(Numbers 21:9)
10 "The _____ facing Joppa"
(Joshua 19:46 NIV)
14 Islands greeting
15 "Cast her ___ heaps"
(Jeremiah 50:26) (2 words)
16 "**LOVE** is _____" (A characteristic
of love from 1 Corinthians 13 NKJV)
17 Grinding tooth
18 "_____ they faint in the way"
(Matthew 15:32)
19 French _____-China
20 "**LOVE**. . ._____" (A characteristic
of love from 1 Corinthians 13:4–7
NKJV) (3 words)
23 German auto
24 "It is _____ on fire of hell"
(James 3:6)
25 "They. . .took no _____ with them"
(Matthew 25:3)
28 In _____ (In its place)
30 Sale inducement
35 Shapeless mass
37 A long, long time
39 Excessive zeal
40 A characteristic of **LOVE** from
1 Corinthians 13:4 NKJV (3 words)
43 "There is one _____ unto all"
(Ecclesiastes 9:3)
44 "Much _____ gold" (Psalm 19:10)
45 "His teeth shall be set on _____"
(Jeremiah 31:30)
46 More crimson
48 In charge of airport security (abbr.)
50 *Auction* or *profit* follower
51 "A _____ for a burnt offering"
(Leviticus 16:3)
53 Suitable for chuch use (abbr.)
55 "**LOVE**. . ._____" (A characteristic
of love from 1 Corinthians 13:4–7
NKJV) (3 words)

62 "Casting all your _____ upon him"
(1 Peter 5:7)
63 "Over Edom will I cast out my
_____" (Psalm 60:8)
64 _____ Gay, famous WWII bomber
65 Get things ready, for short
66 Vietnam neighbor
67 "He looked like glowing _____"
(Ezekiel 1:27 NIV)
68 Follower of Joel
69 Fraternal fellows
70 Wear away

## DOWN

1 Door post
2 Healing succulent
3 Gaucho's cowcatcher
4 Actress Maureen
5 "Then departed Barnabas to
_____" (Acts 11:25)
6 Succeed (3 words)
7 German auto
8 "For his anger _____ only a
moment" (Psalm 30:5 NIV)
9 Hadassah (Esther 2:7)
10 Similar
11 "Put a _____ on his hand, and
shoes on his feet" (Luke 15:22)
12 "The Creator of the _____ of the
earth" (Isaiah 40:28)
13 "Why make ye this _____, and
weep?" (Mark 5:39)
21 *Goodbye* in Lyon
22 List components
25 One who leers
26 "Gaius, whom _____ in the truth"
(3 John 1:1) (2 words)
27 "I have _____ thee" (Isaiah 43:4)
29 "Disobedient and _____ for doing
anything good" (Titus 1:16 NIV)
31 Unit of cotton
32 Positive electrode
33 Slight color

*by David K. Shortess*

34 "The very thing I was _____ to do" (Galatians 2:10 NIV)
36 "For, lo, the wicked _____ their bow" (Psalm 11:2)
38 "The _____ man does not know" (Psalm 92:6 NIV)
41 Cubic meter
42 Respond to a stimulus
47 Fight playfully (dial.)
49 "And you will devise an evil _____" (Ezekiel 38:10 NIV)
52 Taj _____
54 Ocean vessel
55 "Do thyself no _____: for we are all here" (Acts 16:28)
56 Sandwich cookie
57 Energizes (with up)
58 "Which things the angels desire to _____ into" (1 Peter 1:12)

59 "It teaches us to say _____ ungodliness and worldly passions" (Titus 2:12 NIV) (2 words)
60 "Therefore my heart is _____" (Psalm 16:9)
61 "Then let him count the years of the _____ thereof" (Leviticus 25:27)
62 He presents his numbers well (abbr.)

## ACROSS

1 What you do to a drum
5 "The seed should spring and _____" (Mark 4:27)
9 "In Asher and in _____" (1 Kings 4:16)
14 Likewise
15 Salathiel's father (Luke 3:27)
16 Henadad's son (Nehemiah 3:18)
17 Yell
18 So be it
19 Things
20 "Woe to the land _____ with wings" (Isaiah 18:1)
22 "The Amorites would dwell in mount _____" (Judges 1:35)
23 Not dry
24 Hebrew eighth month
25 "Every _____ fled away" (Revelation 16:20)
29 "God created _____ heaven" (Genesis 1:1)
31 "The linen _____ at a price" (1 Kings 10:28)
35 Allotment
36 "Barley, and _____, and lentiles" (Ezekiel 4:9)
38 "But the wheat and the _____ were not smitten" (Exodus 9:32)
39 Cephas
40 Boat paddle
41 Rebuke
43 King Hezekiah's mother (2 Kings 18:2)
44 Honed
46 "The son of _____" (1 Kings 4:10)
47 Suspend
49 Possessive pronoun
50 Tall buildings
51 Have possession
53 "He became the first of the herdsmen _____ live in tents" (Genesis 4:20 NLT)
54 Hurry
57 Looks at (arch.)

63 A gem on the third row of the ephod (Exodus 28:19)
64 "Mahli, and _____" (1 Chronicles 23:23)
65 "_____ the Ahohite" (1 Chronicles 11:29)
66 Reigned
67 "_____ not unto thine own understanding" (Proverbs 3:5)
68 Shoe bottom
69 "If by any _____ I may provoke" (Romans 11:14)
70 Picnic pests
71 "At his holy _____" (Psalm 99:9)

## DOWN

1 "The earth with her _____ was about me for ever" (Jonah 2:6)
2 King Hoshea's father (2 Kings 15:30)
3 Largest continent
4 Spoke
5 Chewed
6 Forgive
7 Jerahmeel's son (1 Chronicles 2:25)
8 "The one _____ of the cherub" (1 Kings 6:24)
9 A son of Aaron (Exodus 6:23)
10 "Aquila, born in Pontus, _____ come from Italy" (Acts 18:2)
11 Opposite of *under*
12 Gentle
13 Snake sound
21 "The life of the _____ thereof" (Proverbs 1:19)
24 "Zechariah, _____, and Jaaziel" (1 Chronicles 15:18)
25 A son of Beriah (1 Chronicles 8:16)
26 The visiting queen at Solomon's court was from here
27 Dead language
28 "_____ there yet the treasures" (Micah 6:10)
29 Product of weeping
30 "The joy of the _____ ceaseth" (Isaiah 24:8)
32 Get up

*by N. Teri Grottke*

33 "The horse and his _____ hath he thrown into the sea" (Exodus 15:1)
34 "And he must _____ go through Samaria" (John 4:4)
36 "None other _____ there" (John 6:22)
37 Instructional place
42 Chop
45 A liquid measure (Leviticus 23:13)
48 "It cannot be _____ for gold" (Job 28:15)
50 "And some fell among _____" (Mark 4:7)
52 Troublesome plants
53 Small bread grain
54 Hurt
55 A chill
56 Heber's father (Luke 3:35)

57 Another name for *Zoar* (Genesis 14:2)
58 First garden
59 "That dippeth with me in the _____" (Mark 14:20)
60 Jesus cried this on the cross
61 Having great height
62 "_____ the Bethelite" (1 Kings 16:34)

## ACROSS

1 Twelve months
5 Kudos
9 "Kingdom was Babel, and Erech, and _____" (Genesis 10:10)
14 "We _____ bear record" (3 John 1:12)
15 "The curse upon mount _____" (Deuteronomy 11:29)
16 Nahash's son (2 Samuel 17:27)
17 Wander
18 "He caused an east _____ to blow in the heaven" (Psalm 78:26)
19 "The stork, the _____ after her kind" (Leviticus 11:19)
20 "It came to pass in the month _____" (Nehemiah 2:1)
22 Framework for carrying (arch.)
24 "A _____, and a stone lay upon it" (John 11:38)
25 "_____ his son, Jehoshua his son" (1 Chronicles 7:27)
27 Spotted
29 Run after
32 "I gave unto _____ mount Seir" (Joshua 24:4)
33 "Thou believest that there is _____ God" (James 2:19)
34 Report
36 "Your old men shall dream _____" (Joel 2:28)
41 "Take thee a _____" (Ezekiel 4:1)
43 "My people _____ know that thou art a virtuous woman" (Ruth 3:11)
45 "The sons of _____ the Netophathite" (Jeremiah 40:8)
46 Fashion
48 Close
50 "Which is the _____, even Christ" (Ephesians 4:15)
51 A prophet son of Amoz (abbr.)
53 Indicator
55 "The wheat and the _____ were not smitten" (Exodus 9:32)
56 Emote
59 Terminate
60 Uproar
62 "All their _____ shall be scattered" (Jeremiah 10:21)
65 Mareshah's father (1 Chronicles 4:21)
69 Obtain
70 "Where the women _____ hangings for the grove" (2 Kings 23:7)
73 "Let all _____ that seek thee rejoice" (Psalm 40:16)
74 Level
75 Salah's son (Genesis 10:24)
76 "Thou _____ cast me into the deep" (Jonah 2:3)
77 Lease
78 Unique
79 "Adam, Sheth, _____" (1 Chronicles 1:1)

## DOWN

1 "Merchants received the linen _____ at a price" (1 Kings 10:28)
2 "_____, lama sabachthani?" (Mark 15:34)
3 "Nevertheless _____ heart was perfect" (1 Kings 15:14)
4 "The _____ shall come" (John 11:48)
5 Not many
6 "Observe the month of _____" (Deuteronomy 16:1)
7 "But hath in due times _____ his word" (Titus 1:3)
8 "Let him call for the _____ of the church" (James 5:14)
9 Wood
10 Verify
11 Polyp
12 Over
13 "So when they had _____" (John 21:15)
21 Substantive
23 Construe
26 Lack
28 Remedy

*by Tonya Vilhauer*

29 "Whether it be oven, or ranges for _____" (Leviticus 11:35)
30 Monad
31 Depend on
35 "Out of the spoils _____ in battles" (1 Chronicles 26:27)
37 Tenth NT book (abbr.)
38 Hushim's father (1 Chronicles 7:12)
39 "Gilalai, _____, Nethaneel, and Judah" (Nehemiah 12:36)
40 Edge
42 "Samuel arose and went to _____" (1 Samuel 3:6)
44 "If a man have long _____" (1 Corinthians 11:14)
47 "He called the name of the well _____" (Genesis 26:20)
49 Rant
52 Response

54 "The Egyptians shall _____ to drink" (Exodus 7:18)
56 "Going _____ strange flesh" (Jude 1:7)
57 "Ruth _____ unto her" (Ruth 1:14)
58 Symbol
61 "_____, the family of the Tahanites" (Numbers 26:35)
63 Coin
64 Always
66 Eleazar's father (2 Samuel 23:9)
67 "Thy King cometh, sitting on an _____ colt" (John 12:15)
68 "Ephron dwelt among the children of _____" (Genesis 23:10)
71 Minor OT prophet (abbr., var.)
72 In time

# PUZZLE 51

## ACROSS

1 Shallum's father (1 Chronicles 9:19)
5 A brother of Arad (1 Chronicles 8:15)
9 _____ and hers towels, for example
12 The Israelites filled _____ with manna (Exodus 16:32)
14 Dwell
15 Arrived
16 King of Syria (Isaiah 7:1)
17 "Brought the heads of _____" (Judges 7:25)
18 "Of Harim, _____" (Nehemiah 12:15)
19 In time past
20 Sister of a parent
22 Joshaviah's father (1 Chronicles 11:46)
24 "They were _____ upon the trees until the evening" (Joshua 10:26)
26 Beg
27 Elderly
28 Abiel's son (1 Samuel 9:1)
29 Female sheep
32 Furious driver (2 Kings 9:20)
35 Garden in Babylon
37 Judge after Jephthah (Judges 12:7–8)
39 "The Spirit of God was hovering _____ its surface" (Genesis 1:2 NLT)
40 Shaving tool
42 Give for temporary use
43 "Traitors, _____, highminded, lovers of pleasures" (2 Timothy 3:4)
45 Grapes grow on this
46 "Used curious _____" (Acts 19:19)
47 "Garments, _____ stood" (Zechariah 3:3)
48 Asa's father (1 Chronicles 3:10)
50 He is good
52 A son of Zebulun (Genesis 46:14)
54 In the opposite direction
58 "_____ sister was Timna" (Genesis 36:22)

60 "Let fall also _____ of the handfuls" (Ruth 2:16)
61 Capable
62 Naum's son (Luke 3:25)
63 Not short
65 A son of Benjamin (1 Chronicles 8:2)
67 A lot
68 Idol
69 Trap
70 "_____ there yet the treasures" (Micah 6:10)
71 "With three _____ of great stones" (Ezra 6:4)
72 The tenth part of an ephah (Exodus 16:36)

## DOWN

1 A son of Esau (Genesis 36:5)
2 The end
3 Eliadah's son (1 Kings 11:23)
4 A son of Gad (Genesis 46:16)
5 "Her maidens walked _____ by the river's side" (Exodus 2:5)
6 Filth
7 First mother
8 "I will purge out from among you the _____" (Ezekiel 20:38)
9 Rehob's son (2 Samuel 8:3)
10 A son of Helem (1 Chronicles 7:35)
11 Jesus' coat didn't have one (John 19:23)
13 "As a _____ which melteth" (Psalm 58:8)
15 Jesus' first miracle was here (John 2:11)
21 Below
23 Location of the spring called Enhakkore (Judges 15:19)
25 It provided shade for Jonah (Jonah 4:6)
26 A duke of Edom (Genesis 36:41)
28 A daughter of Job (Job 42:14)
30 Desire
31 "Pride _____ in humiliation,

*by N. Teri Grottke*

while humility brings honor"
(Proverbs 29:23 NLT)
32 Jediael's brother
(1 Chronicles 11:45)
33 "_____ the death of the cross"
(Philippians 2:8)
34 "He shall bring forth the _____
thereof" (Zechariah 4:7)
36 A son of Jesse (1 Samuel 17:12)
38 "First the _____, then the ear"
(Mark 4:28)
41 A son of Jahdai (1 Chronicles 2:47)
44 "The linen _____ at a price"
(1 Kings 10:28)
49 "Thou shalt _____ thyself: for
then shall the LORD go"
(2 Samuel 5:24)
51 Bread bakes in these
53 Opposite of *hard*

54 "House of the _____" (Ezra 6:1)
55 Jorkoam's father (1 Chronicles 2:44)
56 Meager
57 "Libnah, and _____"
(Joshua 15:42)
58 Tibetan monk
59 A son of Eliphaz (Genesis 36:11)
60 "They are not _____ in giving
birth like Egyptian women"
(Exodus 1:19 NLT)
64 Fuss
66 "Lod, and _____, the valley of
craftsmen" (Nehemiah 11:35)

# PUZZLE 52 — CHRISTMAS GREETINGS

*And the Word was made flesh, and dwelt among us. . .*
*full of grace and truth.*
JOHN 1:14

## ACROSS

1 "And _____ the father of Canaan" (Genesis 9:18) (2 words)
6 "And death rather _____ my life" (Job 7:15)
10 "And after three days _____ again" (Mark 8:31)
14 "Thy neck _____ tower of ivory" (Song of Solomon 7:4) (3 words)
15 "Jesus died and _____ again" (1 Thessalonians 4:14)
16 "_____ in the path of your commands" (Psalm 119:32 NIV) (2 words)
17 "Thy _____ perish with thee" (Acts 8:20)
18 *Mila 18* author
19 "For God did _____ me before you" (Genesis 45:5)
20 Start of a good holiday **REMINDER** for this year (3 words)
23 "Four days _____ I was fasting" (Acts 10:30)
25 Giants' Mel
26 "A bushel, or _____ a bed?" (Mark 4:21)
30 "I have found my lost _____" (Luke 15:9 NIV)
32 Town on the Delaware River
36 "_____ no man any thing" (Romans 13:8)
37 Like a fork
39 Wampum
40 High school equivalent exam (abbr.)
41 **REMINDER**, cont'd from 20 Across (2 words)
45 "And lead us _____ into temptation" (Matthew 6:13)
48 "_____ is this day" (Deuteronomy 4:38) (2 words)
49 Book after Micah
53 "Because they _____ not" (Matthew 2:18)
54 "And to give his life a _____ for many" (Matthew 20:28)
57 "We came to _____, a city of Lycia" (Acts 27:5)
58 "And bread made without _____" (Exodus 12:8 NIV)
60 New (prefix)
62 "_____ her a double portion" (Revelation 18:6 NIV)
63 End of **REMINDER**, cont'd from 41 Across
68 "I know it _____ of a truth" (Job 9:2) (2 words)
71 "Know that it is _____" (Matthew 24:33)
72 "And bound _____ his son" (Genesis 22:9)
75 "His flesh shall wax _____" (Isaiah 17:4)
76 "So Jesus came again into _____" (John 4:46)
77 Nickname for a very timid person: Nervous _____
78 "To sit up _____" (Psalm 127:2)
79 "And in him _____" (2 Corinthians 1:20)
80 Shows shock

## DOWN

1 "And saith unto _____" (Matthew 4:6)
2 Mount _____, Japan
3 "Durst no _____ himself to them" (Acts 5:13) (2 words)
4 "When _____ the blood" (Exodus 12:13) (2 words)
5 "Let not the king _____" (2 Chronicles 18:7) (2 words)
6 "Do not _____ neighbor" (Micah 7:5 NIV) (2 words)
7 "Shaphat the son of _____" (Numbers 13:5)
8 "But such _____ common to man" (1 Corinthians 10:13) (2 words)
9 "And make her _____ on high?" (Job 39:27)
10 "For he is _____" (Matthew 28:6)
11 Anger
12 "Neither light of the _____" (Revelation 22:5)
13 "Even unto the _____" (Psalm 119:112)
21 The Beehive State (abbr.)

*by David K. Shortess*

22 "And his body is _____ a tree"
(Deuteronomy 21:22 NIV) (2 words)
23 "His strange _____" (Isaiah 28:21)
24 "Let me _____ pray thee"
(Jeremiah 40:15) (2 words)
27 "Am I a _____" (1 Samuel 17:43)
28 "Save one little _____ lamb"
(2 Samuel 12:3)
29 "His eyes shall be _____ with wine"
(Genesis 49:12)
31 "And Abner the son of _____"
(2 Samuel 2:12)
33 "Or the leopard his _____?"
(Jeremiah 13:23)
34 "Even _____ men with him"
(Jeremiah 41:1)
35 Lummox
38 "Because of the _____" (Nehemiah 5:3)
42 Jehoshaphat's father (1 Kings 22:41)
43 "Stand in awe, and _____ not"
(Psalm 4:4)
44 "A _____ without blemish out of the
flock" (Leviticus 6:6)
45 "And he said, _____" (Joshua 5:14)
46 "And my people the _____"
(Jeremiah 6:27 NIV)

47 Herbal, for one
50 They are often on the backs of pews
51 "_____, the son of Hur" (Exodus 31:2)
52 Physicist and Nobelist Planck
55 "And _____ and filled a sponge"
(Mark 15:36) (2 words)
56 "Create in _____ clean heart"
(Psalm 51:10) (2 words)
59 "Cast a _____ upon me"
(Lamentations 3:53)
61 "_____ unto the LORD a new song"
(Psalm 96:1) (2 words)
64 Empire conquered by Pizarro
65 "The coat was without _____"
(John 19:23)
66 Rational
67 "Why was it, _____" (Psalm 114:5 NIV)
(2 words)
68 "It shall be _____ with him"
(Isaiah 3:11)
69 "Said unto the _____" (Mark 4:39)
70 "And they _____ down" (Ruth 4:2)
73 High mountain
74 Baseball's Young and namesakes

## ACROSS

1 Solomon's great-grandson (1 Kings 15:8)
4 "Suburbs, and _____" (1 Chronicles 6:73)
8 Zechariah's father (Ezra 5:1)
12 "Used curious _____" (Acts 19:19)
13 Measured (arch.)
15 Action
16 Ebed's son (Judges 9:26)
17 Ribai's son (1 Chronicles 11:31)
18 Give for temporary use
19 "Og the king of Bashan, which dwelt at Astaroth in _____" (Deuteronomy 1:4)
21 "Because of his _____ for wicked men" (Job 34:36)
23 "Tobiah, and _____ the Arabian" (Nehemiah 6:1)
26 Another name for stannum
27 "Thou inhabitant of _____" (Micah 1:11)
28 Best
31 Anub's father (1 Chronicles 4:8)
32 Jacob's God-given name
34 "Set it between Mizpeh and _____" (1 Samuel 7:12)
36 "_____, Hizkijah, Azzur" (Nehemiah 10:17)
38 Tiny insect
39 Certain
40 Uncovered
41 A sweet spice (Exodus 30:34)
44 Prophecy book for Nineveh and the Assyrians (abbr.)
45 "And every _____ fled away" (Revelation 16:20)
47 A daughter of Zelophehad (Numbers 26:33)
49 Hophni's father (1 Samuel 4:4)
50 "Righteousness as a mighty _____" (Amos 5:24)
51 "Ziph, and Telem, and _____" (Joshua 15:24)
54 "The waters of _____" (Isaiah 15:9)
57 Boys
58 Belonging to Shem's father
61 Eat formally
62 "As he saith also in _____" (Romans 9:25)
63 A son of Joseph (Luke 3:26)
64 Night sky illuminator
65 Take care of
66 "_____ shall offer gifts" (Psalm 72:10)
67 "Hundred and _____ years old" (Joshua 24:29)

## DOWN

1 "_____ the Canaanite" (Numbers 21:1)
2 "The astrologers, the _____, the monthly prognosticators" (Isaiah 47:13)
3 Slumbering
4 Patriarch of a family of returned exiles (Ezra 2)
5 Old-time fishers' tool
6 In the edge of the wilderness (Exodus 13:20)
7 "What _____ ye to weep" (Acts 21:13)
8 Laziness
9 "The fallow _____" (Deuteronomy 14:5)
10 Homes of wild animals
11 Strange
12 Get older
14 "Which the clouds do drop and _____ upon man abundantly" (Job 36:28)
20 Rephaiah's father (1 Chronicles 4:42)
22 Christians want to _____ souls for Christ
24 "Behold, Rachel _____ daughter cometh with the sheep" (Genesis 29:6)
25 "I have an _____ to thee, O captain" (2 Kings 9:5)
27 One of Solomon's servants (Nehemiah 7:57)
28 "_____ a calf tender and good" (Genesis 18:7)

*by N. Teri Grottke*

29 "Found Abishag a _____" (1 Kings 1:3)
30 Abraham's father
31 "A _____ of dove's dung" (2 Kings 6:25)
33 No matter which
35 If he was your boss, you could carry your weapon to work (abbr.)
37 Let go
41 "The leeks, and the _____, and the garlick" (Numbers 11:5)
42 "Ye shall point out for you mount _____" (Numbers 34:7)
43 Old
46 "Destroy _____ kings and people" (Ezra 6:12)
48 "Thou _____ affliction upon our loins" (Psalm 66:11)
50 Disgrace

51 "In presence am _____ among you" (2 Corinthians 10:1)
52 Adam and Eve were cast out of here
53 The giant had six of these (2 Samuel 21:20)
55 A son of Judah (1 Chronicles 2:3)
56 Saul's grandfather (1 Chronicles 8:33)
57 Abraham's nephew
59 This NT book has an anonymous author and an unknown time of writing (abbr.)
60 "Of Keros, the children of _____" (Nehemiah 7:47)

# PUZZLE 54 — PRINCE OF EGYPT

*And now abide faith, hope, love, these three;*
*but the greatest of these is love.*
1 CORINTHIANS 13:13 NKJV

## ACROSS

1 "She named him _____, saying, 'I drew him out of the water' " (Exodus 2:10 NIV)
5 Helps solve mysteries (abbr.)
7 "Let there _____ strife" (Genesis 13:8) (2 words)
8 A cry of despair; "_____! I am fainting" (Jeremiah 4:31 NIV)
10 Type of deer
11 Near Ai and east of Bethel: Beth _____ (Joshua 7:2 NIV)
12 "A new king. . .came to power _____ Egypt" (Exodus 1:8 NIV)
13 Paul put many of the _____ in prison (Acts 26:10 NIV)
15 King of Judea, called "that fox" by Jesus (Luke 13:32 NIV)
16 "Is there _____ in the white of an egg?" (Job 6:6 NIV)
18 Another name for Dad
19 A grain offering was baked in one (Leviticus 2:4 NIV)
20 Group of cheerleaders, _____ squad
21 Of the burning bush, Moses said, "I will go _____ and see this strange sight" (Exodus 3:3 NIV)
22 Horn sound
23 Pharaoh's daughter felt sorry for baby Moses because _____ was crying (Exodus 2:6 NIV)
24 Pharaoh was ruler of this country

## DOWN

1 "The LORD said to Moses, 'Come up to _____ the mountain' " (Exodus 24:12 NIV) (2 words)
2 Pharaoh's daughter said, "This is _____ of the Hebrew babies" (Exodus 2:6 NIV)
3 "Let my people go, _____ that they may hold a festival to me in the desert" (Exodus 5:1 NIV)

4 "In the town of David a _____ has been born to you" (Luke 2:11 NIV)
5 Breathe rapidly
6 "The place where you are standing _____ holy ground" (Exodus 3:5 NIV)
7 "The mirth of the wicked is _____" (Job 20:5 NIV)
9 Give for temporary use; Jesus says to _____ to enemies without expecting to get anything back (Luke 6:35 NIV)
11 Moses' brother (Exodus 4:14)
13 A _____ famine struck the distant country where the younger, wasteful son had gone (Luke 15:14 NIV)
14 "Strike you hands together and _____ your feet" (Ezekiel 6:11 NIV)
15 "Invite him to _____ something to eat" (Exodus 2:20 NIV)
17 The Lord is "slow to anger, abounding in _____ and faithfulness" (Exodus 34:6 NIV)
18 A person who writes verse
20 Energy
21 Moses said, "_____, what a great sin these people have committed!" (Exodus 32:31 NIV)
22 Close to; Moses met Zipporah _____ a well in Midian (Exodus 2:15–21)

by John Hudson Tiner

# PUZZLE 55

## ACROSS

1 An idol of Babylon (Isaiah 46:1)
4 Make a correction
9 Possesses
12 "Prepare war, _____ up the mighty men" (Joel 3:9)
13 Priests had to wash here
14 King Hezekiah's mother (2 Kings 18:2)
15 "Abiezer the _____" (1 Chronicles 27:12)
17 "_____ the door after her" (2 Samuel 13:17)
19 Knight
20 "Let him down by the _____ in a basket" (Acts 9:25)
21 A son of Haman (Esther 9:9)
23 A son of Zophah (1 Chronicles 7:36)
24 "If well, why _____ thou me?" (John 18:23)
25 Bed coverings
28 Visiting queen at Solomon's court was from here (2 Chronicles 9:1)
29 "Abraham gave a _____ part of all" (Hebrews 7:2)
30 "Do not _____ the edge" (Ecclesiastes 10:10)
31 Weed of grain fields especially of biblical times
35 Zibeon's daughter (Genesis 36:2)
36 Alemeth's father (1 Chronicles 9:42)
37 Enoch's son (Genesis 4:18)
38 Male sheep
39 "God made a wind to pass _____ the earth" (Genesis 8:1)
40 "They _____ him" (Mark 11:4)
41 "Son of _____, in Aruboth" (1 Kings 4:10)
43 "They shall _____ from sea to sea" (Amos 8:12)
44 Changed
47 "Heavens shall _____ away with a great noise" (2 Peter 3:10)
48 "They who _____ to be somewhat in conference" (Galatians 2:6)
49 Flow
50 A son of Bela (1 Chronicles 7:7)
53 "Helkath, and _____" (Joshua 19:25)
54 Adrammelech and Sharezer's brother (2 Kings 19:37)
57 "Rachel had taken the images. . . and _____ upon them" (Genesis 31:34)
58 Stop
59 Esau's father-in-law (Genesis 26:34)
60 "God created _____ heaven" (Genesis 1:1)
61 Baanah's son (1 Chronicles 11:30)
62 "They are _____ with the showers of the mountains" (Job 24:8)

## DOWN

1 Mighty man of David (2 Samuel 23:36)
2 A son of Ram (1 Chronicles 2:27)
3 Allow
4 Places of sacrifice
5 A son of Merari (Numbers 3:20)
6 Great wickedness
7 Restaurant workers sometimes put a _____ over their hair
8 "As when a thirsty man _____" (Isaiah 29:8)
9 Places to live
10 Stayed in a place
11 Paul's missionary partner
12 "God saw that it _____ good" (Genesis 1:21)
16 Be in debt to (arch.)
18 This NT author took messages to the Corinthian church (abbr.)
22 Eve was made from Adam's
23 "Cart came into the field of Joshua, a _____" (1 Samuel 6:14)
24 "Laban went to _____ his sheep" (Genesis 31:19)
25 Night sky illuminator
26 "_____, and Ivah?" (Isaiah 37:13)
27 "Tappuah, and _____" (Joshua 15:34)
28 Tear repeatedly
30 "May be _____ for a wave offering before the LORD" (Leviticus 7:30)

*by N. Teri Grottke*

32 "Of _____, the family"
(Numbers 26:17)
33 "Who said, _____ it"
(Psalm 137:7)
34 "Mahli, and _____"
(1 Chronicles 23:23)
36 Joshua's father (Haggai 1:1)
40 "Even unto _____" (Genesis 10:19)
42 Before (arch.)
43 "Sow that was _____ to her
wallowing in the mire"
(2 Peter 2:22)
44 Type of tree (Isaiah 44:14)
45 Smallest
46 A descendant of Ephraim
(1 Chronicles 7:22–25)
47 "No scrip, no bread, no money in
their _____" (Mark 6:8)
49 Ebed's son (Judges 9:26)

50 Lazy
51 "_____ of Jesse" (Isaiah 11:10)
52 Motel
55 "_____ that ye refuse"
(Hebrews 12:25)
56 Ground moisture

# PUZZLE 56 — LISTEN UP!

*Hear diligently my speech,*
*and my declaration with your ears.*
JOB 13:17

## ACROSS

1 "If a man _____, will he live again?" (Job 14:14 NIV)
5 Average grades
9 "And let _____ man hearken unto me" (Job 34:34) (2 words)
14 "Sweeter _____ than honey" (Psalm 19:10)
15 "Within as it were an half _____ of land" (1 Samuel 14:14)
16 "That the island was called _____" (Acts 28:1 NIV)
17 Start of Jesus' closing **WORDS** to each of the seven churches (Revelation 2–3) (5 words)
20 "If he _____ satisfy his soul when he is hungry" (Proverbs 6:30) (2 words)
21 "As _____ gone by" (Malachi 3:4 NIV) (2 words)
22 Mineral spring site
23 Town on Lake Murray, NW of Columbia, S.C.
25 **WORDS**, cont'd from 17 Across (4 words)
32 "Eden who were in _____ Assar?" (Isaiah 37:12 NIV)
33 "_____ of faith" (Trust in the unseen) (2 words)
34 What Ezekiel saw in the wall in Ezekiel 8:7 (2 words)
35 "Forgive their sin, and will _____ their land" (2 Chronicles 7:14)
37 "We shall be _____ by his life" (Romans 5:10)
39 "Fine _____ have been poured upon me" (Psalm 92:10 NIV)
40 "Is this how you _____ king over Israel?" (1 Kings 21:7 NIV) (2 words)
42 Trait bearers
44 "The people _____ down to eat and to drink" (Exodus 32:6)
45 **WORDS**, cont'd from 25 Across (3 words)

48 "Can a devil _____ the eyes of the blind?" (John 10:21)
49 Government river project (abbr.)
50 "For they might not be _____ come into the city" (2 Samuel 17:17) (2 words)
54 Mild earthquakes
58 End of **WORDS**, cont'd from 45 Across (3 words)
61 Avant-garde French composer Erik
62 Volunteer service for women in WWII (abbr.)
63 "The body is a _____" (1 Corinthians 12:12 NIV)
64 "And to make _____ of sins" (Daniel 9:24) (2 words)
65 Give off
66 Coal units

## DOWN

1 Dits' companions
2 "In a basket was _____ down by the wall" (2 Corinthians 11:33) (2 words)
3 *This* in Torreon (Sp.)
4 "_____ thou also them that hold" (Revelation 2:15) (2 words)
5 Marsh plants
6 "The woodwork will _____ it" (Habakkuk 2:11 NIV)
7 Mound stat (abbr.)
8 "And _____ them in their place" (Nehemiah 13:11)
9 "If an ox gore _____ woman" (Exodus 21:28) (4 words)
10 Magician's stick
11 Intestinal segments
12 "Neither _____ thou in all the plain" (Genesis 19:17)
13 "His fingers into his _____" (Mark 7:33)
18 "I am _____ and Omega" (Revelation 1:8)
19 "For I will make _____ great nation" (Genesis 21:18) (2 words)

by David K. Shortess

23 "Upon the great confidence which
_____ you" (2 Corinthians 8:22)
(3 words)

24 "Except they _____ of their deeds"
(Revelation 2:22)

25 "The _____ has two daughters"
(Proverbs 30:15 NIV)

26 Make glad

27 *Scant* in Sussex (Brit.)

28 "And _____ will go for us?" (Isaiah 6:8)

29 Crane

30 God of Islam

31 "_____ everything. Hold on to the
good" (1 Thessalonians 5:21 NIV)

32 "There be many _____ say" (Psalm 4:6)

36 _____ Cruces, NM

38 Intentionally destroy

41 "Hating even the garment _____ by
the flesh" (Jude 1:23)

43 Frugal person

46 City north of Kuala Lumpur, Malaysia

47 "Then I said, _____ off"
(Lamentations 3:54) (3 words)

50 "An edict was issued in _____"
(Esther 9:14 NIV)

51 "Ahira the son of _____"
(Numbers 1:15)

52 Follows *sermon* or *kitchen* (suffix)

53 "_____ no wise" (Romans 3:9)
(2 words)

54 Siamese language

55 Expression of incredulity (2 words)

56 "Give free _____ to my complaint"
(Job 10:1 NIV)

57 Concordes, for example (abbr.)

59 "Save one little _____ lamb"
(2 Samuel 12:3)

60 Moving machine component

**ACROSS**

1 Having great height
5 Possessive pronoun
8 What you do with clothes
12 "As he saith also in _____"
   (Romans 9:25)
13 Large lake
14 Damaged
16 Curses
18 43,560 sq. ft. x 2
20 He was a shepherd from Tekoa in
   Judah (abbr.)
21 Hushim's husband
   (1 Chronicles 8:8)
23 Book written by John while exiled
   on Patmos (abbr.)
24 "_____ upon mount Zion"
   (Obadiah 1:17)
25 Steal
26 "Even of _____ my people is risen
   up as an enemy" (Micah 2:8)
27 Whole
30 Tenth Jewish month (Esther 2:16)
32 There was none at the inn
33 Ghost
35 A son of Gad (Genesis 46:16)
36 "Ungodly sinners have spoken
   _____ him" (Jude 1:15)
38 Writing tool
41 Opposite of *autumn*
42 "Whosoever shall say to his brother,
   _____, shall be in danger of the
   council" (Matthew 5:2)
43 One of David's wives
   (1 Chronicles 3:3)
45 "_____ out into the deep"
   (Luke 5:4)
47 Hananiah's father (Jeremiah 28:1)
48 "Who gave himself _____ our sins"
   (Galatians 1:4)
50 Abdiel's son (1 Chronicles 5:15)
51 Nahor's firstborn
   (Genesis 22:20–21)
52 Broken pieces
56 King Hezekiah's mother
   (2 Kings 18:2)

57 "Dwelling was from _____"
   (Genesis 10:30)
58 "Plucked up by the _____"
   (Jude 1:12)
60 "My sword shall be _____ in
   heaven" (Isaiah 34:5)
62 This prophet's name means "God
   strengthens" (abbr.)
64 Daniel had a vision by this river
65 Basketball team Miami _____
66 Boy
67 "Through faith also _____ herself
   received strength to conceive seed"
   (Hebrews 11:11)

**DOWN**

1 Also
2 "Nevertheless _____ heart"
   (1 Kings 15:14)
3 "A _____ek of barley"
   (Hosea 3:2 NIV)
4 A son of Mizraim (Genesis 10:13)
5 Rhode _____ (abbr.)
6 Rip
7 Ahiam's father (1 Chronicles 11:35)
8 "God saw that it _____ good"
   (Genesis 1:21)
9 Judah's firstborn (Numbers 26:19)
10 Resting place of Noah's ark
11 "And _____, and Engannim"
   (Joshua 19:21)
14 "Your lusts that war in your
   _____?" (James 4:1)
15 Bird from the ark sent out three
   times
17 "Wilderness of _____"
   (Exodus 15:22)
19 "Not in _____ and drunkenness"
   (Romans 13:13)
22 Partook
26 Allow
27 Before (arch.)
28 "_____ was an hair of their head"
   (Daniel 3:27)
29 "When _____ king" (2 Samuel 8:9)
31 This is used to control a horse

*by N. Teri Grottke*

33 "The company in ships, and
   _____" (Revelation 18:17)
34 Bowling target
36 Capable
37 "Wert _____ in among them"
   (Romans 11:17)
38 Cooking vessel
39 The author of this book calls himself
   "the Preacher" (abbr.)
40 Jonah would have loved this biblical
   book (abbr.)
41 Knight
42 "It shall be a _____ heap"
   (Isaiah 17:1)
43 Caleb's wife (1 Chronicles 2:18)
44 "Elihu the son of Barachel the
   _____" (Job 32:2)
45 Book by the weeping prophet (abbr.)

46 "Sons of _____"
   (1 Chronicles 7:12)
47 Jezebel's husband
49 "_____ weeping for her children"
   (Jeremiah 31:15)
53 "I will send a fire on the wall of
   _____" (Amos 1:6)
54 Puah's son (Judges 10:1)
55 Night sky illuminator
57 Became acquainted
59 "Of Keros, the children of _____"
   (Nehemiah 7:47)
61 Used to express joy
63 An altar (Joshua 22:34)

# PUZZLE 58

**ACROSS**

1 Save
5 "The sons of _____"
   (1 Chronicles 7:39)
9 "I reap where I _____ not"
   (Matthew 25:26)
14 "_____ the Ahohite"
   (1 Chronicles 11:29)
15 "Goeth out to Remmonmethoar to
   _____" (Joshua 19:13)
16 Reprove
17 Neb
18 "Prepare war, _____ up the mighty
   men" (Joel 3:9)
19 Grassland
20 "There was a continual _____
   given him" (Jeremiah 52:34)
21 Thought
22 "Stingeth like an _____"
   (Proverbs 23:32)
23 Agreement
25 Lade
27 Flog
30 Holler
33 "_____ ye, and believe the gospel"
   (Mark 1:15)
38 "Her children _____ up"
   (Proverbs 31:28)
40 "Dwelt at Michmash, and _____"
   (Nehemiah 11:31)
42 "Whom thou slewest in the valley of
   _____" (1 Samuel 21:9)
43 Hyssop
44 "What _____ thee, O thou sea"
   (Psalm 114:5)
45 Citron
46 "Sons of Merari by Jaaziah; _____"
   (1 Chronicles 24:27)
47 Esau's mother-in-law
   (Genesis 36:2)
48 Old-time anesthesia
49 "He carried into the land of _____"
   (Daniel 1:2)
51 "From the vessels of _____"
   (Isaiah 22:24)
53 Utilize
54 Cainan's father (Genesis 5:9)

56 "Samuel arose and went to _____"
   (1 Samuel 3:6)
58 "_____ the sacrifices of the dead"
   (Psalm 106:28)
61 "I would not write with paper and
   _____" (2 John 1:12)
62 Carmine
66 "The inhabitants of _____"
   (Isaiah 10:31)
68 Zoheth's father (1 Chronicles 4:20)
70 Maim
71 "Absalom made _____ captain of
   the host" (2 Samuel 17:25)
72 Gera's son (Judges 3:15)
73 "They shall say in all the highways,
   _____!" (Amos 5:16)
74 "Bakbakkar, Heresh, and _____"
   (1 Chronicles 9:15)
75 A son of Cush (Genesis 10:7)
76 Male red deer

**DOWN**

1 "Be ye _____ one to another"
   (Ephesians 4:32)
2 "_____, lama sabachthani?"
   (Mark 15:34)
3 "Woe to them that are at _____ in
   Zion" (Amos 6:1)
4 Devotion
5 "O foolish people and _____?"
   (Deuteronomy 32:6)
6 Guide
7 Salina is one
8 Leading
9 "He took him a potsherd to _____
   himself" (Job 2:8)
10 "Jemuel, and Jamin, and _____"
   (Genesis 46:10)
11 "He caused an east _____ to blow
   in the heaven" (Psalm 78:26)
12 Rim
13 Whitetail
24 Look at
26 "Unto Enoch was born _____"
   (Genesis 4:18)
27 "The _____ are for thy clothing"
   (Proverbs 27:26)

*by Tonya Vilhauer*

28 "King's house, with Argob and
   _____" (2 Kings 15:25)
29 "The kingdoms of Ararat, _____,
   and Ashchenaz" (Jeremiah 51:27)
31 "I have _____ still and been quiet"
   (Job 3:13)
32 Syringa
34 Beat
35 Barachel's son (Job 32:2)
36 "I will take away the _____ of
   Baalim" (Hosea 2:17)
37 Yonder
39 Gem
41 Hanani's son (1 Kings 16:1)
44 "Is not _____ the Levite thy
   brother?" (Exodus 4:14)
48 "The son of _____, which was the
   son of Nagge" (Luke 3:25)
50 Bestial
52 "Sophereth, the children of _____"
   (Nehemiah 7:57)

55 "Thick clouds of the _____"
   (2 Samuel 22:12)
57 Micaiah's father (1 Kings 22:8)
58 King of the Amalekites
   (1 Samuel 15:8)
59 "The troops of _____" (Job 6:19)
60 "The curse upon Mount _____"
   (Deuteronomy 11:29)
62 "All the mingled people, and
   _____" (Ezekiel 30:5)
63 "Which was the son of _____"
   (Luke 3:35)
64 "Duke Teman, duke _____"
   (Genesis 36:15)
65 "Thou shouldest make thy _____ as
   high as the eagle" (Jeremiah 49:16)
67 A prophet son of Amoz (abbr.)
69 "But if _____ bear a maid child"
   (Leviticus 12:5)

123

**ACROSS**

1 Retained
5 "_____, and Shema"
(Joshua 15:26)
9 Binea's son (1 Chronicles 8:37)
14 "_____ the Ahohite"
(1 Chronicles 11:29)
15 Travel other than on foot
16 "_____ whose fruit" (Jude 1:12)
17 "In whose eyes a vile person is
_____" (Psalm 15:4)
19 The king of Assyria took Israel
here in their captivity
(2 Kings 17:6)
20 Ethan's father
(1 Chronicles 6:44)
21 "And _____ away much people
after him" (Acts 5:37)
23 "As the serpent beguiled _____
through his subtilty"
(2 Corinthians 11:3)
24 Chicken products
26 Idols
29 Ahijah's son (2 Kings 9:9)
32 Joseph mourned for Jacob at his
threshing floor (Genesis 50:10)
33 "To meet the Lord in the _____"
(1 Thessalonians 4:17)
34 "For three transgressions of _____,
and for four" (Amos 1:9)
37 Burdened
41 Teacher of Judaism
43 "_____ there yet the treasures"
(Micah 6:10)
44 "Like a _____ or a swallow"
(Isaiah 38:14)
45 Allotment
46 "The well of _____" (2 Samuel 3:26)
48 Not cooked
49 "And with the _____"
(Deuteronomy 28:27)
51 "_____ builders did hew them"
(1 Kings 5:18)
53 Shinrath's father (1 Chronicles 8:21)
56 Greek form of *aware* (Acts 14:6)
57 "They departed from _____,

and pitched in Dibongad"
(Numbers 33:45)
58 "_____ shall offer gifts"
(Psalm 72:10)
61 Absalom's captain (2 Samuel 17:25)
65 A raisin is first this
68 "From Mithcah, and pitched in
_____" (Numbers 33:29)
70 Ishmael's mother (Genesis 16:16)
71 "I have stretched out my hands
_____ thee" (Psalm 88:9)
72 "And in the _____"
(Deuteronomy 1:7)
73 Belonging to them
74 Perished
75 Salah's son (Genesis 10:24)

**DOWN**

1 Strike with the foot
2 Jesus cried this on the cross
(Mark 15:34)
3 "Baked it in _____" (Numbers 11:8)
4 "In _____ and offerings"
(Malachi 3:8)
5 This is attached to the shoulder
6 "Lest ye be wearied and faint in your
_____" (Hebrews 12:3)
7 A brother of Arad
(1 Chronicles 8:15)
8 Darius was one
9 "If thou depart to the _____, then I
will go to the left" (Genesis 13:9)
(2 words) (abbr.)
10 A son of Jether (1 Chronicles 7:38)
11 A son of Eber (Genesis 10:25)
12 Haul
13 Fire product
18 "The four hundred and _____
year" (1 Kings 6:1)
22 "To _____, that God was in Christ,
reconciling the world unto himself"
(2 Corinthians 5:19)
25 Happy (arch.)
27 "_____ also, and Pedaiah"
(1 Chronicles 3:18)
28 Twelfth Hebrew month (Esther 3:7)
29 "The earth with her _____ was

by N. Teri Grottke

about me for ever" (Jonah 2:6)
30  A son of Zibeon (1 Chronicles 1:40)
31  Anak's father (Joshua 15:13)
32  Greek form of *Asher* (Revelation 7:6)
35  Hasty
36  "Shallum, and Telem, and _____"
    (Ezra 10:24)
38  A son of Zerah (1 Chronicles 2:6)
39  "Tappuah, and _____"
    (Joshua 15:34)
40  Current events
42  "And they filled them up to the
    _____" (John 2:7)
47  "Against Jerusalem, _____"
    (Ezekiel 26:2)
50  King Saul's father (Acts 13:21)
52  "Though I have all faith, so that I
    could _____ mountains, and have
    not charity, I am nothing"
    (1 Corinthians 13:2)
53  Vision

54  "A certain Adullamite, whose name
    was _____" (Genesis 38:1)
55  Idol
56  Garbage
59  A judge of Israel (Judges 3:15)
60  Mighty man of David
    (2 Samuel 23:36)
62  A Canaanite city (Joshua 11:21)
63  "_____ of his patrimony"
    (Deuteronomy 18:8)
64  "Sons of _____"
    (1 Chronicles 7:12)
66  "Name of his city was _____"
    (1 Chronicles 1:50)
67  Make a mistake
69  "Bezer, and _____"
    (1 Chronicles 7:37)

# PUZZLE 60 — CAREER CHANGE

*Therefore if any man be in Christ, he is a new creature:*
*old things are passed away; behold, all things are become new.*
2 CORINTHIANS 5:17

## ACROSS

1 Messy people
6 "Put it into a _____ with holes" (Haggai 1:6)
9 "Ye shall offer _____ your own will" (Leviticus 19:5) (2 words)
13 "_____ Israel: the LORD" (Deuteronomy 6:4) (2 words)
14 "And Joseph _____ goodly person" (Genesis 39:6) (2 words)
15 "From the _____ of his foot unto his crown" (Job 2:7)
16 "And he shall _____ the left hand" (Isaiah 9:20) (2 words)
17 "Things the angels desire to look _____" (1 Peter 1:12)
18 "The _____ of this command is love" (1 Timothy 1:5 NIV)
19 Start of **QUOTE** taken from Mark 1:17 NIV (3 words)
22 DeMille's *Ten Commandments*, for example
25 Folklore little guy
26 Add on
27 Reduced in rank
29 "Laid he up in the _____" (Genesis 41:48)
31 "That dress doesn't _____ for you." (3 words)
32 Metric foot
33 Occupants of UFOs (abbr.)
36 **QUOTE**, cont'd from 19 Across (5 words)
39 Wind direction (abbr.)
40 Blue dye
41 "He marketh it out with a _____ fitteth it" (Isaiah 44:13) (2 words)
42 An NCO (abbr.)
43 "Since you _____ all my advice" (Proverbs 1:25 NIV)
44 Alter to advantage
47 "It _____ meat offering" (Leviticus 2:6) (2 words)
48 "Shew _____ pray thee" (Judges 1:24) (2 words)

49 End of **QUOTE**, cont'd from 36 Across (3 words)
53 "Even in laughter the heart may _____" (Proverbs 14:13 NIV)
54 Sicilian peak
55 It may go with tea
59 Brain canal
60 "For a _____ of shoes" (Amos 2:6)
61 "According to the _____ of these words" (Genesis 43:7)
62 "More _____ than the gold of Ophir" (Isaiah 13:12 NIV)
63 "Brass, _____ tinkling cymbal" (1 Corinthians 13:1) (2 words)
64 "Knit together _____ man" (Judges 20:11) (2 words)

## DOWN

1 "_____ seeketh wool" (Proverbs 31:13)
2 Meadow in a poem
3 Dobbin's morsel
4 Plant from which buds are eaten
5 "But will do _____ more" (Job 27:19 NIV) (2 words)
6 Alberta resort
7 "I speak _____ wise men" (1 Corinthians 10:15) (2 words)
8 British pokey
9 "The thing _____ from me" (Daniel 2:5) (2 words)
10 "And came _____ large flocks" (Genesis 30:43 NIV) (2 words)
11 "A blind man, or _____" (Leviticus 21:18) (2 words)
12 This preceded the fax
14 "As if a rod were to _____ him who lifts it up" (Isaiah 10:15 NIV)
20 "Even the solemn _____" (Isaiah 1:13)
21 Dear small child
22 Collections of old Norse poems
23 Unskilled laborers in Mexico
24 "_____ me great works" (Ecclesiastes 2:4) (2 words)

*by David K. Shortess*

28 "They will begin _____ away under the oppression" (Hosea 8:10 NIV) (2 words)
29 America's uncle
30 Mercury alloy often found in the mouth
32 "Or have any _____ blemish" (Deuteronomy 15:21)
33 Oglers
34 "Any that can skill _____ timber" (1 Kings 5:6) (2 words)
35 Soft-napped leather
37 "Your lightning _____ up the world" (Psalm 77:18 NIV)
38 Pronounces with great clarity
42 Domain
43 "But their heart _____ from me" (Matthew 15:8) (2 words)

44 "She was a woman of _____ countenance" (2 Samuel 14:27) (2 words)
45 Pronouncements
46 "And she called his name _____" (Genesis 30:13)
47 Region in ancient western Asia Minor
50 It may be the result of a payment default (slang)
51 "Shall come a _____ out of Jacob" (Numbers 24:17)
52 ¿Cómo _____ usted?
56 "March _____ warriors—men of Cush" (Jeremiah 46:9 NIV) (2 words)
57 "_____ his son, Jehoshua his son" (1 Chronicles 7:27)
58 "_____ it was chewed" (Numbers 11:33)

# PUZZLE 61

## ACROSS

1 "So many _____ of voices in the world" (1 Corinthians 14:10)
6 Drinking vessels
10 Father (Galatians 4:6)
14 Abraham's heir
15 Zibeon's daughter (Genesis 36:2)
16 "Rewardeth the proud _____" (Psalm 31:23)
17 "Found Abishag a _____" (1 Kings 1:3)
19 Shammai's brother (1 Chronicles 2:28)
20 "And the Midianites sold _____ into Egypt unto Potiphar" (Genesis 37:36)
21 "The whole world _____ in wickedness" (1 John 5:19)
22 A son of Jerahmeel (1 Chronicles 2:25)
23 "Jonah was in the _____ of the fish three days" (Jonah 1:17)
24 "_____ nor sown" (Deuteronomy 21:4)
25 Military clergyman, for example (abbr.)
27 Make good _____ of time
28 Complete
29 Depend
31 "Resen between Nineveh and _____" (Genesis 10:12)
33 "We _____ our bread" (Lamentations 5:9)
36 A son of Jether (1 Chronicles 7:38)
37 Jorkoam's father (1 Chronicles 2:44)
38 Make a mistake
39 The book that started it all (abbr.)
40 A son of Bela (1 Chronicles 8:5)
41 Jacob's brother
42 Spirit
44 A son of Bani (Ezra 10:34)
46 Its capital is Augusta (abbr.)
47 "_____ great bulwarks" (Ecclesiastes 9:14)
48 "The children of _____, the children of Meunim" (Nehemiah 7:52)
50 Prepared

51 Peter's mother-in-law was healed of this
52 Sharp-toothed tool
55 "_____ him vehemently" (Luke 11:53)
56 "There was no _____ in the land" (Judges 18:7)
58 "Punish the men that are settled on their _____" (Zephaniah 1:12)
59 "Shelesh, and _____" (1 Chronicles 7:35)
60 "In _____ for all Israel" (Malachi 4:4)
61 "The third river. . .goeth toward the _____ of Assyria" (Genesis 2:14)
62 Peter's occupation required these
63 "One day is with the Lord as a thousand _____" (2 Peter 3:8)

## DOWN

1 Saul's father (1 Samuel 9:1–2)
2 Rephaiah's father (1 Chronicles 4:42)
3 Amos's father (Luke 3:25)
4 A son of Jacob
5 "His _____ are his pride" (Job 41:15)
6 Humpbacked animal
7 Accord
8 Way
9 "And _____ lay at his feet until the morning" (Ruth 3:14)
10 Charge with an oath (Matthew 26:63)
11 Sons of thunder (Mark 3:17)
12 Hadad's father (Genesis 36:35)
13 A son of Ulla (1 Chronicles 7:39)
18 "Shall compel thee to go a _____, go with him twain" (Matthew 5:41)
22 Place to get clean
23 Purchase
24 "The rock _____" (Judges 15:11)
25 Rocky outcropping
26 In this place
28 A son of Sheresh (1 Chronicles 7:16)
30 "O people, nations, and _____" (Daniel 3:4)

*by N. Teri Grottke*

31 Small wagon
32 "Against Jerusalem, _____"
(Ezekiel 26:2)
34 A son of Shem (Genesis 10:22)
35 Not false
37 Decomposing metal
40 Pure
41 Taught the child Samuel
(1 Samuel 3:1)
43 Obscure from sight (arch.)
44 Makes use of
45 "The first man is of the earth,
_____" (1 Corinthians 15:47)
47 Paul and Silas were sent by night
here (Acts 17:10)
48 "Of his own will _____ he us
with the word of truth"
(James 1:18)

49 "For innumerable _____ have
compassed me" (Psalm 40:12)
50 "According to this _____"
(Galatians 6:16)
51 Reknown
52 "Through faith also _____ herself
received strength to conceive seed"
(Hebrews 11:11)
53 "_____, Hizkijah, Azzur"
(Nehemiah 10:17)
54 Spiders spin these
56 Adam was the first
57 Small deer

# PUZZLE 62

**ACROSS**

1 Call on
6 "Jerusalem shall become _____"
(Micah 3:12)
11 "The Syrians of Zoba, and of
Rehob, and _____"
(2 Samuel 10:8)
14 "The son of _____, keeper of the
wardrobe" (2 Chronicles 34:22)
15 "Parmashta, and _____, and
Aridai" (Esther 9:9)
16 Undivided
17 Thrash
18 "The prophets of God _____
them" (Ezra 5:2)
21 "The son of _____, which was the
son of Noe" (Luke 3:36)
22 "Of Gad the king's _____"
(2 Chronicles 29:25)
24 "Micah his son, _____ his son"
(1 Chronicles 5:5)
25 "In the wilderness of mount _____"
(Acts 7:30)
26 Eliasaph's father (Numbers 3:24)
28 Dark
29 Lease
30 "_____ the son of a Canaanitish
woman" (Exodus 6:15)
32 "He cast four _____"
(Exodus 38:5)
33 Spume
34 Remnants
35 Entry
39 "The priest's office shall be _____"
(Exodus 29:9)
43 Single
44 "And _____ him up into the
mount" (Exodus 24:18)
46 Gullet
47 Blemish
48 "Perform unto the Lord thine
_____" (Matthew 5:33)
50 Rescue
51 Venomous snakes
53 Bed covering
54 Shammah's father (2 Samuel 23:11)

55 "The children of Ziha, the children
of _____" (Ezra 2:43)
57 Clothing
59 "If any be a _____ of the word"
(James 1:23)
60 "The _____ of the people"
(Hebrews 9:7)
61 "Pekod, and _____" (Ezekiel 23:23)
62 Effortless

**DOWN**

1 Phials
2 "One of the king of _____
servants" (2 Kings 3:11)
3 Jonathan's father (2 Samuel 21:21)
4 "That which groweth of _____
own accord" (Leviticus 25:5)
5 "The son of Eliel, the son of _____"
(1 Chronicles 6:34)
6 Loll
7 Established (abbr.)
8 "The king _____ from the
banquet" (Esther 7:7)
9 Mothers and fathers
10 Jewish confession of faith
12 Feretory
13 Restore
14 "The gods of Sepharvaim, _____,
and Ivah? (2 Kings 18:34)
19 "Thou in thy mercy hast _____
forth the people" (Exodus 15:13)
20 "Baalah, and _____, and Azem"
(Joshua 15:29)
23 Ratiocinate
25 "Gave the _____" (Nehemiah 8:8)
27 "Not given to filthy _____"
(Titus 1:7)
29 Dextral
31 "They of Persia and of _____ and
of Phut" (Ezekiel 27:10)
32 Rodent
35 "And the trumpet in _____"
(Hosea 5:8)
36 Shaphan's son (Jeremiah 29:3)
37 Cadavers
38 Charge
40 Statues

by Tonya Vilhauer

41 Blackbirds

42 "The mountains shall drop _____ wine" (Amos 9:13)

44 "The children of Giddel, the children of _____" (Ezra 2:47)

45 Yonder

48 Nun's son (Numbers 13:8)

49 Gaze

50 "The next day we arrived at _____" (Acts 20:15)

52 "The sons of Zophah; _____" (1 Chronicles 7:36)

56 Expert

58 "_____ also the Jairite" (2 Samuel 20:26)

# PUZZLE 63

## ACROSS

1 Market
5 Fleecy ruminant
10 Cain's victim
14 King Hoshea's father (2 Kings 15:30)
15 A son of Reuben (Exodus 6:14)
16 "_____; God hath numbered thy kingdom, and finished it" (Daniel 5:26)
17 Dwell
18 "But _____ foolish questions" (Titus 3:9)
19 At once (Mark 1:30)
20 A son of Ram (1 Chronicles 2:27)
21 "The _____ chamber was five cubits broad" (1 Kings 6:6)
23 A baptismal site of John the Baptist (John 3:23)
25 "Wilt thou _____ the prey for the lion?" (Job 38:39)
26 Enemies
29 A son of David (2 Samuel 5:13–14)
34 "_____, Reuse, Recycle"
37 Wound covering
39 "_____ him vehemently" (Luke 11:53)
40 "And he will take your daughters to be _____" (1 Samuel 8:13)
45 Melchi's father (Luke 3:28)
46 "Say unto them which _____ it" (Ezekiel 13:11)
47 Became acquainted
48 "_____, O isles, unto me" (Isaiah 49:1)
51 "Being _____ together" (Colossians 2:2)
53 Heber's father (Luke 3:35)
56 "He shall _____ his flesh in water" (Numbers 19:7)
60 "The outgoings thereof are in the valley of _____" (Joshua 19:14)
66 "Set it between Mizpeh and _____" (1 Samuel 7:12)
67 Daniel had a vision by this river
68 To the side

69 "And in process of _____" (Genesis 4:3)
70 Verbalize
71 This Hararite was father to Jonathan in David's army (1 Chronicles 11:34)
72 "Tappuah, and _____" (Joshua 15:34)
73 Exhaust
74 "Came to_____" (Isaiah 30:4)
75 Refuse to admit

## DOWN

1 Menan's son (Luke 3:31)
2 Similar
3 First bird out of the ark
4 "They shall give account _____ in the day of judgment" (Matthew 12:36)
5 Breadth
6 Own
7 "He built _____, and restored it to Judah" (2 Chronicles 26:2)
8 Elkanah's grandfather (1 Samuel 1:1)
9 "Eubulus greeteth thee, and _____, and Linus" (2 Timothy 4:21)
10 "_____, and Shema" (Joshua 15:26)
11 A brother of Shoham (1 Chronicles 24:27)
12 Seth's son (Genesis 4:26)
13 Gave a loan
22 Not left hand but _____ (abbr.)
24 Smelling orifice
27 This book's key verse: "Vanity of vanities; all is vanity" (abbr.)
28 "A certain blind man _____ by the way side begging" (Luke 18:35)
30 "Altogether for _____ sakes?" (1 Corinthians 9:10)
31 "And they filled them up to the _____" (John 2:7)
32 Shammah's father (2 Samuel 23:11)
33 First place
34 "Even unto Ithiel and _____" (Proverbs 30:1)
35 Gaddiel's father (Numbers 13:10)

*by N. Teri Grottke*

36 "The LORD will judge the _____ of the earth" (1 Samuel 2:10 NKJV)
38 Send (Zephaniah 1:7)
41 "To the plough and looking back, is _____ for the kingdom of God" (Luke 9:62)
42 Strong wood
43 Joshua's father
44 First Hebrew month (Exodus 34:18)
49 Aka Hadassah (abbr.)
50 Saul defeated him in his first battle as king (1 Samuel 11)
52 Experienced flavor
54 "Even unto _____" (Genesis 10:19)
55 A son of Shemidah (1 Chronicles 7:19)
57 Yours (arch.)
58 "_____, and Chalcol" (1 Kings 4:31)

59 Foe
60 Fair
61 "_____ the Ahohite" (1 Chronicles 11:29)
62 Couple
63 Pelt
64 Furthest part
65 "Punish the men that are settled on their _____" (Zephaniah 1:12)

# PUZZLE 64 — IT'S ALL RELATIVE

*Each theme answer (17, 26, 47, and 61 Across) describes*
*one of the four people listed in the clue. The circled letter in*
*the answer provides the identity of the correct person.*

## ACROSS

1 Kind of metabolism
6 Ex-New York governor Mario
11 Mr. Baba
14 Godly love
15 Late Chilean-born pianist Claudio
16 "That he might _____ him out of their hands" (Genesis 37:22)
17 A. Bathsheba
   B. Abigail
   C. Ahinoam
   D. Michal
20 Fencing weapon
21 "Round about the _____ thereof" (Exodus 28:33)
22 Pond plant
23 Olympic gold medal runner Sebastian
25 Leeds trolly
26 A. Jehu
   B. Ahab
   C. Ahaziah
   D. Jehoshaphat
34 Prefix for the birds
35 "According to the _____ of the king" (Esther 1:7)
36 Indonesian island
37 Engrossed
39 Bergen's dummy Mortimer
41 Royal address
42 Figure of speech
44 "He has a _____" (Matthew 11:18 NIV)
46 Agency that issues nine-digit ID numbers (abbr.)
47 A. Rachel
   B. Bilhah
   C. Zilpah
   D. Leah
50 *Trinity* author Leon
51 "Then answered I, and said, So be _____ LORD" (Jeremiah 11:5) (2 words)
52 Sports stadiums
55 "He said, _____ is a lion's whelp" (Deuteronomy 33:22)
57 "And not in _____ speeches" (Numbers 12:8)
61 A. Levi
   B. Reuben
   C. Simeon
   D. Naphtali
64 "He planteth an _____, and the rain doth nourish it" (Isaiah 44:14)
65 Edmonton hockey player
66 "And of _____ oil a hin" (Exodus 30:24)
67 Follows *pi* in the Greek alphabet
68 "With _____ both the grayheaded and very aged men" (Job 15:10) (2 words)
69 "And _____ a right spirit within me" (Psalm 51:10)

## DOWN

1 "All that her mother in law _____ her" (Ruth 3:6)
2 "And not _____ was left in it" (Nehemiah 6:1 NIV) (2 words)
3 "Any god, _____ unto the LORD only" (Exodus 22:20)
4 "Neither have two coats _____" (Luke 9:3)
5 "And be _____ forth with peace" (Isaiah 55:12)
6 _____ au lait
7 "There stood up a priest with _____ and Thummim" (Nehemiah 7:65)
8 NHL's Bobby
9 Capital of Lesotho, formerly part of South Africa
10 "They will set _____, under their standards" (Numbers 2:31 NIV) (2 words)
11 "It goes through _____ places" (Matthew 12:43 NIV)
12 "For with thee is the fountain of _____" (Psalm 36:9)
13 "But you have no _____ where I come from" (John 8:14 NIV)
18 "Then shall ye give me thirty _____" (Judges 14:13)

*by David K. Shortess*

19 "The fruit of the _____ his reward" (Psalm 127:3) (2 words)
24 Gyns. partners (abbr.)
25 Heat units
26 A son of Simeon (1 Chronicles 4:24)
27 Give the slip
28 Make a fast stop at the mini-mart (2 words)
29 "And the _____ defiled" (Leviticus 18:25) (2 words)
30 Dutch painter Jan
31 Pennsylvania sect
32 Scandinavian
33 Cheerless, to Wordsworth
38 Ode written by Horace for a Roman goddess
40 R & B pianist "Fats"
43 Large African stork
45 "Ye shall _____ surely die" (Genesis 3:4)
48 "A _____ as good as a mile"

49 Walk unsteadily, as a baby (2 words)
52 "There is not _____ left" (2 Kings 4:6 NIV)
53 "Be not _____ with thy mouth" (Ecclesiastes 5:2)
54 "Their calls will _____ through the windows" (Zephaniah 2:14 NIV)
55 "Her princes are like _____ that find no pasture" (Lamentations 1:6 NIV)
56 "As it were an half _____ of land" (1 Samuel 14:14)
58 "And there is _____ not unto death" (1 John 5:17) (2 words)
59 Peregrinate
60 "But they _____ not him" (Genesis 42:8)
62 Patty Hearst's former organization (abbr.)
63 "Thou, _____ thy son" (Exodus 20:10)

## ACROSS

1 City of the priests (1 Samuel 22:19)
4 After eight
8 In this manner
12 A son of Benjamin (Genesis 46:21)
13 "Mountains shall reach unto _____" (Zechariah 14:5)
14 Igdaliah's son (Jeremiah 35:4)
16 Adoniram's father (1 Kings 4:6)
17 "Of _____, the family" (Numbers 26:17)
18 Similar
19 Eliasaph's father (Numbers 3:24)
20 "These are the families of the _____" (Numbers 26:14)
22 "_____ whose fruit" (Jude 1:12)
24 Prophet for forty years (abbr.)
25 Her name means "star" (abbr.)
26 Jehoshua's father (1 Chronicles 7:27)
28 Snare
31 "He _____ Uriah unto a place" (2 Samuel 11:16)
36 The butler's cellmate (Genesis 40:2–3)
40 Capture tactic
41 "Dip the _____ of his finger in water" (Luke 16:24)
43 Not dead
44 You do this to bread
45 "Which _____ the people of the land" (2 Kings 25:19)
47 Dogs do this
50 Partook
51 Patriarch of a family of returned exiles (Ezra 2:57)
54 Petroleum product
56 Increased
60 Force to do something (arch.)
64 "Day of _____ birth" (Ecclesiastes 7:1)
66 "At _____" (1 Chronicles 4:29)
67 The beast and the false prophet will be cast here
68 Jacob's brother
69 Trap
70 Great wickedness
71 "According to this _____" (Galatians 6:16)
72 "Set it between Mizpeh and _____" (1 Samuel 7:12)
73 Refuse to admit
74 To place

## DOWN

1 Jeroboam's father (1 Kings 11:26)
2 "Set in _____ the things that are wanting" (Titus 1:5)
3 "People that were with him from _____ of Judah" (2 Samuel 6:2)
4 Salmon's father (Luke 3:32)
5 "Fourth to _____" (1 Chronicles 25:11)
6 Ruth's mother-in-law
7 Firstborn
8 "Now the serpent was more subtil _____ any beast" (Genesis 3:1)
9 "Helkath, and _____" (Joshua 19:25)
10 Bring together
11 "They are beloved for the fathers' _____" (Romans 11:28)
12 Girl (slang)
15 Bird home
21 Boat paddle
23 "Dwelt in strong holds at _____" (1 Samuel 23:29)
27 Short name for the system linking computers around the world
29 "Waters were _____ from off the earth" (Genesis 8:11)
30 Little color
31 Pose a question
32 Transgression
33 "_____that ye refuse" (Hebrews 12:25)
34 Son of Nathan of Zobah (2 Samuel 23:36)
35 Opposite of *bright*
37 The people of Syria shall go into captivity here (Amos 1:5)

*by N. Teri Grottke*

38 "She would become the mother of all the living" (Genesis 3:20 NIV)
39 Color of blood
42 Issachar's son (Numbers 26:23)
46 "Satest upon a _____ bed" (Ezekiel 23:41)
48 One of Paul's four "prison epistles" (abbr.)
49 Slayed
51 Only NT history book
52 "Her new _____, and her sabbaths" (Hosea 2:11)
53 Micaiah's father (1 Kings 22:8)
55 "Intreat me not to _____ thee" (Ruth 1:16)
57 Accomplishers
58 "Let him seek peace, and _____ it" (1 Peter 3:11)
59 Doled out
61 Cut back
62 First garden
63 Epidermis
65 Take to court

# PUZZLE 66

## ACROSS

1 "Which was the son of _____" (Luke 3:35)
5 "They _____ us with such things as were necessary" (Acts 28:10)
10 Reserve
12 Astonished
14 Emeritus
15 "_____ the word of the LORD came unto me" (Zechariah 4:8)
17 "Went out to the cities of mount _____" (Joshua 15:9)
19 Endeavor
20 Amusement
21 Spoil
23 Espy
24 "Judah went to the top of the rock _____" (Judges 15:11)
26 "Having understood that he was a _____" (Acts 23:27)
28 "That no man might buy or _____" (Revelation 13:17)
29 "Which is _____ in knowledge" (Colossians 3:10)
31 Dressing gown
33 "_____, she is broken" (Ezekiel 26:2)
34 Pekoe
35 Cord
37 "Fed them with bread and water?" (1 Kings 18:13)
39 "Southward were Kabzeel, and _____" (Joshua 15:21)
41 Jabal's mother (Genesis 4:20)
45 Opulent
47 Office
48 "Hariph, Anathoth, _____" (Nehemiah 10:19)
50 "There was war between _____ and Baasha" (1 Kings 15:16)
52 "If thy father at all _____ me" (1 Samuel 20:6)
54 Discover
55 "The Amorites would dwell in mount _____" (Judges 1:35)
57 Zoheth's father (1 Chronicles 4:20)

## DOWN

58 "Written in the story of the prophet _____" (2 Chronicles 13:22)
59 A son of Gad (Genesis 46:16)
60 Next
61 Eliasaph's father (Numbers 3:24)
62 "After they were come to _____" (Acts 16:7)
63 "Glean _____ of corn" (Ruth 2:2)
64 "So is thy praise unto the _____ of the earth" (Psalm 48:10)

1 "Who shall _____ him up" (Numbers 24:9)
2 "Is not _____ the Levite thy brother?" (Exodus 4:14)
3 "Though ye have _____ among the pots" (Psalm 68:13)
4 Also
5 Flog
6 "Saying _____ hath conspired against thee" (Amos 7:10)
7 "To quench all the fiery _____" (Ephesians 6:16)
8 Son of the ruler of Mizpah (Nehemiah 3:19)
9 Concoct
10 Putative
11 "Zereth, and Jezoar, and _____" (1 Chronicles 4:7)
13 Grow
14 Point
16 "They _____ to and fro" (Psalm 107:27)
18 Gypsy
21 Pole
22 _____ and feather
25 "_____ that is beside the Sidonians" (Joshua 13:4)
26 "The plowman shall overtake the _____" (Amos 9:13)
27 Letter
28 "So shall the _____ be calm unto you" (Jonah 1:12)
30 "That he _____ loveth God love his brother" (1 John 4:21)

by Tonya Vilhauer

32 "Sent Jerubbaal, and _____"
(1 Samuel 12:11)

36 "Hadad the _____" (1 Kings 11:14)

37 "His flesh shall be _____ than a
child's" (Job 33:25)

38 "Remembering mine affliction and
my _____" (Lamentations 3:19)

40 "Elijah went with _____ from
Gilgal" (2 Kings 2:1)

42 "He would not _____ himself"
(Daniel 1:8)

43 Gideoni's son (Numbers 10:24)

44 "While he is weary and weak
_____" (2 Samuel 17:2)

45 Shema's son (1 Chronicles 2:44)

46 "And _____ of this life"
(Luke 21:34)

49 Graven images

51 "Stayed in _____ for a season"
(Acts 19:22)

53 "For the remission of _____"
(Acts 2:38)

56 "Samuel arose and went to _____"
(1 Samuel 3:6)

# PUZZLE 67

## ACROSS

1 Peaceful
5 A king of Midian (Numbers 31:8)
8 "Valley of _____" (Psalm 84:6)
12 "As he saith also in _____"
   (Romans 9:25)
13 "God hath numbered thy kingdom, and finished it" (Daniel 5:26)
15 Naum's son (Luke 3:25)
16 "For ye tithe _____ and rue and all manner of herbs" (Luke 11:42)
17 "To _____ all that call on thy name" (Acts 9:14)
18 "I travail in _____ again until Christ be formed in you" (Galatians 4:19)
20 Consume food
21 Cooking vessel
22 Happy (arch.)
24 Expert
25 Son of Nathan of Zobah
   (2 Samuel 23:36)
27 Arioch was king here (Genesis 14:1)
29 "The howling thereof unto _____"
   (Isaiah 15:8)
31 Lucre
32 "They _____ to and fro"
   (Psalm 107:27)
33 Gihon was this river coming out of Eden (Genesis 2:13)
36 Possessive pronoun
37 Children of aunts and uncles
39 "No man, having put his hand to the plow, and looking back, is _____ for the kingdom of God"
   (Luke 9:62)
42 "Live delicately, are in kings'
   _____" (Luke 7:25)
43 Mud
44 "With a _____, with the voice of the archangel" (1 Thessalonians 4:16)
46 "The inhabitant of _____ came not forth" (Micah 1:11)
48 Bright red
50 Nagge's son (Luke 3:25)
51 Are (arch.)
52 Test
53 Where the mercy seat was

54 "And _____ lay at his feet until the morning" (Ruth 3:14)
57 A tenth
59 Thorny flower
61 Jezebel's husband
62 "Touched the _____" (Luke 7:14)
63 Gaal's father (Judges 9:26)
64 "And _____ destroyed of the destroyer" (1 Corinthians 10:10)
65 Type of trees
66 A son of Jether (1 Chronicles 7:38)
67 "Tower of _____" (Genesis 35:21)

## DOWN

1 "_____ up before me" (Jonah 1:2)
2 Largest continent
3 "Then Jacob gave Esau bread and pottage of _____" (Genesis 25:34)
4 "The angels of God _____ him"
   (Genesis 32:1)
5 "Then Joseph directed the physicians in his service to _____ his father Israel" (Genesis 50:2 NIV)
6 Blood vessel
7 Motel
8 "For then the king of _____ army besieged Jerusalem" (Jeremiah 32:2)
9 Patriarch of a family of returned exiles (Ezra 2:57)
10 Dead body
11 "Sheep going _____" (1 Peter 2:25)
14 Furthest part
19 "Ye shall point out for you mount _____" (Numbers 34:7)
21 "Name of his city was _____"
   (1 Chronicles 1:50)
23 "And _____ with her suburbs; four cities" (Joshua 21:18)
26 This equals four quarts (abbr.)
28 "Garments, _____ stood"
   (Zechariah 3:3)
29 A son of Gad (Genesis 46:16)
30 Acquire
33 A temple gate (2 Kings 11:6)
34 Mordecai's charge (abbr.)
35 King Saul's father (Acts 13:21)

by N. Teri Grottke

37 "For the _____, and for the forks" (1 Samuel 13:21)
38 "Cast ye the unprofitable servant into _____ darkness" (Matthew 25:30)
39 "When he had received the drink, Jesus said, 'It is _____'" (John 19:30 NIV)
40 "Helez the Paltite, _____" (2 Samuel 23:26)
41 "Hundred and _____ years old" (Joshua 24:29)
42 This book of First and Second addressed problems with immorality in the church (abbr.)
43 This prophet's name means "messenger of the Lord" (abbr.)
44 "Where is the wise? where is the _____?" (1 Corinthians 1:20)
45 "The children of Shephatiah, the children of _____" (Nehemiah 7:59)

46 Jeroboam the son of Nebat was from here (1 Kings 11:26)
47 Pose a question
48 "There came an angel of the LORD, and _____ under an oak which was in Ophrah" (Judges 6:11)
49 "And Herod was highly displeased with them of _____ and Sidon" (Acts 12:20)
53 Greek form of *Asher* (Revelation 7:6)
55 "Habor, and _____" (1 Chronicles 5:26)
56 Salah's son (Genesis 10:24)
58 Edge of a garment
60 This book was written to the Edomites and Judah's Jews, among others (abbr.)
61 Reverent fear

# PUZZLE 68 — THE FIRST WOMAN

## ACROSS

1 "Adam named his wife _____"
(Genesis 3:20 NIV)

4 During a storm, Jesus was asleep
in the back, or _____, of the ship
(Mark 4:38 NIV)

8 Rearrange letters of the name of the
main heart artery

10 "Do you watch when the _____
bears her fawn?" (Job 39:1 NIV)

11 Expression meaning "okay"

12 Precious stones

13 Child's plaything

14 "How often I have longed to gather
your children together, as a _____
gathers her chicks under her wings"
(Luke 13:34 NIV)

15 "Prophesy to us, Christ. Who
_____ you?" (Matthew 26:68 NIV)

18 "God _____ granted me another
child in place of Abel"
(Genesis 4:25 NIV)

19 While walking beside the _____ of
Galilee, Jesus saw Peter and Andrew
(Matthew 4:18 NIV)

21 "Whatever you do, whether in word
or _____, do it all in the name
of the Lord Jesus"
(Colossians 3:17 NIV)

23 Bird (abbr.)

24 Natural gas organization (abbr.)

25 This is now bone of my _____ and
flesh of my flesh (Genesis 2:23 NIV)

26 Eve became the _____ of all the
living (Genesis 3:20 NIV)

27 To Cain, God said, "If you _____
what is right, will you not be
accepted?" (Genesis 4:7 NIV)

## DOWN

1 "God had planted a garden in the
_____, in Eden" (Genesis 2:8 NIV)

2 The sound a vehicle's engine makes

3 Jesus said, "For my yoke is _____ ,
and my burden is light"
(Matthew 11:30)

4 During creation, God separated the
water, "and it was _____"
(Genesis 1:7)

5 What God prepared for Adam
and Eve

6 This book expounds on justification
by faith alone (abbr.)

7 "Like a bird that strays from its
_____ is a man who strays from his
home" (Proverbs 27:8 NIV)

9 "It is not good for the man _____
be alone" (Genesis 2:18 NIV)

12 "How long will you lie there, you
sluggard? When will you _____ up
from your sleep?" (Proverbs 6:9 NIV)

14 "God created man in _____ own
image" (Genesis 1:27)

15 "God saw all that he _____ made,
and it was very good"
(Genesis 1:31 NIV)

16 "So they _____ fig leaves
together and made coverings"
(Genesis 3:7 NIV)

17 "The first man _____ became a living being" (1 Corinthians 15:45 NIV)

18 The sun in the desert brings
scorching _____

19 Cain was Eve's first _____
(Genesis 4:1)

20 "He _____ made the stars"
(Genesis 1:16 NIV)

22 Self-esteem

23 The garden had "trees that were
pleasing to the eye and good _____
food" (Genesis 2:9 NIV)

25 God said, "Let there _____ light"
(Genesis 1:3)

*by John Hudson Tiner*

# PUZZLE 69

## ACROSS

1 Ground moisture
4 Darling
8 Before (arch.)
11 A king of Midian (Numbers 31:8)
12 "Sound of the _____" (Job 21:12)
14 Livestock feed
15 A son of Bani (Ezra 10:34)
16 Place of the dead
17 Common tree
18 Right hand (abbr.)
20 A daughter of Zelophehad (Joshua 17:3)
23 Foreigner
26 "Helez the Paltite, _____" (2 Samuel 23:26)
27 Roman emperor
30 "The Lord knoweth how to deliver the _____ out of temptations" (2 Peter 2:9)
32 Petroleum product
33 These First and Second books have an unknown author (abbr.)
34 Fight between countries
35 Cut
37 Elevate
39 "God _____ tempt Abraham" (Genesis 22:1)
40 "And _____ with her suburbs, and Rehob" (1 Chronicles 6:75)
42 A brother of Uz (Genesis 10:23)
43 Acquire
44 Conquered by Joshua (Joshua 8)
45 Hophni's father (1 Samuel 4:4)
46 Philistine idol (Judges 16:23)
48 Give (Psalm 116:12)
50 Exclamation of affirmation
51 "_____ of Judah" (2 Samuel 6:2)
53 "Until ye be _____ with power from on high" (Luke 24:49)
55 "Shall be astonished, and _____ his head" (Jeremiah 18:16)
58 Entrance
61 A city in Benjamin (Joshua 18:25)
64 Steal
66 Night flier
67 Idol
68 "_____ there yet the treasures" (Micah 6:10)
69 Color of blood
70 Show (arch.)
71 Zephaniah's son (Zechariah 6:14)

## DOWN

1 This book is quoted more than 80 times in the NT (abbr.)
2 Always
3 "Knowing that thou _____ also do more than I say" (Philemon 1:21)
4 Canine
5 Make a mistake
6 A gem on the third row of the ephod (Exodus 28:19)
7 "Filled his holes with prey, and his dens with _____" (Nahum 2:12)
8 A son of Benjamin (Genesis 46:21)
9 "And _____ greedily after the error of Balaam" (Jude 1:11)
10 "But the _____ of their God was upon the elders of the Jews" (Ezra 5:5)
13 Saul's grandfather (1 Chronicles 8:33)
17 A son of Reuben (Genesis 46:9)
19 Possesses
21 "_____; nine cities" (Joshua 15:54)
22 Naaman's brother (Numbers 26:40)
24 The beast and the false prophet will be cast here
25 A son of Bela (1 Chronicles 7:7)
27 This book talks about giving and church discipline, among other topics (abbr.)
28 A son of Zibeon (1 Chronicles 1:40)
29 Achim's son (Matthew 1:14)
30 A son of Jacob (Genesis 30:11)
31 "Be ye not unequally _____ together with unbelievers" (2 Corinthians 6:14)
34 "To _____, that God was in Christ, reconciling the world unto himself" (2 Corinthians 5:19)

by N. Teri Grottke

36 "Upon a _____" (Numbers 21:8)
38 Killer (arch.)
39 "As a lion in his _____"
   (Psalm 10:9)
40 "_____ the Bethelite"
   (1 Kings 16:34)
41 The people of Syria shall go into
   captivity here (Amos 1:5)
43 Prod
44 A son of Jether (1 Chronicles 7:38)
47 Book of the patriarchs (abbr.)
49 Roosevelt had a _____ Deal during
   the 1930s
51 "Who layeth the _____ of his
   chambers" (Psalm 104:3)
52 "Shall I make thee as _____?"
   (Hosea 11:8)
54 "Shallum, and Telem, and _____"

(Ezra 10:24)
56 A son of Ulla (1 Chronicles 7:39)
57 Pierce with horns
58 "Borders of _____" (Joshua 11:2)
59 Be indebted to
60 Elderly
62 Get older
63 Chop (arch.)
65 Zechariah, _____"
   (1 Chronicles 15:18)

145

*And Ruth the Moabitess said unto Naomi,*
*Let me now go to the field, and glean ears of corn.*
RUTH 2:2

## ACROSS

1 Ollie's friend
5 "And Zaavan, and _____"
(Genesis 36:27)
9 "_____ darkness lies in wait for his
treasures" (Job 20:26 NIV)
14 Mercury or Saturn
15 Estee's rival
16 "According to the days _____ king"
(Isaiah 23:15) (2 words)
17 "But grievous words _____ up anger"
(Proverbs 15:1)
18 "But _____ was a tiller of the
ground" (Genesis 4:2)
19 Bismarck and Preminger
20 "For we have treasures in _____"
(Jeremiah 41:8) (4 words)
23 " '_____ ghost,' they said"
(Matthew 14:26 NIV) (2 words)
24 "That we love _____ another"
(2 John 1:5)
25 Whippets and greyhounds
28 "Why make ye this _____, and
weep?" (Mark 5:39)
30 Follows *pro-* or *mo-*
34 "As _____ that is told" (Psalm 90:9)
(2 words)
35 "Blessed ____ the meek" (Matthew 5:5)
36 _____ Rica
37 "My arms can _____ bow of bronze"
(Psalm 18:34 NIV) (2 words)
38 "And cast him into the _____ of
lions" (Daniel 6:16)
39 "Arise, cry _____ the night"
(Lamentations 2:19) (2 words)
40 "To go _____ to lodge in Gibeah"
(Judges 19:15) (2 words)
41 "If _____ man will come after me"
(Matthew 16:24)
42 "He esteemeth iron as _____"
(Job 41:27)
43 _____ *contendere* (Lat.)
44 A son of Jether (1 Chronicles 7:38)
45 "Whilst we are _____ in the body"
(2 Corinthians 5:6) (2 words)

46 Boring routine
48 University employee (abbr.)
49 "As the ox licketh up the _____"
(Numbers 22:4) (4 words)
57 Hindu queen
58 Attention getter
59 Ancient Greek colony in Italy
60 "He shall not _____ it"
(Leviticus 27:10)
61 "More _____ desired are they than
gold" (Psalm 19:10) (2 words)
62 "Neither shall I know the _____ of
children" (Isaiah 47:8)
63 "Ye do the _____ of your father"
(John 8:41)
64 Hard beef fat
65 "That dippeth with me in the _____"
(Mark 14:20)

## DOWN

1 "Saying, Proclaim a _____"
(1 Kings 21:9)
2 Great-grandmother of David
(Matthew 1:5–6)
3 Nobody won; it ended in _____
(2 words)
4 "Neither have we vineyard, _____"
(Jeremiah 35:9) (4 words)
5 "By whom also we have _____ by
faith" (Romans 5:2)
6 Teddy bear from down under
7 Sulfuric or nitric
8 "And your _____" (James 5:12 NIV)
(2 words)
9 "The man. . .came _____ large
flocks" (Genesis 30:43 NIV) (2 words)
10 "Prophesy against the forest _____"
(Ezekiel 20:46) (4 words)
11 Lug
12 Celebes buffalo
13 "Neither shall ye touch it, _____ ye
die" (Genesis 3:3)
21 "And fastened to the cross. _____:
JESUS" (John 19:19 NIV) (2 words)
22 Egg _____ yong

*by David K. Shortess*

25 Israeli general and prime minister
26 "I _____ choice food" (Daniel 10:3 NIV) (2 words)
27 "I was beside the Ulai _____" (Daniel 8:2 NIV)
28 "To die in the _____" (1 Corinthians 4:9 NIV)
29 "Let him _____ himself" (Matthew 16:24)
31 Houston athlete
32 "And so become unclean through _____ the LORD" (Leviticus 22:8 NIV) (3 words)
33 "And how _____ know the way?" (John 14:5) (2 words)
35 Twelfth Jewish month (Esther 9:1)
36 "Who sinned at the _____ their lives" (Numbers 16:38 NIV) (2 words)
44 From _____ Z (2 words)

45 "Mercy and truth _____ together" (Psalm 85:10) (2 words)
47 Computer operators
48 "I commend unto you _____ our sister" (Romans 16:1)
49 New alum
50 Lung noise
51 Preceding (prefix)
52 Jazzman Domino
53 "_____ art worthy, O Lord" (Revelation 4:11)
54 "Jesus cried with a loud voice, saying, _____" (Mark 15:34)
55 "The _____ is blessed of the better" (Hebrews 7:7)
56 "Lest thou _____ thy foot against a stone" (Psalm 91:12)

## ACROSS

1 Accomplish
3 Began prophesying "in the year that king Uzziah died" (abbr.)
6 "My speech distill as the _____" (Deuteronomy 32:2 NKJV)
9 Cut
10 "Now the serpent was more subtil _____ any beast" (Genesis 3:1)
12 In chemistry, a colorless liquid belonging to alkanes
14 Single
15 "The _____ after her kind" (Leviticus 11:19)
17 Incident
18 "And the herdmen of _____" (Genesis 26:20)
20 "Lod, and _____, the valley of craftsmen" (Nehemiah 11:35)
21 "I travail in _____ again until Christ be formed in you" (Galatians 4:19)
22 Solomon's great-grandson (1 Kings 15:8)
23 "Cuth made _____" (2 Kings 17:30)
25 Partook
26 Conquered by Joshua (Joshua 8)
27 Agreement
31 "To meet the Lord in the _____" (1 Thessalonians 4:17)
32 "Take unto thee sweet spices, _____, and onycha" (Exodus 30:34)
35 "Name of his city was _____" (1 Chronicles 1:50)
36 Tiger Woods: golf _____
37 "The name of the other _____" (1 Samuel 14:4)
38 Empty talk is _____ air
39 "Came to Joel the _____" (Joel 1:1)
40 "They shall _____ one against another" (Nahum 2:4)
41 This is attached to the shoulder
42 Response
44 Judah's firstborn (Numbers 26:19)

45 "Between Bethel and _____" (Genesis 13:3)
46 King of Damascus (2 Corinthians 11:32)
49 Obese
50 "No more _____" (Hosea 2:16)
53 "And a river went _____ of Eden to water the garden" (Genesis 2:10)
54 A son of David (1 Chronicles 3:5–6)
57 Bend
58 Bring together
60 A son of Caleb (1 Chronicles 4:15)
61 Moses' father-in-law (Exodus 2:18–21)
62 "And his _____ drew" (Revelation 12:4)
63 This is connected to the foot
64 Watch for this color of heifer near the end
65 Commanded militarily
66 An altar (Joshua 22:34)

## DOWN

1 "For he hath _____ marvellous things" (Psalm 98:1)
2 "And there are diversities of _____" (1 Corinthians 12:6)
3 Amasa's father (2 Samuel 17:25)
4 "And _____ lay at his feet until the morning" (Ruth 3:14)
5 Priesthood
6 Demons
7 A son of Ram (1 Chronicles 2:27)
8 Desire
9 A measurement for oil (Leviticus 14:10)
11 Not any
12 "Didst _____ thyself even unto hell" (Isaiah 57:9)
13 "To the _____ degree" (common phrase)
16 "_____ was an hair of their head" (Daniel 3:27)
19 Greek form of *Asher* (Revelation 7:6)
24 "All faces shall _____ blackness"

*by N. Teri Grottke*

(Joel 2:6)

25 Moses' brother
26 "And shall _____ our hearts before him" (1 John 3:19)
28 Elkanah was one (1 Samuel 1:1)
29 Ruth's mother-in-law
30 This biblical author took up the offering for Jerusalem's poor believers (abbr.)
33 Tiny insect
34 "The glory of the _____ is one" (1 Corinthians 15:40)
36 A biblical book of poetry (abbr.)
40 A son of Tola (1 Chronicles 7:2)
41 Jezebel's husband
43 The cities are great and _____ up to heaven" (Deuteronomy 1:28)
47 King of Hamath (1 Chronicles 18:9)
48 Sister of parent

49 "Shepherds abiding in the _____" (Luke 2:8)
50 Barrier
51 A brother of Eshcol (Genesis 14:13)
52 Fever
55 "Of _____, the family" (Numbers 26:17)
56 "For ye tithe mint and _____" (Luke 11:42)
59 Bind

# PUZZLE 72 — BIBLICAL ILLUMINATION

*For these commands are a lamp,*
*this teaching is a light.*
PROVERBS 6:23 NIV

## ACROSS

1 Seth's father (Genesis 4:25)
5 "They _____ walls like soldiers" (Joel 2:7 NIV)
10 Swiss river
14 "The devil threw him down, and _____ him" (Luke 9:42)
15 Sugar stalks
16 Noah's oldest son (Genesis 5:32)
17 "As the camp _____ set forward" (Numbers 4:15) (2 words)
18 Playful prank
19 "It is a _____ offering" (Leviticus 2:6)
20 Start of **QUOTE** from Psalm 119:105, with 48 Across and 37 Across, in that order (5 words)
23 E.T.'s ship, for example
24 "The _____ of the scribes is in vain" (Jeremiah 8:8)
25 Gold purity units
29 "_____ is written" (Romans 3:10) (2 words)
31 RR stop
34 "The rest of all the acts _____" (1 Kings 15:23)
35 *Years* in Yucatan
36 Cornelia _____ Skinner
37 End of **QUOTE** (4 words)
40 "Either make the _____ good" (Matthew 12:33)
41 "And at _____, will I pray" (Psalm 55:17)
42 "The way of an _____ in the air" (Proverbs 30:19)
43 Socioeconomic status (abbr.)
44 "The Man" Musial
45 Jaw whalebone
46 _____ Lanka
47 _____ *Miniver* (WWII film)
48 Part 2 of **QUOTE** (5 words)
56 "This great thing _____ hath been heard like it?" (Deuteronomy 4:32) (2 words)
57 "Hide not thine _____ my breathing" (Lamentations 3:56) (2 words)

58 "And when the new _____ was come" (1 Samuel 20:24)
59 "There he _____ Jew named Aquila" (Acts 18:2 NIV) (2 words)
60 Argentine plain
61 "He goeth _____ meet the armed men" (Job 39:21) (2 words)
62 "And _____ of cedar beams" (1 Kings 6:36) (2 words)
63 "Of Nebat, who was _____ Egypt" (1 Kings 12:2) (2 words)
64 "The evidence of things not _____" (Hebrews 11:1)

## DOWN

1 "And ye have snuffed _____" (Malachi 1:13) (2 words)
2 "Lest thou _____ thy foot against a stone" (Psalm 91:12)
3 Affectedly or showily artistic
4 Cat call
5 Buffet runners
6 "For without me ye _____ nothing" (John 15:5) (2 words)
7 Against (prefix)
8 Island souvenirs
9 Daydreaming, perhaps
10 "Or seest thou _____ seeth?" (Job 10:4) (2 words)
11 Attention getter
12 "They that sow in tears shall _____ in joy" (Psalm 126:5)
13 CPR provider (abbr.)
21 "And they went _____ noon" (1 Kings 20:16) (2 words)
22 "And God said, _____ there be light" (Genesis 1:3)
25 "Thirty milch camels with their _____" (Genesis 32:15)
26 "_____ goeth before him, and burneth" (Psalm 97:3) (2 words)
27 "The fool _____ and scoffs, and there is no peace" (Proverbs 29:9 NIV)
28 "Simon the Leper, _____ sat at meat" (Mark 14:3) (2 words)

*by David K. Shortess*

29 Composer and pianist Rubinstein
30 "Now as _____ as it was day" (Acts 12:18)
31 "And ran at flood _____ as before" (Joshua 4:18 NIV)
32 "And Pilate wrote a _____" (John 19:19)
33 Pale
35 Celebes buffalo
36 Lustrous gem
38 "Like the _____ birth of a woman" (Psalm 58:8)
39 "Eat nothing made with _____" (Exodus 12:20 NIV)
44 Sign of a success (abbr.)
45 Cape _____, Nova Scotia
46 "I will not give you _____" (Exodus 5:10)
47 "If you had known what these words _____ desire mercy" (Matthew 12:7 NIV) (2 words)
48 Computer operator
49 "It teaches us to say _____ ungodliness" (Titus 2:12 NIV)
50 Elihu's school
51 Greek organiation (abbr.)
52 Book after Joel
53 "Because it is _____ of his" (Job 18:15)
54 "And they shall _____" (Jeremiah 50:36)
55 "And _____ they tell him of her" (Mark 1:30)
56 "And _____ man with smooth skin" (Genesis 27:11 NIV) (2 words)

## ACROSS

1 "Between Bethel and _____" (Genesis 13:3)
4 "_____, Hadid, and Ono" (Ezra 2:33)
7 Opposite of *her*
10 "Restore all that was _____" (2 Kings 8:6)
11 Seth's son (Genesis 4:26)
13 A son of Jahdai (1Chronicles 2:47)
15 Greek form of *Hagar* (Galatians 4:24)
16 Jesus' garden trial
18 A son of Raamah (Genesis 10:7)
20 Bed covering
21 Allow
22 Peter cut one off
24 A king of Midian (Numbers 31:8)
25 "_____, Bethzur, and Gedor" (Joshua 15:58)
28 "Ointment and _____ rejoice the heart" (Proverbs 27:9)
33 A son of Benjamin (Genesis 46:21)
34 Consume food
36 Beloved hymn: "_____, My God, to Thee"
37 "Thee in this _____" (2 Kings 9:26)
38 Exclamation of affirmation
40 Exhaust
41 Rescue (arch.)
44 This book includes two censuses (abbr.)
46 "_____ mouth is smoother than oil" (Proverbs 5:3)
47 Azareel's son (Nehemiah 11:13)
49 "Aquila, born in Pontus, _____ come from Italy" (Acts 18:2)
51 To furnish with equipment, or a body part
52 "Borders of _____" (Joshua 11:2)
53 "Against Jerusalem, _____" (Ezekiel 26:2)
56 Snake poison
59 "Jozabad, and _____" (2 Chronicles 31:13)
63 "He stood by the lake of _____" (Luke 5:1)
66 Nagge's son (Luke 3:25)
67 A son of Zabad (1 Chronicles 7:21)
68 A son of Caanan (Genesis 10:15)
69 "And your feet _____ with the preparation of the gospel of peace" (Ephesians 6:15)
70 "O ye _____ bones, hear the word of the LORD" (Ezekiel 37:4)
71 Buzzing stinger
72 Transgression

## DOWN

1 The king's chamberlain (Esther 2:3)
2 "_____ the Canaanite" (Numbers 21:1)
3 Jacob's descendants
4 Appendage
5 "Day of _____ birth" (Ecclesiastes 7:1)
6 "What _____ the LORD require of thee" (Micah 6:8)
7 Edge of a garment
8 Son of Nathan of Zobah (2 Samuel 23:36)
9 "_____. God hath numbered thy kingdom, and finished it" (Daniel 5:26)
10 "He _____ horns" (Habakkuk 3:4)
12 Fleecy ruminant
13 Go to sleep
14 Became acquainted
17 Popular biblical number
19 Prophecy book only three chapters long (abbr.)
23 "For ye tithe mint and _____" (Luke 11:42)
25 David fought the Syrians here (2 Samuel 10:17)
26 Ezra proclaimed a fast there (Ezra 8:21)
27 Beat down
29 "To visit the _____ and widows" (James 1:27)
30 Michaiah's father (2 Chronicles 13:2)
31 Happy
32 Before (arch.)
35 "Hundred and _____ years old" (Joshua 24:29)

*by N. Teri Grottke*

37 This book was written between the times of Moses and Babylonian captivity (abbr.)
39 Another way to spell *awl*
42 Shorn
43 Weeds
45 Insane
48 Asher's firstborn (1 Chronicles 7:30)
50 This is connected to the foot
53 Get older
54 Gripped
55 A brother of Eshcol (Genesis 14:13)
57 "Brought the heads of _____" (Judges 7:25)
58 Measure (arch.)
60 Rephaiah's father (1 Chronicles 4:42)
61 Esau's father-in-law (Genesis 26:34)

62 "Bored a hole in the _____ of it" (2 Kings 12:9)
64 No (arch.)
65 "_____ word of the Lord was precious in those days" (1 Samuel 3:1)

# PUZZLE 74 — WHAT'S HIS LINE?

What was the occupation of each person named in all caps?

*The labourer is worthy of his hire.*
LUKE 10:7

## ACROSS

1 Asner and Ames
4 "_____ in a poke" (2 words)
8 **ESAU** (Genesis 25:27)
14 "Fifteen in a _____" (1 Kings 7:3)
15 1947 biochemistry Nobel laureate
16 Gunsmoke actor James
17 Hophni's father (1 Samuel 1:3)
18 Shades
19 Fifth part of an act in a Roman play (2 words)
20 **ALEXANDER** (2 Timothy 4:14)
23 Pile driver head
24 "Nor on any _____" (Revelation 7:1)
25 School founded by Henry VI
26 Doctrinal ending (suffix)
28 "There is a _____ here" (John 6:9)
30 Winding in and out
34 "If you have _____ with men on foot" (Jeremiah 12:5 NIV)
37 Basic bread spread
39 Just barely got by
40 Good Judean king (1 Kings 15:9, 11)
41 **MALCHUS** (John 18:10)
44 "Sir, come down _____ my child die" (John 4:49)
45 "Neither shall they learn war any _____" (Isaiah 2:4)
47 "Waters to _____ in" (Ezekiel 47:5)
48 Island of western Scotland
50 "But a wise man will _____ it" (Proverbs 16:14 NIV)
52 "Blessed _____ . . ." (Matthew 5:3–11)
53 "Firm unto the _____" (Hebrews 3:6)
54 "And I saw when the _____ opened one of the seals" (Revelation 6:1)
57 "The open _____ between the side rooms" (Ezekiel 41:9 NIV)

61 "Then Gideon took _____ men of his servants" (Judges 6:27)
63 **DEMETRIUS** (Acts 19:24)
66 Choose (2 words)
68 _____ vera
69 "Was _____ unto him" (Matthew 18:34)
70 _____ Nevadas
71 "The _____ of the scornful" (Psalm 1:1)
72 Harem room
73 **EZRA** (Nehemiah 8:1)
74 Spreads hay
75 "I have _____ you with milk" (1 Corinthians 3:2)

## DOWN

1 "And do not _____ a sacred stone" (Deuteronomy 16:22 NIV)
2 Sorrow
3 Filch
4 "Even in laughter the heart may _____" (Proverbs 14:13 NIV)
5 "His fury is _____ out like fire" (Nahum 1:6)
6 "I was not in safety, neither had _____" (Job 3:26) (2 words)
7 Gadget (var.)
8 "_____ thou eaten of the tree" (Genesis 3:11)
9 Street youngster
10 Compass point between N and NE
11 **AQUILA** (Acts 18:2–3)
12 "But _____ have I hated" (Romans 9:13)
13 Request for a formal answer (abbr.)
21 Soccer great
22 Pant leg length
27 "And if any man will _____ thee at the law" (Matthew 5:40)
29 Classifieds
31 H+ or OH–

32 Trillion (prefix)
33 "On the east of _____" (Genesis 4:16)
34 "With the _____ third of a hin" (Numbers 28:14 NIV) (2 words)
35 "He it is, to whom I shall give _____" (John 13:26) (2 words)
36 **JESUS** (Mark 6:3–4)
37 *1984* author
38 CXII ÷ II
42 Follows *heir-* or *host-*
43 "Of stone, and _____ for mortar" (Genesis 11:3 NIV)
46 Follows *hallow-* or *eight-*
49 Enlarge a hole
51 Accumulate on a surface
52 "Now when this was noised _____" (Acts 2:6)
55 Nautical halt

56 Brawl
58 "Houses may be _____ the frogs" (Exodus 8:9 NIV) (2 words)
59 Piece for the piano
60 "My messenger _____ of you" (Mark 1:2 NIV)
61 "Waves thereof _____ themselves" (Jeremiah 5:22)
62 Heroic narrative
64 "*Dies* _____" (Latin hymn of mourning)
65 "So if the Son _____ you free" (John 8:36 NIV)
67 Day before Saturday (abbr.)

# PUZZLE 75

## ACROSS

1 Melchi's father (Luke 3:28)
5 Uri's son (1 Kings 4:19)
10 "We _____ our bread" (Lamentations 5:9)
13 "Baalah, and _____" (Joshua 15:29)
14 Stayed in a place
15 Shammah's father (2 Samuel 23:11)
17 "Tappuah, and _____" (Joshua 15:34)
18 "This only would I _____ of you" (Galatians 3:2)
19 "_____ which is lent" (1 Samuel 2:20)
20 Sugar plant
21 Made a mistake
22 "_____ the waters" (Exodus 15:25)
23 "Who shall lay any thing to the _____ of God's elect?" (Romans 8:33)
25 Pass away
26 More or _____
27 Strange
29 "The wheat and the _____ were not smitten" (Exodus 9:32)
31 "An he _____ also" (Proverbs 30:31)
34 Strong wood
37 Gave a loan
40 "Take thy _____" (Luke 16:7)
41 "At his holy _____" (Psalm 99:9)
43 A son of Gad (Genesis 46:16)
45 Great wickedness
46 "Is not _____" (Isaiah 10:9)
48 City in Egypt (Hosea 10:8)
49 Book of ceremonial law (abbr.)
50 Jediael's brother (1 Chronicles 11:45)
51 "What _____ ye to weep" (Acts 21:13)
52 "The other _____" (Nehemiah 7:33)
54 King Hezekiah's mother (2 Kings 18:2)
56 "Wherefore _____ up the loins of your mind" (1 Peter 1:13)
57 Put it to good _____
59 "Shimei, and _____" (1 Kings 1:8)
61 A son of Lotan (1 Chronicles 1:39)
64 Solomon's great-grandson (Matthew 1:7)
67 One who stood at Ezra's right hand (Nehemiah 8:4)
72 A son of Joktan (Genesis 10:26–29)
73 "Jonah was gone down into the _____ of the ship" (Jonah 1:5)
75 Rephaiah's father (1 Chronicles 4:42)
76 Desire
77 Walked (arch.)
78 Precipitation

## DOWN

2 Jacob and Leah's daughter (Genesis 30:16–21)
3 Pagan goddess of the Ephesians (Acts 19:35)
4 Pashur's father (Jeremiah 20:1)
5 What Jacob called Jegarsahadutha (Genesis 31:47)
6 Salah's son (Genesis 10:24)
7 "Under every _____ two sockets" (Exodus 36:30)
8 "Og the king of Bashan, which dwelt at Astaroth in _____" (Deuteronomy 1:4)
9 Give
10 "Nathanael of Cana in _____" (John 21:2)
11 "Three days _____ I fell sick" (1 Samuel 30:13)
12 "Lament for the _____" (Isaiah 32:12)
16 Seth's son (Genesis 4:26)
17 One of the books likely written by Solomon (abbr.)
24 Received
28 Accomplish
30 Sick
31 "Not _____ to filthy lucre" (Titus 1:7)
32 Oily fruit
33 "Destroy _____ kings and people" (Ezra 6:12)
35 Asher didn't drive out the inhabitants of this town (Judges 1:31)

by *N. Teri Grottke*

36 Relatives
38 "For if ye do these things, ye shall _____ fall" (2 Peter 1:10)
39 Walk
40 A god of Babylon (Isaiah 46:1)
42 "For, _____, as soon as the voice of thy salutation" (Luke 1:44)
44 Motel
46 Rocky Mountain state (abbr.)
47 "Against Jerusalem, _____" (Ezekiel 26:2)
48 Patriarch of a family of returned exiles (Ezra 2:57)
50 Moses' successor (abbr.)
53 "And _____ great" (Ecclesiastes 9:14)
55 "Children of _____" (1 Chronicles 7:12)
56 "_____ is for him?" (Amos 3:5)

58 Direction of the rising sun
60 Comfort
61 "_____ shall we" (Hebrews 2:3)
62 Edom will be destroyed in its only chapter (abbr.)
63 "_____ greedily after the error of Balaam" (Jude 1:11)
65 Knight
66 Fuss
68 "To meet the Lord in the _____" (1 Thessalonians 4:17)
69 This prophet had a son named Shear-jashub (abbr.)
70 Abdiel's son (1 Chronicles 5:15)
71 A liquid measure (Leviticus 23:13)
74 An altar (Joshua 22:34)

157

*And he laid hold on the dragon, that old serpent,*
*which is the Devil, and Satan, and bound him a thousand years.*
REVELATION 20:2

## ACROSS

1 "A _____ answer turneth away wrath"
(Proverbs 15:1)
5 "Cometh to me I will in no wise
_____ out" (John 6:37)
9 Danish physicist Niels and family
14 "Shammah the son of _____"
(2 Samuel 23:11)
15 Quechuan
16 Nebraska cow town
17 "Now the coat was without _____"
(John 19:23)
18 "Our end is _____"
(Lamentations 4:18)
19 German city on the Moselle near
Luxembourg
20 **IT SWEET-TALKED:** "And the
woman said, The _____ me, and I
did eat" (Genesis 3:13) (2 words)
23 _____ la-la
24 Entertainer Mineo
25 "When anyone went to a wine
_____" (Haggai 2:16 NIV)
28 Singing brothers of yesteryear
31 Bay off the west coast of France
36 Islands in the Seine
38 Where Pearl Harbor is located
40 "Is he a homeborn _____?"
(Jeremiah 2:14)
41 **IT HAD BEEN A ROD:** "And it
became a _____ fled from before it"
(Exodus 4:2–3) (3 words)
44 Halos
45 Countertenor
46 "I would thou _____ cold or hot"
(Revelation 3:15)
47 Posture
49 "And led him out of the _____"
(Mark 8:23)
51 Precedes -*king*, -*ring*, or -*wing*
52 "Stand in _____, and sin not"
(Psalm 4:4)
54 "Thou shalt _____ kill" (Exodus 20:13)
56 **IT WAS ON A POLE:** "And Moses
made _____" (Numbers 21:9) (4 words)

65 "Sent away Paul and Silas by night
unto _____" (Acts 17:10)
66 "As _____ large number of God-
fearing Greeks" (Acts 17:4 NIV)
(2 words)
67 "That an _____ is nothing in the
world" (1 Corinthians 8:4)
68 Cooped up
69 City on the Oka
70 "But the tongue can no man _____"
(James 3:8)
71 "And Jacob _____ away unawares to
Laban the Syrian" (Genesis 31:20)
72 "For my flesh is _____ food"
(John 6:55 NIV)
73 "Leah was tender _____"
(Genesis 29:17)

## DOWN

1 Back talk
2 S-shaped curve
3 "And in thy _____ will I worship"
(Psalm 5:7)
4 "Wherefore do ye _____ the LORD?"
(Exodus 17:2)
5 "Calamus and _____"
(Song of Solomon 4:14)
6 "For he is cast into _____ by his own
feet" (Job 18:8) (2 words)
7 Sign of healing
8 "Then appeared the _____ also"
(Matthew 13:26)
9 Food poisoning
10 "But _____ wrought evil in the eyes
of the LORD" (1 Kings 16:25)
11 "And the _____ shall sweep away"
(Isaiah 28:17)
12 Post-WWII Korean dictator Syngman
13 A semiprecious form of reddish
chalcedony
21 Pitcher's stat (abbr.)
22 Chatter
25 Passport add-ons
26 Alaskan native
27 Precedes *cotta* or *firma*

*by David K. Shortess*

29 "That they may _____ whole month" (Numbers 11:21) (2 words)

30 "Thou _____ not kill" (Exodus 20:13)

32 "The LORD is _____ to anger" (Nahum 1:3)

33 "Is not under bondage in such _____" (1 Corinthians 7:15)

34 "Can consecrated meat _____ your punishment?" (Jeremiah 11:15 NIV)

35 "_____ your amazement he will show him" (John 5:20 NIV) (2 words)

37 "And children of a _____ long?" (Lamentations 2:20)

39 "And it shall be opened _____ you" (Matthew 7:7)

42 Foolhardy, reckless adventure

43 "Your sins have been your _____!" (Hosea 14:1 NIV)

48 "One _____ lamb of the first year without blemish" (Leviticus 14:10)

50 "And _____, the city of the priests" (1 Samuel 22:19)

53 "There is a woman that hath a familiar spirit at _____" (1 Samuel 28:7)

55 Hackneyed

56 Fundamentals

57 "I prepared my _____ in the street!" (Job 29:7)

58 Consequently

59 "The earth shall _____ to and fro" (Isaiah 24:20)

60 "Bind the _____ of thine head upon thee" (Ezekiel 24:17)

61 Greek theaters

62 "It is _____ of blowing the trumpets unto you" (Numbers 29:1) (2 words)

63 "The devil shall cast _____ of you into prison" (Revelation 2:10)

64 Winter coaster

# PUZZLE 77

## ACROSS

1 "The fenced cities are Ziddim, _____, and Hammath" (Joshua 19:35)
4 Shiphi's son (1 Chronicles 4:37)
8 Interpreted by Daniel to mean "Thy kingdom is divided" (Daniel 5:28)
13 "Of Hena, and _____?" (2 Kings 19:13)
15 "_____, Hizkijah, Azzur" (Nehemiah 10:17)
16 A son of Elioenai (1 Chronicles 3:24)
17 "Gedaliah, and _____" (1 Chronicles 25:3)
18 "Whosoever shall say to his brother, _____, shall be in danger of the council" (Matthew 5:22)
19 A son of Eliphaz (Genesis 36:11)
20 A son of Eliab (Numbers 26:9)
22 "She waited on _____ wife" (2 Kings 5:2)
24 Verbalize
25 "Everything on _____ land that had the breath of life in its nostrils died" (Genesis 7:22 NIV)
26 Uzziah broke down this Philistine wall (2 Chronicles 26:6)
30 Largest continent
32 Barrier
35 "Myrrh and _____" (Song of Solomon 4:14)
36 "The LORD dwelleth in _____" (Joel 3:21)
37 Mighty man of David (2 Samuel 23:36)
38 Cook
39 Fuss
40 "_____ it, and smote the Philistine in his forehead" (1 Samuel 17:49)
41 Injured
42 "Though ye have _____" (Psalm 68:13)
43 A son of Ephraim (1 Chronicles 7:22–25)
44 Increase
45 Master

46 "Thou _____ up mine iniquity" (Job 14:17)
47 This book ends with Moses' death (abbr.)
48 Kona, Hawaii (airport code)
49 "From the _____ of the sea" (Isaiah 11:11)
53 Firstborn
57 Disburse
58 Load (arch.)
60 The city Lot fled to (Genesis 19:17–22)
62 Spear
63 A son of Shem (Genesis 10:22)
64 "According to this _____" (Galatians 6:16)
65 Come in
66 "The linen _____ at a price" (1 Kings 10:28)
67 Commanded militarily

## DOWN

1 "Go ye down against them: behold, they come up by the cliff of _____" (2 Chronicles 20:16)
2 "_____ the death of the cross" (Philippians 2:8)
3 Not easily found
4 "At Enrimmon, and at _____, and at Jarmuth" (Nehemiah 11:29)
5 Country of Rome
6 Most apocalyptic and messianic book of all minor prophets (abbr.)
7 Uz's brother (1 Chronicles 1:42)
8 "Thence unto _____" (Acts 21:1)
9 Foe
10 "In _____ was there a voice" (Matthew 2:18)
11 Ahira's father (Numbers 1:15)
12 Iniquities
14 "They asked _____, 'Then who are you? Are you Elijah?' " (John 1:21 NIV)
21 Use (arch.)
23 Patriarch of a family of returned exiles (Ezra 2:15)
26 Attai's father (1 Chronicles 2:35)

*by N. Teri Grottke*

27 With the speaking voice
28 "Under every _____ two sockets" (Exodus 36:30)
29 Bird home
30 Helped
31 "Not _____ angry" (Titus 1:7)
32 "_____ of Judah" (2 Samuel 6:2)
33 "_____ and Caiaphas being the high priests" (Luke 3:2)
34 "If you do what is _____, will you not be accepted?" (Genesis 4:7 NIV)
36 Where Joram smote the Edomites (2 Kings 8:21)
37 What the wind did at the parting of the Red Sea
40 In place of (arch.)
42 "There will be _____ wailing throughout Egypt" (Exodus 11:6 NIV)
45 "The borrower is servant to the _____" (Proverbs 22:7)
46 "Call a _____ assembly" (Joel 2:15)
47 One way to praise the Lord
48 "The tents of _____!" (Psalm 120:5)
49 Island
50 Breadth
51 Gave a loan
52 Kill
54 This prophet's name means "help" (abbr.)
55 Human being
56 Story
59 Jether's son (1 Chronicles 7:38)
61 Color of blood

# PUZZLE 78 — FOLLOW THE LEADER

*By this shall all men know that ye are my disciples,*
*if ye have love one to another.*
JOHN 13:35

## ACROSS

1 Start of **VERSE** from John 15:12
5 "It is only _____ from the burn" (Leviticus 13:28 NIV) (2 words)
10 Israeli folk dance
14 "Be not _____ with thy mouth" (Ecclesiastes 5:2)
15 A silly one
16 "No, nor _____ shall be" (Matthew 24:21)
17 **VERSE**, cont'd from 1 Across (3 words)
20 Hot dog man Oscar
21 "Forbear, what am I ____?" (Job 16:6)
22 Nutritional intake guidelines (abbr.)
23 "The trees of the LORD are full of _____" (Psalm 104:16)
25 Lbs. or kgs. (abbr.)
27 **VERSE**, cont'd from 17 Across (3 words)
33 _____ Romeo
37 "And he shall smite the earth with the _____ of his mouth" (Isaiah 11:4)
38 "And when she had _____ it" (Exodus 2:6)
39 Durocher and Tolstoy
40 What most of the earth's people are
42 Prof's aides (abbr.)
43 "Let us _____ rebuilding" (Nehemiah 2:18 NIV)
44 "Six thousand shekels of gold and ten _____ of clothing" (2 Kings 5:5 NIV)
45 Cause to put on weight
47 "For God, said _____, hath appointed me" (Genesis 4:25)
48 "Wherein thou _____ been instructed" (Luke 1:4)
49 **VERSE**, cont'd from 27 Across (2 words)
51 "And all that handle the _____" (Ezekiel 27:29)
53 "Unto thee, O LORD, _____ lift up my soul" (Psalm 25:1) (2 words)
54 "The custom of the ____" (Luke 2:27)
57 "Tell me, art thou a _____?" (Acts 22:27)

61 Zoo favorite
65 End of **VERSE**, cont'd from 49 Across (5 words)
68 "Sir, your _____ has earned five more" (Luke 19:18 NIV)
69 Rub out
70 Tight
71 "For my yoke is _____" (Matthew 11:30)
72 "And _____ between Nineveh and Calah" (Genesis 10:12)
73 "Come back _____ his own head" (Esther 9:25 NIV)

## DOWN

1 "_____ her nails" (Deuteronomy 21:12 NIV)
2 "He _____ demon" (Luke 7:33 NIV) (2 words)
3 "What _____ strength, that I should hope?" (Job 6:11) (2 words)
4 Most bashful
5 "But also to be forward a year _____" (2 Corinthians 8:10)
6 "And _____ fell among thorns" (Mark 4:7)
7 Stupor
8 "The events of _____ reign" (2 Chronicles 16:11 NIV)
9 "And be _____ in the spirit of your mind" (Ephesians 4:23)
10 "Round about the _____ thereof" (Exodus 28:33)
11 "And passed _____, and came into his own city" (Matthew 9:1)
12 "And _____ your heart" (Joel 2:13)
13 "For thou _____ near kinsman" (Ruth 3:9) (2 words)
18 Colorful drawing implement
19 It was banned in the US in 1972
24 Brio
26 "Eaten without _____?" (Job 6:6)
27 Refuse
28 Book after Daniel
29 Mine openings

*by David K. Shortess*

30 "Is pleased with me, _____ order be written" (Esther 8:5 NIV) (2 words)
31 First governor of New Mexico
32 The brightest asteroid
34 "Or put him on a _____ for your girls?" (Job 41:5 NIV)
35 "_____ was above all the people" (Nehemiah 8:5) (2 words)
36 Fall bloomer
41 "Had no leisure so much _____ eat" (Mark 6:31) (2 words)
43 Forty winks
45 "Been with me _____ a year" (1 Samuel 29:3 NIV) (2 words)
46 "There shall be no _____" (Luke 1:33)
50 "Are to be _____ the rings" (Exodus 28:28 NIV) (2 words)
52 One of the three sons of Jether (1 Chronicles 7:38)

54 "And the _____ walk" (Matthew 11:5)
55 "Which are in _____" (Revelation 1:4)
56 "He who _____ souls is wise" (Proverbs 11:30 NIV)
58 "A _____ man" (Romans 2:3 NIV)
59 "_____, my lord" (Numbers 12:11)
60 "The rings, and _____ jewels" (Isaiah 3:21)
62 "Confirmed it _____ oath" (Hebrews 6:17) (2 words)
63 "Shoot your arrows and _____ them" (Psalm 144:6 NIV)
64 Ford, for example
66 "Stones, wood, _____, stubble" (1 Corinthians 3:12)
67 Neighbor of Brazil (abbr.)

# PUZZLE 79

## ACROSS

1 "_____ of truth shall be established for ever" (Proverbs 12:19)
4 Assist
8 "Zelah, _____, and Jebusi" (Joshua 18:28)
13 Thummim's partner (Exodus 28:30)
15 Cain's victim
16 A son of Ulla (1 Chronicles 7:39)
17 "For he hath _____ marvellous things" (Psalm 98:1)
18 "For in him we live, and _____, and have our being" (Acts 17:28)
19 "Go on your way _____ in the morning" (Genesis 19:2 NIV)
20 A son of Asaph (1 Chronicles 25:2)
23 "But the wheat and the _____ were not smitten" (Exodus 9:32)
24 No matter which
25 "On the east side of _____" (Numbers 34:11)
27 Belonging to Sarai's husband
31 Sunrise
33 "Bore his _____ through with a thorn?" (Job 41:2)
36 Elkanah's grandfather (1 Samuel 1:1)
37 People
38 Naomi wanted to be called this
39 Bellybutton
40 The people of one of the greatest empires (abbr.)
41 "Name of _____" (Judges 1:11)
42 Ancient Hebrew unit of dry capacity, 1/10 ephah
43 Hearing organs
44 Elevate
45 Saul's grandfather (1 Chronicles 8:33)
46 Weeks are made of these
47 "Now as _____ and Jambres withstood Moses" (2 Timothy 3:8)
48 Biblical spy turned leader (abbr.)
49 Plant seed
50 "Helez the Paltite, _____" (2 Samuel 23:26)
52 "Stones of _____" (Isaiah 34:11)

58 Hurt
60 A son of Dishan (Genesis 36:28)
61 Tubs
63 "Argob and _____" (2 Kings 15:25)
64 "In vain you rise early and stay up _____" (Psalm 127:2 NIV)
65 "_____ the Ahohite" (1 Chronicles 11:29)
66 "I would hasten my escape from the _____ storm and tempest" (Psalm 55:8)
67 Looked at
68 Are (arch.)

## DOWN

1 A son of Shem (1 Chronicles 1:17)
2 Strong metal
3 Common tree
4 Belonging to Esther's enemy
5 "Ivory and _____" (Ezekiel 27:15)
6 Tribe of the priesthood
7 Guilty or not guilty
8 Before (arch.)
9 "This only would I _____ of you" (Galatians 3:2)
10 Chelub's son (1 Chronicles 27:26)
11 Heap
12 Livestock feed
14 Became acquainted
21 A son of Pharez (Genesis 46:12)
22 "Doth the _____ fly by thy wisdom" (Job 39:26)
26 Fort Wayne's state (abbr.)
27 Baptismal site of John the Baptist (John 3:23)
28 "Holy and without _____" (Ephesians 1:4)
29 The Jordan is the main one in Israel
30 "Sons of _____" (1 Chronicles 7:12)
31 Entrances
32 Charity
33 "Until they had destroyed _____ king of Canaan" (Judges 4:24)
34 Get up
35 Goods

*by N. Teri Grottke*

37 "None shall _____ them away"
    (Jeremiah 7:33)
38 "What _____ ye to weep"
    (Acts 21:13)
41 "Drink of that which the young men
    have _____" (Ruth 2:9)
43 Comfort
46 Accomplish
47 "The whole body fitly _____
    together" (Ephesians 4:16)
48 Maleleel's son (Luke 3:37)
49 "In whatsoever _____"
    (Philippians 4:11)
50 Zaccur's father (Nehemiah 3:2)
51 Precipitation
53 Not female
54 "_____ for the peace"
    (Psalm 122:6)
55 A king of Midian (Numbers 31:8)

56 Heber's father (Luke 3:35)
57 Night sky illuminator
58 Sharp-toothed tool
59 "So shall _____ seed be"
    (Romans 4:18)
62 "Turn aside, _____ down here"
    (Ruth 4:1)

# PUZZLE 80 — THE LORD'S COMPASSIONS

*Strength for today and bright hope for tomorrow—*
*blessings all mine and ten thousand beside!*

THOMAS O. CHISHOLM

## ACROSS

1 "And he was in his presence, as in times _____" (1 Samuel 19:7)
5 "Every man by his own _____" (Numbers 1:52)
9 "Behold, thou art but _____ man" (Genesis 20:3) (2 words)
14 "It is time for you to _____ LORD" (Psalm 119:126 NIV) (2 words)
15 "Which gendereth to bondage, which is _____" (Galatians 4:24)
16 Arbor _____ (Asian evergreen shrub)
17 Start of **VERSE:** Lamentations 3:23 (4 words)
20 "About the _____ of the robe to minister in" (Exodus 39:26)
21 "A tight _____ on his tongue" (James 1:26 NIV)
22 Rubs out
23 "To seek an _____" (Ezekiel 21:21 NIV)
24 "How much _____ man, that is a worm?" (Job 25:6)
25 **VERSE**, cont'd from 17 Across
28 Keats product
29 "The weasel, the _____" (Leviticus 11:29 NIV)
32 "Sort of error that _____ from a ruler" (Ecclesiastes 10:5 NIV)
33 Oriental sauce
34 "In _____ was there a voice" (Matthew 2:18)
35 "The choicest of its _____" (Isaiah 37:24 NIV)
36 "_____ ye here while I go and pray" (Matthew 26:36)
37 "Son of Ammiel in Lo _____" (2 Samuel 9:4 NIV)
38 "She had waited, and her hope was _____" (Ezekiel 19:5)
39 "Is he then his _____?" (Mark 12:37)
40 "Arose, and led him unto _____" (Luke 23:1)

41 Follows *ethyl-* or *methyl-*
42 Bad joke, often
43 **VERSE**, cont'd from 25 Across (2 words)
44 "So that the earth _____ again" (1 Samuel 4:5)
45 Rubicund
46 Toward the back of the boat
49 Small restaurant
50 Sheep-speak
53 End of **VERSE**, cont'd from 43 Across (2 words)
56 Recorded
57 "Whose faith is weak, _____ only vegetables" (Romans 14:2 NIV)
58 Beehive state
59 "How right they are to _____ you!" (Song of Solomon 1:4 NIV)
60 Altar location
61 Back of the neck

## DOWN

1 "They mar my _____" (Job 30:13)
2 "Even in laughter the heart may _____" (Proverbs 14:13 NIV)
3 "Out of the _____ of Jesse" (Isaiah 11:1)
4 Trifle
5 Drives recklessly
6 Getting old in Great Britain (var.)
7 Educator Horace
8 Prefix meaning "prior to"
9 "Securely as men _____ from war" (Micah 2:8)
10 Operatic prima donnas
11 Seine summers (Fr.)
12 Alpine river
13 Tunisian rulers
18 "He sent for his _____, and destroyed" (Matthew 22:7)
19 Like an unkept garden
23 Beginning
24 "They have been made _____" (Isaiah 42:22 NIV)

*by David K. Shortess*

25 Syrup source
26 "Or loose the bands of _____?" (Job 38:31)
27 Washer cycle
29 Capital of Morocco
30 He taught Stradivarius
31 "Then appeared the _____ also" (Matthew 13:26)
33 "The wilderness of _____" (Exodus 16:1)
34 Track event
36 "I was the _____ of the drunkards" (Psalm 69:12)
37 Type of engine
39 Branch of Islam
40 Copious
42 "They _____ their sin like Sodom" (Isaiah 3:9 NIV)
43 Nursery methods
44 "I _____ to those" (1 John 5:16 NIV)
46 "_____ boy!"

47 Roe source
48 Steno's error
49 Become raw
50 Follows *alpha*
51 Urgency letters
52 "Even _____ is pure" (1 John 3:3) (2 words)
54 It's in the bag, sometimes
55 Joshua's father (Exodus 33:11)

## ACROSS

1 A son of Judah (1 Chronicles 2:3)
5 She met Peter at the door
10 "Go, wash in the _____ of Siloam" (John 9:7)
14 Rabbit
15 "_____, and Hara" (1 Chronicles 5:26)
16 This priest rebuilt the temple
17 "Alammelech, and _____" (Joshua 19:26)
18 "And _____ it, that the tent lay along" (Judges 7:13)
20 "David _____ of him how Joab did" (2 Samuel 11:7)
22 "Into my _____" (Lamentations 3:13)
23 "Ye have _____ rebellious against the LORD" (Deuteronomy 31:27)
24 Timothy's grandmother
26 A set of steps
29 A son of Shimei (1 Chronicles 23:10)
30 Take action
33 "Habor, and _____" (1 Chronicles 5:26)
34 "Shall be your _____" (Ezekiel 45:12)
35 The Assyrians' fall is predicted in this book (abbr.)
36 Elkanah's grandfather (1 Samuel 1:1)
38 Before (arch.)
39 Take an oath (biblical sp.)
41 Buzzing stinger
42 Ishmael and Hagar lived in this wilderness
44 "Day of _____ birth" (Ecclesiastes 7:1)
45 Type of tree (Isaiah 44:14)
46 "Ho, _____ a one!" (Ruth 4:1)
47 "Shall it break in pieces and _____" (Daniel 2:40)
49 "He shall grow as the _____" (Hosea 14:5)
50 Apostle to the Gentiles
51 Loaded (arch.)

54 "Every neighbour will walk with _____" (Jeremiah 9:4)
58 Jacob's descendants
61 King Hoshea's father (2 Kings 15:30)
62 A son of Zibeon (1 Chronicles 1:40)
63 Bathsheba's first husband (2 Samuel 11:3)
64 Very (arch.)
65 Worn-out clothing
66 "Chalcol, and _____" (1 Kings 4:31)
67 Bound

## DOWN

1 "Jamin, and _____" (Genesis 46:10)
2 "That at the _____" (Philippians 2:10)
3 A son of Shem (Genesis 10:22)
4 A son of Jeconiah (1 Chronicles 3:17–18)
5 "Unto _____, and from thence unto Patara" (Acts 21:1)
6 Place of refuge
7 Ruth's son (Ruth 4:13–17)
8 "Borders of _____" (Joshua 11:2)
9 Are (arch.)
10 Part of the handwriting on the wall (Daniel 5:28)
11 A child of Gad (Numbers 26:16–18)
12 A son of Jerahmeel (1 Chronicles 2:25)
13 Boys
19 Belonging to Bathsheba's first husband
21 Saul's grandfather (1 Chronicles 8:33)
24 Flax cloth
25 Single
26 The visiting queen at Solomon's court was from here
27 Stories
28 "Argob and _____" (2 Kings 15:25)
29 Pharez' twin brother (Genesis 38:27–30)

by N. Teri Grottke

30 A son of Elioneai
   (1 Chronicles 3:24)
31 Concerns
32 "Thought on _____ things"
   (Matthew 1:20)
34 Undeserved favor
37 "These that have turned the world
   _____ down" (Acts 17:6)
40 "If thou _____seek unto God"
   (Job 8:5)
43 Awl (biblical sp.)
47 Ahijah's son (2 Kings 9:9)
48 Sprint
49 Belonging to Jacob's first wife
50 Beg
51 "If we say that we have not sinned,
   we make him a _____"
   (1 John 1:10)
52 Largest continent

53 Pull
54 Mix
55 Jesus cried this on the cross
   (Mark 15:34)
56 Not easily found
57 Slough off
59 A child of Shem (1 Chronicles 1:17)
60 "The sixth captain for the sixth
   month was _____"
   (1 Chronicles 27:9)

# PUZZLE 82

## ACROSS

1 "Straightway the spirit _____ him" (Mark 9:20)
5 City
9 "Jaresiah, and _____" (1 Chronicles 8:27)
14 "Duke Teman, duke _____" (Genesis 36:15)
15 Solomon's grandson (Matthew 1:7)
16 House
17 Zaccur's father (Nehemiah 3:2)
18 Menahem's father (2 Kings 15:17)
19 "Sons of Shemaiah; Hattush, and _____" (1 Chronicles 3:22)
20 "The whole world _____ in wickedness" (1 John 5:19)
22 Besides
24 "With a strong _____" (Jeremiah 21:5)
25 "Woe to them that are at _____ in Zion" (Amos 6:1)
28 "In that day shall this song be _____" (Isaiah 26:1)
30 "Thou shalt not _____ thyself" (Matthew 5:33)
34 Absalom's father (2 Samuel 3:3)
38 NT book after Galatians (abbr.)
39 "At the brook of _____" (Psalm 83:9)
41 "Whose name was _____ an Israelite" (2 Samuel 17:25)
42 Hushim's father (1 Chronicles 7:12)
44 "Whose soever sins ye _____, they are remitted unto them" (John 20:23)
46 "_____ stones and coals of fire" (Psalm 18:12)
47 "_____ between Nineveh and Calah" (Genesis 10:12)
49 "Offer a great sacrifice unto _____" (Judges 16:23)
51 A prophet son of Amoz (abbr.)
52 Servants
54 "Which was the son of _____" (Luke 3:27)
55 Hachaliah's son (Nehemiah 10:1) (abbr.)
56 "Out of the spoils _____ in battles" (1 Chronicles 26:27)
58 Lease

60 "They that followed, cried, saying, _____" (Mark 11:9)
64 "Which is neither _____ nor sown" (Deuteronomy 21:4)
68 Celeste
69 "My belly is as wine which hath no _____" (Job 32:19)
73 Beor's son (Genesis 36:32)
74 "He made narrowed _____ round about" (1 Kings 6:6)
75 "_____, lama sabachthani?" (Mark 15:34)
76 "Over the camels also was _____ the Ishmaelite" (1 Chronicles 27:30)
77 Awry
78 "Thy land shall be divided by _____" (Amos 7:17)
79 Level (arch.)

## DOWN

1 Travail
2 "Say ye unto your brethren, _____" (Hosea 2:1)
3 Unique
4 "Of Eri, the family of the _____" (Numbers 26:16)
5 License plate
6 Minor prophet who wrote an OT book (abbr.)
7 Broad
8 "His _____ of brass" (Daniel 7:19)
9 And _____, and Zilthai, and Eliel" (1 Chronicles 8:20)
10 Timber
11 Thought
12 "This _____ is mount Sinai" (Galatians 4:25)
13 Wheel
21 Falcon
23 Addition total
26 "When thou wentest out of _____" (Judges 5:4)
27 "Though I forbear, what am I _____?" (Job 16:6)
29 "Fought against _____" (2 Kings 12:17)
30 "Delivered me from all my _____" (Psalm 34:4)

170

*by Tonya Vilhauer*

31 "The Nethinims dwelt in _____"
   (Nehemiah 3:26)
32 "Which was the son of _____"
   (Luke 3:27)
33 "Having understood that he was a
   _____" (Acts 23:27)
35 Shackles
36 "Her children _____ up"
   (Proverbs 31:28)
37 "Brought them unto _____"
   (1 Chronicles 5:26)
40 "Simeon that was called _____"
   (Acts 13:1)
43 Accelerate
45 Torus
48 Novelty
50 Adam lived _____ hundred and
   thirty years (Genesis 5:5)
53 Offspring
57 Belly button

59 "The coast reacheth to _____"
   (Joshua 19:22)
60 "Brought them unto Halah, and Habor,
   and _____" (1 Chronicles 5:26)
61 "Oren, and _____, and Ahijah"
   (1 Chronicles 2:25)
62 Gaddi's father (Numbers 13:11)
63 "Used curious _____ brought their
   books" (Acts 19:19)
65 "_____, which were dukes"
   (Joshua 13:21)
66 Asked for a double portion of Elijah's
   spirit (abbr.)
67 "Which is in the king's _____"
   (2 Samuel 18:18)
70 "Samuel arose and went to _____"
   (1 Samuel 3:6)
71 "_____ his son, Jehoshua his son"
   (1 Chronicles 7:27)
72 Bind

171

## ACROSS

1 "His _____; on the eighth" (Exodus 22:30)
4 A king of Midian (Numbers 31:8)
7 Walk
12 Phares's brother (Matthew 1:3)
13 Before (arch.)
14 A son of Gad (Genesis 46:16)
15 Strong metal
16 "Will cause them to be _____ there" (1 Kings 5:9)
19 Strange
20 "To possess the land of the _____" (Amos 2:10)
21 "That _____ him up from the dead" (1 Peter 1:21)
24 Male sheep
25 "God created _____ heaven" (Genesis 1:1)
28 Astatine (sym.)
29 Possessive pronoun
30 "Shall be astonished, and _____ his head" (Jeremiah 18:16)
31 A son of David (1 Chronicles 3:5–6)
33 Snake sound
37 Refrain
39 "From the _____ of the sea" (Isaiah 11:11)
40 Palm Sunday praise
41 Metal pegs
42 Caleb's son (1 Chronicles 4:15)
43 This prophet's name means "festive" (abbr.)
45 Maine (abbr.)
46 Single
47 "God saw that it _____ good" (Genesis 1:21)
48 Not male
52 Joab's brother (2 Samuel 2:18)
55 A large salty body of water
56 Elkanah was one (1 Samuel 1:1)
59 "Nevertheless _____ heart" (1 Kings 15:14)
60 Adina's father (1 Chronicles 11:42)
61 Last book of the OT (abbr.)
62 Decomposing metal
63 Caused by or relating to tides
64 Increase
65 Are (arch.)

## DOWN

1 "Chalcol, and _____" (1 Kings 4:31)
2 A son of Gad (Genesis 46:16)
3 Adam was the first
4 "As men go to _____" (Ezekiel 47:15)
5 Thummim's partner (Deuteronomy 33:8)
6 "And the people _____ unto him again" (Mark 10:1)
7 Specific one
8 Not easily found
9 Chicken product
10 Get older
11 "God _____ tempt Abraham" (Genesis 22:1)
12 "_____; nine cities" (Joshua 15:54)
17 "A great _____ from the hills" (Zephaniah 1:10)
18 "This time. . .the bird returned to _____ with a fresh olive leaf in its beak" (Genesis 8:11 NLT)
22 A son of Cush (1 Chronicles 1:9)
23 A son of Zerah (1 Chronicles 2:6)
25 Esau and Jacob were these
26 "The Lord is at _____" (Philippians 4:5)
27 These are sometimes painted for Easter
29 Tehinnah's son (1 Chronicles 4:12)
31 "An _____ of blood twelve years" (Mark 5:25)
32 Word preceding Psalm 119:121
34 He predicted the Messiah's birth to Ahaz (abbr.)
35 "Daubed it with _____ and with pitch" (Exodus 2:3)
36 "Melchisedec, king of _____" (Hebrews 7:1)
37 A son of Jehiel (1 Chronicles 9:35–37)
38 "When he was _____" (Hebrews 11:23)
44 An idol of Hamath (2 Kings 17:30)

*by N. Teri Grottke*

47 "To _____, that God was in Christ, reconciling the world unto himself" (2 Corinthians 5:19)

48 "Shepherds abiding in the _____" (Luke 2:8)

49 Esarhaddon was king here (Ezra 4:2)

50 Smallest

51 "The LORD God stationed mighty angelic beings to the _____ of Eden" (Genesis 3:24 NLT)

52 Steward of Zimri's house in Tirzah (1 Kings 16:9)

53 "Remnant of _____" (Zephaniah 1:4)

54 Joseph mourned for Jacob at this threshing floor (Genesis 50:11)

56 Jewish queen (abbr.)

57 Twenty-first letter of the Greek alphabet

58 "Jacob _____ them under the oak which was by Shechem" (Genesis 35:4)

59 Jether's son (1 Chronicles 7:38)

# PUZZLE 84 — CLIMBING THE WALLS

*May there be peace within your walls
and security within your citadels.*
PSALM 122:7 NIV

## ACROSS

1 "_____ a mocker" (Proverbs 19:25 NIV)
5 "A swelling, _____ or a bright spot" (Leviticus 14:56 NIV) (2 words)
10 "Rehob, toward _____ Hamath" (Numbers 13:21 NIV)
14 "The scarlet _____ in the window" (Joshua 2:21)
15 French river up north
16 "By _____ and living way" (Hebrews 10:20) (2 words)
17 Location of Rahab's house (Joshua 2:15) (4 words)
20 "Upon the great _____ of his right foot" (Leviticus 8:23)
21 "Have we not all _____ father?" (Malachi 2:10)
22 Formerly Shima Province, Japan, _____ prefecture
23 "And I _____ a vision" (Daniel 8:2) (2 words)
26 Follows *novel-* or *romantic-*
28 "_____ younger men as brothers" (1 Timothy 5:1 NIV)
30 What Ezekiel saw by the door of the court (Ezekiel 8:7) (5 words)
33 "Were cast into the _____ of fire" (Revelation 20:14)
34 "Behold, I will _____ new thing" (Isaiah 43:19) (2 words)
35 "To him that weareth the _____ clothing" (James 2:3)
36 Lincoln
37 Carnival workers
39 "I am like an _____ of the desert" (Psalm 102:6)
42 Sound from a massage recipient
43 Orthodontist's degree (abbr.)
44 "Am I _____, or a whale" (Job 7:12) (2 words)
45 Where they put the body of Saul (1 Samuel 31:10) (3 words)
49 Salsa base
50 Another northern French river

51 "Thou hast asked _____ thing" (2 Kings 2:10) (2 words)
52 Follows *switcher-* and *tab-*
53 G. H. W. Bush was once its director
55 Greek *h*
56 Where Ezekiel saw cherubims and palm trees (Ezekiel 41:20)
63 "The ants _____ people not strong" (Proverbs 30:25) (2 words)
64 "All of you be on the _____" (Joshua 8:4 NIV)
65 Relative of altitude (abbr.)
66 Hardy heroine
67 "From the tower of _____ shall they fall" (Ezekiel 30:6)
68 "And they shall _____" (Jeremiah 50:36)

## DOWN

1 Winter bug
2 "They shoot out the _____" (Psalm 22:7)
3 "Beth Aven, lead _____ Benjamin" (Hosea 5:8 NIV) (2 words)
4 "And also of the _____" (Romans 2:9)
5 "_____ that setteth snares" (Jeremiah 5:26) (2 words)
6 "As light of foot as a wild _____" (2 Samuel 2:18)
7 Relative of quantity (abbr.)
8 "And I am a _____ man" (Genesis 27:11)
9 "Was _____ in stone" (Luke 23:53)
10 "Will not do the _____ of thy God" (Ezra 7:26)
11 Cloisonné covering
12 "The children of _____" (2 Chronicles 13:7)
13 Hooting chick
18 "Be with you now and change my _____" (Galatians 4:20 NIV)
19 "With so many the _____ not torn" (John 21:11 NIV) (2 words)
23 "Which was the son of _____" (Luke 3:35)
24 Omri's son (1 Kings 16:28)

*by David K. Shortess*

25 "Then I _____ up" (Genesis 41:21 NIV)
26 "Took thee _____ naked" (Matthew 25:38) (2 words)
27 "Which say, _____ thyself" (Isaiah 65:5) (2 words)
29 "Without a _____ of brightness?" (Amos 5:20 NIV)
31 Utah neighbor
32 Discharge
37 Multicolored cat
38 July 15, for one
39 Government safety group (abbr.)
40 "Thou wilt surely _____ away" (Exodus 18:18)
41 "Rowed hard to bring it to the _____" (Jonah 1:13)
42 "Hear, _____ ye people" (Micah 1:2)
44 Opposite of *proud*
45 "And said, _____ those with thee?" (Genesis 33:5) (2 words)

46 Bridal paths
47 Categorically
48 "For either he will _____ the one" (Matthew 6:24)
49 "Every _____ that which is before her" (Amos 4:3) (2 words)
54 "_____ one people speaking the same language" (Genesis 11:6 NIV) (2 words)
55 Suffix meaning "little one"
57 _____ Cruces, NM
58 Haw's TV partner
59 Directional suffix
60 Arafat's group
61 "_____ there be light" (Genesis 1:3)
62 Cain's mother (Genesis 4:1)

## ACROSS

1 In this place
5 Pay scale
9 "Ye also, as lively stones, are built up a spiritual _____, an holy priesthood" (1 Peter 2:5)
14 David hid by this stone (1 Samuel 20:19)
15 Jacob gave Esau two hundred of these (Genesis 32:13–14)
16 "Believed the master and the _____ of the ship" (Acts 27:11)
17 "_____ the Canaanite" (Numbers 21:1)
18 "God hath given thee all them that _____ with thee" (Acts 27:24)
19 Below
20 Cut back
21 "And let him down through the _____ with his couch into the midst before Jesus" (Luke 5:19)
23 "Either good _____ bad" (Genesis 31:24)
24 "The same excess of _____" (1 Peter 4:4)
26 A son of Benjamin (Genesis 46:21)
28 A son of Korah (Exodus 6:24)
30 "Let not thy left hand know what thy _____ doeth" (Matthew 6:3) (2 words) (abbr.)
32 Lower often as a sign of respect
36 King Hezekiah's mother (2 Kings 18:2)
37 Chelub's son (1 Chronicles 4:11)
39 "Your brethren, _____" (Hosea 2:1)
40 "Melchizedek. . .was the priest of the most _____ God" (Genesis 14:18)
42 "The heathen _____" (Psalm 46:6)
44 Rabbit
45 "Of Harim, _____" (Nehemiah 12:15)
46 Belonging to them
48 Unhappy
49 First place
50 Haman was her archenemy (abbr.)

51 A pause or musical note used in the Psalms
53 "Her _____ was to light" (Ruth 2:3)
55 "_____ thee out of my mouth" (Revelations 3:16)
56 Arsenic (sym.)
58 A son of Reuben (Genesis 46:9)
61 "Dominion and power, _____ now and ever" (Jude 1:25)
65 Zattu's son (Ezra 10:27)
67 "Other _____ there" (John 6:22)
68 Asa's father (1 Chronicles 3:10)
69 Ephraim didn't drive out the Canaanites who lived here (Judges 1:29)
70 "_____ not the world" (1 John 2:15)
71 Salathiel's father (Luke 3:27)
72 Selected ones
73 A son of Ram (1 Chronicles 2:27)
74 Arad's brother (1 Chronicles 8:15)

## DOWN

1 "For in so doing thou shalt _____ coals of fire on his head" (Romans 12:20)
2 This priest rebuilt the temple
3 "Thou shalt _____ up the tabernacle according to the fashion thereof" (Exodus 26:30)
4 "Ordain _____ in every city" (Titus 1:5)
5 "He shall be unto thee a _____ of thy life" (Ruth 4:15)
6 Expect
7 "Shall be eaten: as a _____ tree" (Isaiah 6:13)
8 Nagge's son (Luke 3:25)
9 "Thou shalt _____ their horses" (Joshua 11:6)
10 Possess
11 "I will _____ all that afflict thee" (Zephaniah 3:19)
12 Prophet (arch.)
13 Make a mistake
22 Iranian wine tester (abbr.)

by *N. Teri Grottke*

25 "And they departed from _____,
and pitched in Dibongad"
(Numbers 33:45)
27 "Of Hena, and _____?"
(2 Kings 19:13)
28 Live with
29 Indicators
30 "Shall not the Judge of all the earth
do _____?" (Genesis 18:25)
31 "Rest yourselves under the _____"
(Genesis 18:4)
33 Absalom's captain (2 Samuel 17:25)
34 A son of Zophah
(1 Chronicles 7:36)
35 Told an untruth
36 Jezebel's husband
38 Head covers
41 "That which _____ been"
(Ecclesiastes 6:10)

43 "Where is the _____ of this
world?" (1 Corinthians 1:20)
47 Peleg's son (Genesis 11:18)
50 Paul wrote this book about AD 62
(abbr.)
52 Patriarch of a family of exiles
(Nehemiah 7:48)
54 Separate
55 Serf
56 "And _____ had six sons"
(1 Chronicles 9:44)
57 Dimensions
59 Capable
60 See
62 Ruth's son (Ruth 4:13–17)
63 Exhaust
64 Delilah cut Samson's
65 Get older
66 Contemporary of the prophet
Haggai (abbr.)

177

# PUZZLE 86 — WHO'S THE GREATEST?

*In the world ye shall have tribulation:*
*but be of good cheer; I have overcome the world.*
JOHN 16:33

## ACROSS

1 *Olé* in the USA
4 Group of plotters
9 Like the sound of *m* or *n*
14 E.T.'s transport
15 "Man shall not live by bread _____"
(Matthew 4:4)
16 *Così fan tutte*, for example
17 2 and 3, for example (abbr.)
18 Lariat
19 Yea or nay
20 Start of **QUOTE** from 1 John 4:4
(4 words)
23 "Good comfort, when I know your
_____" (Philippians 2:19)
24 "On the head or on the _____"
(Leviticus 13:29 NIV)
25 Isle of exile
28 "And laid him in a _____" (Luke 2:7)
33 "There is a _____ here" (John 6:9)
36 "King of _____, which is, King of
peace" (Hebrews 7:2)
39 "No man can _____ two masters"
(Matthew 6:24)
40 **QUOTE**, cont'd from 20 Across
(2 words)
42 "And their words seemed to them as
idle _____" (Luke 24:11)
44 "Ye shall find a colt _____" (Mark 11:2)
45 Office notes
47 "But to _____ my right hand, and on
my left" (Matthew 20:23) (2 words)
49 For (prefix)
50 Hippodromes
52 Celebes buffalo
54 "Flew the _____" (on the lam)
57 "Who are _____ with thee?"
(Genesis 33:5)
61 **QUOTE**, cont'd from 40 Across
(5 words)
67 **QUOTE**, cont'd from 61 Across
(2 words)
68 Copland opus
69 "_____ calling Elijah"
(Matthew 27:47 NIV)
70 Skirt feature
71 Shaq of the court
72 "For Adam was first formed, then
_____" (1 Timothy 2:13)
73 Digestive and circulatory (abbr.)
74 End of **QUOTE**, cont'd from 67
Across
75 Actor Harrison

## DOWN

1 Ladder parts
2 "And build _____ against it"
(Ezekiel 4:2) (2 words)
3 Book after Daniel
4 Consortia
5 "That they should believe _____"
(2 Thessalonians 2:11) (2 words)
6 "The _____ out of the wood doth
waste it" (Psalm 80:13)
7 Tomfoolery
8 "Or put him on a _____ for your
girls?" (Job 41:5 NIV)
9 Catholic nine-day prayer cycles
10 "He maketh the deep to boil like
_____" (Job 41:31) (2 words)
11 Cainan's grandfather
(Luke 3:37–38)
12 "The entire _____ will be holy"
(Ezekiel 45:1 NIV)
13 "So the _____ shall be first"
(Matthew 20:16)
21 "I _____ no pleasant bread"
(Daniel 10:3)
22 "What things ye have need of, before
ye ask _____" (Matthew 6:8)
26 "After her kind, and the lapwing, and
the _____" (Leviticus 11:19)
27 "_____ for the day! for the day of the
LORD is at hand" (Joel 1:15)
29 "Yet was not the _____ broken"
(John 21:11)
30 "Days of suffering _____ me"
(Job 30:16 NIV)
31 "For his mercy endureth for _____"
(see Psalm 136)

*by David K. Shortess*

32 Decorate again
33 South American capital
34 Anna's tribe (Luke 2:36)
35 FDR is on it
37 Samuel's mentor (1 Samuel 3:1)
38 "There he _____ Jew named Aquila" (Acts 18:2 NIV) (2 words)
41 "_____ his son" (1 Chronicles 7:27)
43 "For I have born him a _____ in his old age" (Genesis 21:7)
46 Clothes scenters
48 "For Zion's sake will I _____ my peace" (Isaiah 62:1) (2 words)
51 "Iron sharpeneth iron; _____ man sharpeneth" (Proverbs 27:17) (2 words)
53 "_____, our eye hath seen it" (Psalm 35:21)
55 "In Flanders fields the poppies blow, between the crosses, row _____" (McCrae)

56 Where platters used to spin, briefly
58 "Smite thee on thy right cheek, turn to him the _____ also" (Matthew 5:39)
59 "Like as corn is sifted in a _____" (Amos 9:9)
60 Suburb east of Baltimore
61 Puppy sounds
62 "And he said, Take now thy son, thine _____ son Isaac" (Genesis 22:2)
63 Utah, Colorado, Arizona, and New Mexico residents of yore
64 "And all _____ is within me" (Psalm 103:1)
65 A son of Mushi (1 Chronicles 23:23)
66 Dark blue-green

# PUZZLE 87

## ACROSS

1 "Go, wash in the _____ of Siloam" (John 9:7)
5 "And drew to the _____" (Mark 6:53)
10 "Mordecai for _____?" (Esther 6:3)
14 "_____, their brethren" (Nehemiah 12:9)
15 A baptismal site of John the Baptist (John 3:23)
16 "Who said, _____ it" (Psalm 137:7)
17 "Whosoever shall say to his brother, _____, shall be in danger of the council" (Matthew 5:22)
18 Achish's father (1 Samuel 27:2)
19 Haniel's father (1 Chronicles 7:39)
20 Green gem
22 A Levite upon the stairs (Nehemiah 9:4)
24 "_____ ye tribute" (Romans 13:6)
25 "He may _____ the tip of his finger" (Luke 16:24)
26 "He _____ in the valley" (Job 39:21)
30 "_____ of spices" (Song of Solomon 6:2)
32 "Helez the Paltite, _____" (2 Samuel 23:26)
35 Naum's son (Luke 3:25)
36 "The _____, were over the work" (1 Chronicles 9:19)
38 "Rend the _____ of their heart" (Hosea 13:8)
39 "The well of _____" (2 Samuel 3:26)
40 Opposite of *fat*
41 "God will _____ my darkness" (Psalm 18:28)
43 Jesus' first miracle was here
44 Unhappy
45 Told an untruth
46 King of Gath (1 Samuel 21:10)
48 Book after Zechariah (abbr.)
49 Fuss
50 "Thou _____ up mighty rivers" (Psalm 74:15)
54 "Lachish, and _____, and Eglon" (Joshua 15:39)
59 "Michmash, and _____" (Nehemiah 11:31)
60 Ishmael's mother (Genesis 16:16)
62 Rephaiah's father (1 Chronicles 4:42)
63 "_____ your lusts" (James 4:3)
64 Absalom's captain (2 Samuel 17:25)
65 King of the jungle
66 Not straight
67 "_____, and to Tobijah" (Zechariah 6:14)
68 "Praise the Lord, all ye Gentiles; and _____ him, all ye people" (Romans 15:11)

## DOWN

1 "A _____ language" (Zepheniah 3:9)
2 A child of Shobal (Genesis 36:23)
3 The earth was destroyed by a flood this many times
4 "A _____ giveth ear to a naughty tongue" (Proverbs 17:4)
5 "And Hadad died, and _____ of Masrekah reigned" (Genesis 36:36)
6 "Traitors, _____, highminded, lovers of pleasures" (2 Timothy 3:4)
7 "Lod, and _____, the valley of craftsmen" (Nehemiah 11:35)
8 "That _____ was Christ" (1 Corinthians 10:4)
9 "And Remeth, and Engannim, and _____" (Joshua 19:21)
10 "In the twinkling of an eye, at the last _____" (1 Corinthians 15:52)
11 "Helkath, and _____" (Joshua 19:25)
12 Island
13 Closure
21 Capable
23 "That dippeth with me in the _____" (Mark 14:20)
26 "Had gone six _____, he sacrificed oxen and fatlings" (2 Samuel 6:13)
27 "Look from the top of _____" (Song of Solomon 4:8)
28 "They _____ no doubt have continued with us" (1 John 2:19)
29 Nagge's son (Luke 3:25)

by N. Teri Grottke

30 "The priest took a chest, and
   _____ a hole in the lid of it"
   (2 Kings 12:9)
31 "Shuthelah: of _____"
   (Numbers 26:36)
32 Ribai's son (1 Chronicles 11:31)
33 "He hath caused the arrows of his
   quiver to enter into my _____"
   (Lamentations 3:13)
34 "The children of _____"
   (Ezra 2:50)
36 "_____ after his kind"
   (Leviticus 11:14)
37 "And with the _____"
   (Deuteronomy 28:27)
39 A son of Zophah
   (1 Chronicles 7:36–37)
42 "Ye may be _____ also with
   exceeding joy" (1 Peter 4:13)

46 "And _____ was over"
   (2 Samuel 20:24)
47 Anub's father (1 Chronicles 4:8)
48 "But God _____ it"
   (Genesis 50:20)
49 To humble
50 "Say unto them which _____ it"
   (Ezekiel 13:11)
51 "Harvest is _____" (Joel 3:13)
52 "And smote _____, and Dan"
   (1 Kings 15:20)
53 Gentle
55 Slay
56 Largest continent
57 You (arch.)
58 Female red deer
61 Classical Austrian composer
   Bernhard

181

# PUZZLE 88

## ACROSS

1 Vestige
5 Ahithophel's son (2 Samuel 23:34)
10 Crush
14 Ahira's father (Numbers 10:27)
15 A son of Hosah (1 Chronicles 26:10)
16 "Enter thou _____ the joy of thy lord" (Matthew 25:21)
17 Mellow
18 "Whom _____ bare unto Judah" (Ruth 4:12)
19 Fastener
20 "The sons of _____ his brother" (1 Chronicles 8:39)
22 "_____, which were dukes" (Joshua 13:21)
23 "As the camel, and the _____" (Deuteronomy 14:7)
24 "Ye are _____ unto the day of redemption" (Ephesians 4:30)
26 Shorelines
28 Agreement
30 Type of fruit
31 "_____ the people be ensnared" (Job 34:30)
35 "Now is our salvation _____" (Romans 13:11)
37 "_____ him out" (Genesis 39:12)
40 "By the river of _____" (Daniel 8:2)
41 Protected
42 "God shall _____ away all tears from their eyes" (Revelation 21:4)
43 Small underground animals
45 Covers
47 "The land is as the garden of _____" (Joel 2:3)
48 Crater
49 "The son of _____, keeper of the wardrobe" (2 Chronicles 34:22)
51 "He _____ him away to his house" (Mark 8:26)
52 "God formed _____ of the dust" (Genesis 2:7)
53 In time
54 "Their great _____ cut off" (Judges 1:7)
55 "He sold them into the hand of _____" (1 Samuel 12:9)
58 Selvage
59 Terminate
60 Ishbah's son (1 Chronicles 4:17)
62 Zaccur's father (Nehemiah 3:2)
64 Hint
65 Lodging
66 Cave
67 Care for
68 "Darius the _____" (Daniel 5:31)

## DOWN

1 "Tarshish, _____, Marsena, and Memucan" (Esther 1:14)
2 Dill seed
3 "Nohah the fourth, and _____ the fifth" (1 Chronicles 8:2)
4 Genuflect
5 Estimate (abbr.)
6 One who is untruthful
7 Zadok's father (Nehemiah 3:29)
8 "_____, and Dumah, and Eshean" (Joshua 15:52)
9 Marvel
10 "The sons of Elpaal; Eber, and _____" (1 Chronicles 8:12)
11 "_____ and Caiaphas being the high priests" (Luke 3:2)
12 Inception
13 "For which _____ sake" (Acts 26:7)
21 Cay
25 "In _____ and caves of the earth" (Hebrews 11:38)
27 "_____ God is merciful" (Psalm 116:5)
29 Chairs
30 "That they may _____ a city" (Psalm 107:36)
31 "The same _____ to make one vessel" (Romans 9:21)
32 "_____, lama sabachthani?" (Mark 15:34)
33 Seasoning

*by Tonya Vilhauer*

34 Bind

36 "She is come _____" (Mark 14:8)

37 Abidan's father (Numbers 10:24)

38 Unlocked

39 "Abode we in _____ three days" (Ezra 8:15)

42 Occidental

44 To give a part of something

46 "Of _____, the family of the Shemidaites" (Numbers 26:32)

50 "Mizraim begat Ludim, and _____" (1 Chronicles 1:11)

52 "A nation _____ out and trodden down" (Isaiah 18:2)

55 "Which is the _____ of the Sadducees" (Acts 5:17)

56 "Ye inhabitants of the _____" (Isaiah 23:6)

57 Reject

61 "Thou believest that there is _____ God" (James 2:19)

63 "The young _____ from their musick" (Lamentations 5:14)

# PUZZLE 89

## ACROSS

1 "Doth the _____ fly by thy wisdom" (Job 39:26)
5 Jesus' first miracle was here
9 A son of Ishmael (1 Chronicles 1:30–31)
14 Patriarch of a family of returned exiles (Ezra 2:15)
15 Salah's son (Genesis 10:24)
16 Audibly
17 Load (arch.)
18 Move quickly
19 A son of Jehaleleel (1 Chronicles 4:16)
20 "Being a servant, is the Lord's _____" (1 Corinthians 7:22)
22 "I am among you as he that _____" (Luke 22:27)
24 A son of Jether (1 Chronicles 7:38)
25 "_____ that ye refuse" (Hebrews 12:25)
26 Belonging to Esther's enemy
30 Opposite of easy
32 "Against Jerusalem, _____" (Ezekiel 26:2)
35 "Ivory and _____" (Ezekiel 27:15)
36 A brother of Shoham (1 Chronicles 24:27)
37 Ruth's son (Ruth 4:17)
38 Jesus turned water into it (John 2:1–11)
39 A son of Lotan (1 Chronicles 1:39)
40 "Thou, being a _____ olive tree, wert graffed in among them" (Romans 11:17)
41 "Mahli, and _____" (1 Chronicles 23:23)
42 A son of Ulla (1 Chronicles 7:39)
43 Serf
44 Opposite of night
45 A brother of David (1 Chronicles 2:15)
46 "All his bowels _____ out" (Acts 1:18)
47 Fuss
48 Bowling target

49 "Ye ought to _____ the weak" (Acts 20:35)
53 "Hammath, _____, and Chinnereth" (Joshua 19:35)
58 Elkanah's grandfather (1 Samuel 1:1)
59 A son of Jerahmeel (1 Chronicles 2:25)
61 Rephaiah's father (1 Chronicles 4:42)
62 "Nor _____ the thing" (Psalm 89:34)
63 "Ye shall not fulfil the _____ of the flesh" (Galatians 5:16)
64 Perished
65 Responsibilities
66 Opposite of more
67 Identical

## DOWN

1 "Unto the _____ of my kingdom" (Mark 6:23)
2 Twelfth Hebrew month (Esther 9:1)
3 Opposite of narrow
4 "Every _____ should bow" (Philippians 2:10)
5 "His countenance is as Lebanon, excellent as the _____" (Song of Solomon 5:15)
6 A river of Damascus (2 Kings 5:12)
7 Saul's grandfather (1 Chronicles 8:33)
8 "Used curious _____" (Acts 19:19)
9 Mezahab's daughter (Genesis 36:39)
10 Not dead
11 Very (arch.)
12 Set of clothing
13 Jabal's mother (Genesis 4:20)
21 Multiple
23 Phares's son (Luke 3:33)
26 Chopped (arch.)
27 "Henoch, and _____, and Eldaah" (1 Chronicles 1:33)
28 Lucre
29 A brother of Eshcol (Genesis 14:13)
30 A child of Lotan (Genesis 36:22)
31 Zibeon's daughter (Genesis 36:2)
32 Hezron's wife (1 Chronicles 2:24)

*by N. Teri Grottke*

33 "Slippeth from the _____"
   (Deuteronomy 19:5)
34 Increased
36 Dig
37 "I am a brother to dragons,
   and a companion to _____"
   (Job 30:29)
39 Sisera was captain of this host
   (1 Samuel 12:9)
43 "He _____ down with sleep"
   (Acts 20:9)
45 Smells (var.)
46 Goliath and his brothers were these
47 There a wall fell upon 27,000 men
   (1 Kings 20:30)
48 "I _____ toward the mark for the
   prize" (Philippians 3:14)
49 Resting place

50 Haniel's father (1 Chronicles 7:39)
51 Deep holes
52 "It shall not be lawful to impose
   _____" (Ezra 7:24)
54 Baby goats
55 Largest continent
56 Others
57 Pelt
60 "For ye tithe mint and _____"
   (Luke 11:42)

# PUZZLE 90

## ACROSS

1 "Thy word is a _____ unto my feet"
(Psalm 119:105)
5 Mien
9 "Bind the chariot to the swift
_____" (Micah 1:13)
14 "The burning _____"
(Leviticus 26:16)
15 "Bare a son; and she called his name
_____" (Genesis 38:4)
16 "_____ also, and Aphek, and Rehob"
(Joshua 19:30)
17 "Lieth upon the top of a _____"
(Proverb 23:34)
18 "Ye _____ as sheep" (1 Peter 2:25)
19 "Blood, and fire, and pillars of
_____" (Joel 2:30)
20 "Rams of the _____ of Bashan"
(Deuteronomy 32:14)
22 Espy
24 "_____ with her suburbs"
(1 Chronicles 6:73)
25 Costas
28 "They were _____ asunder"
(Hebrews 11:37)
30 "Also I shook my _____"
(Nehemiah 5:13)
33 Prod
35 "Thou hast _____ me"
(Psalm 119:102)
39 Gaal's father (Judges 9:35)
41 Adam lived _____ hundred and
thirty years (Genesis 5:5)
43 "Beriah, and _____ their sister"
(Genesis 46:17)
44 Heart
45 "So is thy praise unto the _____ of
the earth" (Psalm 48:10)
46 Bail
47 Azmaveth's father
(1 Chronicles 27:25)
49 "Bunah, and _____, and Ozem"
(1 Chronicles 2:25)
52 Short for tarpaulin
53 "The LORD _____ me"
(Psalm 118:13)
55 Office
56 In time

57 "I _____, My strength and my hope is
perished" (Lamentations 3:18)
59 Haze
61 "The name of his city was _____"
(1 Chronicles 1:50)
64 Resemble
66 Turret
70 "The sons of Gershom; _____"
(1 Chronicles 6:17)
72 Buss
75 "Take thee a _____" (Ezekiel 4:1)
76 "Is not _____ the Levite thy
brother?" (Exodus 4:14)
77 Range
78 "_____ with joy receiveth it"
(Matthew 13:20)
79 "No good _____ will he withhold
from them" (Psalm 84:11)
80 "I _____ where I sowed not"
(Matthew 25:26)
81 Imprest

## DOWN

1 "The LORD will feed them as a
_____" (Hosea 4:16)
2 "This _____ is mount Sinai"
(Galatians 4:25)
3 Meditate
4 "Simon _____ having a sword drew
it" (John 18:10)
5 Humble
6 "Thou believest that there is _____
God" (James 2:19)
7 Paddles
8 "He kneeled upon his _____"
(Daniel 6:10)
9 Jitney
10 "They shall call his name _____"
(Matthew 1:23)
11 Josiah's father (Jeremiah 1:2)
12 "I intreated for the children's
_____" (Job 19:17)
13 "Have the preeminence among
_____" (3 John 1:9)
21 Lade
23 Dine
26 "Neither shall ye break a _____"
(Exodus 12:46)

*by Tonya Vilhauer*

27 Epidermis
29 "It _____ infinite" (Nahum 3:9)
30 "The sons of Shelah. . .were, Er the father of _____" (1 Chronicles 4:21)
31 "_____ there three days" (Ezra 8:32)
32 Danger
34 "The inhabitants of _____ and her towns" (Joshua 17:11)
36 Grind
37 "Achbor died, and _____ reigned in his stead" (Genesis 36:39)
38 Yonder
40 "All the _____ of the river" (Zechariah 10:11)
42 Aram's father (Matthew 1:3)
48 Renting
50 "Samuel arose and went to _____" (1 Samuel 3:6)
51 "Thou shouldest make thy _____ as high as the eagle" (Jeremiah 49:16)
54 "Neither shall ye touch it, lest ye _____" (Genesis 3:3)

58 "The son of _____, in Makaz" (1 Kings 4:9)
60 Aggregate
61 "Cast him into the _____ of ground" (2 Kings 9:26)
62 Rizpah's father (2 Samuel 21:8)
63 "Zaccur, and _____" (1 Chronicles 24:27)
65 Mud
67 Drink
68 "_____, and Thimnathah, and Ekron" (Joshua 19:43)
69 "They _____ every one his mantle" (Job 2:12)
71 "_____ his son, Jehoshua his son" (1 Chronicles 7:27)
73 "So shall the _____ be calm unto you" (Jonah 1:12)
74 "The trees of the LORD are full of _____" (Psalm 104:16)

187

# PUZZLE 91

## ACROSS

1 Sack
4 A god of Babylon (Isaiah 46:1)
7 Mattathias's son (Luke 3:26)
12 A son of Judah (1 Chronicles 2:3)
14 Seth's son (Genesis 4:26)
16 Ribai's son (1 Chronicles 11:31)
17 Sea rhythm
18 "The joy of the_____ ceaseth" (Isaiah 24:8)
19 "This only would I _____ of you" (Galatians 3:2)
20 Show (arch.)
21 "Weeping may _____ for a night" (Psalm 30:5)
23 Sleeping place
24 Total
26 Resting place
27 Type of tree (Isaiah 44:14)
30 The giving of this revealed Jesus' betrayer (John 13:21–27)
32 "The woman took the child, and _____ it" (Exodus 2:9)
37 "Shall be proclaimed upon the _____" (Luke 12:3)
41 A son of Merari (Numbers 3:20)
42 Land measurement
43 Gomer's husband (Hosea 1:2–3)
45 "A little _____; and she waited on Naaman's wife" (2 Kings 5:2)
46 "Howbeit there came other _____ from Tiberias" (John 6:23)
48 "Some remove the _____" (Job 24:2)
50 "Haphraim, and _____, and Anaharath" (Joshua 19:19)
52 This is connected to the foot
53 Consume food
54 "A _____ of Jesse" (Isaiah 11:10)
57 Right hand (abbr.)
59 Diana was the goddess of this people (abbr.)
62 "He went forth with his disciples over the brook _____" (John 18:1)
64 "_____ for the day!" (Joel 1:15)
68 "_____ of Judah" (2 Samuel 6:2)
70 Comfort
71 Tibetan monk
72 Mistake
73 "There was a continual _____ given him of the king of Babylon" (Jeremiah 52:34)
74 Image
75 Prepared
76 This man served Artaxerxes (abbr.)
77 This man prophesied the destruction of Solomon's temple (abbr.)

## DOWN

1 "And their _____ shall be broken" (Psalm 37:15)
2 Zibeon's daughter (Genesis 36:2)
3 "Abraham _____ the tenth of the spoils" (Hebrews 7:4)
4 "Behold now _____" (Job 40:15)
5 Ahira's father (Numbers 1:15)
6 "Made a supper to his _____" (Mark 6:21)
7 "Trophimus have I left at _____ sick" (2 Timothy 4:20)
8 Partook
9 Omri's son who reigned after his death (1 Kings 16:28)
10 Type of weed
11 Female red deer
13 Current events
15 "_____ thee out of my mouth" (Revelations 3:16)
22 "And _____ greedily after the error of Balaam" (Jude 1:11)
25 Make good _____ of something
27 "Letters in _____ name" (1 Kings 21:8)
28 "Shamir, and Jattir, and _____" (Joshua 15:48)
29 "_____ of the brooks of Gaash" (1 Chronicles 11:32)
31 "Go, wash in the _____ of Siloam" (John 9:7)
33 "In _____ was there a voice" (Matthew 2:18)
34 Allotment
35 A Harodite guard of David (2 Samuel 23:25)

*by N. Teri Grottke*

36 Did (arch.)
38 Cain and Abel's brother
39 150 sections make up this book (abbr.)
40 Caused to go to a destination
44 "As a bride _____ herself with her jewels" (Isaiah 61:10)
47 "Which beforetime in the same city used _____" (Acts 8:9)
49 Became acquainted
51 Greek form of *Noah* (Luke 17:27)
55 Azariah's father (2 Chronicles 15:1)
56 "_____ up a child" (Proverbs 22:6)
58 "Helkath, and _____" (Joshua 19:25)
59 Salah's son (Genesis 10:24)
60 Cut back

61 "Habor, and _____" (1 Chronicles 5:26)
63 "As he saith also in _____" (Romans 9:25)
65 Load (arch.)
66 Isaiah's father (Isaiah 1:1)
67 "_____ of his patrimony" (Deuteronomy 18:8)
69 "_____, Hadid, and Ono" (Ezra 2:33)

## ACROSS

1 Mother of the Savior
4 "_____ will be great and will be called the Son of the Most High" (Luke 1:32 NIV)
6 Pleasant smell
8 Types of offerings are described in this OT book (abbr.)
9 Divide number of days Jesus fasted (Matthew 4:2) by the number of men who carried the man let down through the roof (Mark 2:3)
10 Christians have something to _____ about (happy expression)
12 Joseph was the husband _____ Mary
13 Mary's _____ would be called Immanuel, meaning "God with us" (Matthew 1:23 NIV)
14 Mary was pledged _____ be married
15 Calendar year (abbr.)
17 Informal expression for money; starts with the sound a cow makes
18 "_____ the holy one to be born will be called the Son of God" (Luke 1:35 NIV)
19 Better than okay
20 A close friend
21 "Mary treasured up _____ these things" (Luke 2:19 NIV)
22 Simeon told Mary, "This child is destined to cause the falling and rising of _____ in Israel" (Luke 2:34 NIV)
23 Mary's Son

## DOWN

1 First day of the work week (abbr.)
2 Morning hours (abbr.)
3 Reckless
4 "Levi _____ a great banquet for Jesus" (Luke 5:29 NIV)
5 Mother of Abel and Seth (Genesis 4:1–2, 25 NIV)
6 Small particle that makes up matter
7 One who calls the shots (abbr.)
8 "I am a rose of Sharon, a _____ of the valleys" (Song of Songs 2:1 NIV)
11 A transparent, sheetlike mineral
13 One who prepares a meal
14 "Tubal-Cain, who forged all kinds of _____ out of bronze and iron" (Genesis 4:22 NIV)
16 Mary "was found to be with child through the _____ Spirit" (Matthew 1:18 NIV)
17 Gender of man
18 The foolish man built his house on _____ (Matthew 7:26)
20 Informal name for "Father"
21 _____ is to apple juice what OJ is to orange juice

by John Hudson Tiner

# PUZZLE 93

## ACROSS

1 Possessive pronoun
4 Methuselah's father (Genesis 5:21)
9 "Stand in the _____" (Ezekiel 22:30)
12 "Cursed is every one that hangeth on a _____" (Galatians 3:13)
13 A son of Hodesh (1 Chronicles 8:9)
14 Anak's father (Joshua 15:13)
15 "Not in chambering and _____" (Romans 13:13)
17 Flesh food
18 Strange
19 "Jealous for his land, and _____ his people" (Joel 2:18)
20 "He shall _____ with his teeth" (Psalm 112:10)
21 Cain and Abel's brother
22 The other Simon of the twelve (Luke 6:15)
24 Serious lack of food
27 "At Lydda and _____" (Acts 9:35)
28 A son of Jehiel (1 Chronicles 9:37)
29 "See, here is _____; what doth hinder me to be baptized?" (Acts 8:36)
30 Take to court
33 Bread from heaven
35 Take action
36 Give up
38 A young prophet, he was twenty-five when the Babylonians arrived (abbr.)
39 Saruch's father (Luke 3:35)
41 Not female
42 "A _____ went out to sow his seed" (Luke 8:5)
43 "Tread the _____" (Nahum 3:14 NIV)
45 "Carry these ten _____ unto the captain" (1 Samuel 17:18)
48 A son of Zophah (1 Chronicles 7:36)
49 Haul
50 Arrived
51 A tree of Isaiah 44
54 Otherwise
55 "A living sacrifice, holy, acceptable unto God, which is your _____ service" (Romans 12:1)
58 Always

59 "Believed the master and the _____ of the ship" (Acts 27:11)
60 "Though ye have _____" (Psalm 68:13)
61 Scarlet
62 Tired
63 "Sin is the transgression of the _____" (1 John 3:4)

## DOWN

1 Enoch's son (Genesis 4:18)
2 Take care of
3 To place
4 "The same was Adino the _____" (2 Samuel 23:8)
5 "In the _____ day" (Leviticus 23:32)
6 Carry out directions
7 King Saul's father (Acts 13:21)
8 Possesses
9 Large
10 To humble
11 Trails
12 "_____ wings of a great eagle" (Revelation 12:14)
14 David's incestous son (2 Samuel 13:1–14)
16 Opposite of *closed*
20 Honor and praise
21 "Come out of _____" (Romans 11:26)
22 Elioenai's father (Ezra 10:27)
23 Before (arch.)
24 Renown
25 "Jotham, _____" (Hosea 1:1)
26 Belonging to me
27 Ahiam's father (1 Chronicles 11:35)
29 Employment pay
30 Resting place
31 Haniel's father (1 Chronicles 7:39)
32 "The sons of Mushi; Mahli, and _____" (1 Chronicles 23:23)
34 Jesus did this at the resurrection
37 Zaccur's father (Nehemiah 3:2)
40 Reverent fear
42 Cut off
43 What we remember with

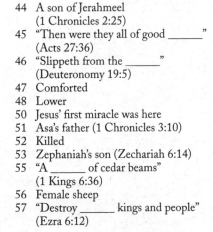

by N. Teri Grottke

44 A son of Jerahmeel
   (1 Chronicles 2:25)
45 "Then were they all of good _____"
   (Acts 27:36)
46 "Slippeth from the _____"
   (Deuteronomy 19:5)
47 Comforted
48 Lower
50 Jesus' first miracle was here
51 Asa's father (1 Chronicles 3:10)
52 Killed
53 Zephaniah's son (Zechariah 6:14)
55 "A _____ of cedar beams"
   (1 Kings 6:36)
56 Female sheep
57 "Destroy _____ kings and people"
   (Ezra 6:12)

# PUZZLE 94 — A PLEA FROM JESUS

*The promise is unto you, and to your children, and to all*
*that are afar off, even as many as the Lord our God shall call.*
ACTS 2:39

## ACROSS

1 "_____ know that my redeemer liveth" (Job 19:25) (2 words)
5 "The woodwork will _____ it" (Habakkuk 2:11 NIV)
9 "I will go out _____ other times before" (Judges 16:20) (2 words)
13 "That in the _____ to come he might show" (Ephesians 2:7)
14 "For they shall see eye _____" (Isaiah 52:8) (2 words)
16 "Shave her head, and _____ her nails" (Deuteronomy 21:12)
17 Ingrid's role in *Casablanca*
18 Intense feeling
19 Formerly Persia
20 Beginning of a **PLEA** from Jesus in John 14:1 (4 words)
23 One of the eleven dukes of Edom (Genesis 36:43)
24 Yearns
25 Jesus' **PLEA**, cont'd from 20 Across (3 words)
31 "Do you fix your _____ such a one?" (Job 14:3 NIV) (2 words)
32 Notable periods
33 "And a _____ of oil" (Leviticus 14:21)
36 A son of Dishan (1 Chronicles 1:42)
37 "And he shall be for an _____ of ships" (Genesis 49:13)
39 "I will arise and _____ my father" (Luke 15:18) (2 words)
40 *Pro* _____ (for the time being)
41 "More majestic than mountains rich with _____" (Psalm 76:4 NIV)
42 Slow in music
43 Jesus' **PLEA**, cont'd from 25 Across (3 words)
46 "I have been an _____ in a strange land" (Exodus 18:3)
49 "That _____ down and wept" (Nehemiah 1:4) (2 words)
50 End of Jesus' **PLEA**, cont'd from 43 Across (4 words)

57 "And the third beast had a face as _____" (Revelation 4:7) (2 words)
58 "A wholesome tongue is _____ of life" (Proverbs 15:4) (2 words)
59 "And a little child shall _____ them" (Isaiah 11:6)
60 "Than for a man to hear the _____ of fools" (Ecclesiastes 7:5)
61 "But such as is common _____" (1 Corinthians 10:13) (2 words)
62 Sea eagle
63 "And their words unto the _____ of the world" (Romans 10:18)
64 Relative of AMEX (abbr.)
65 "For it is _____ cut off" (Psalm 90:10)

## DOWN

1 "He will not _____ thee" (Deuteronomy 31:6)
2 Stare amorously
3 "And I will give you _____" (Matthew 11:28)
4 "And thy neck _____ sinew" (Isaiah 48:4) (3 words)
5 HT (Greek equivalent)
6 Flat-topped flower cluster
7 "The works that I do shall _____ also" (John 14:12) (2 words)
8 "Lift up your heads, _____ gates" (Psalm 24:7 NIV) (2 words)
9 "Neither have two coats _____" (Luke 9:3)
10 "But _____ shall her name be" (Genesis 17:15)
11 "And it is _____ thing" (Daniel 2:11) (2 words)
12 "Dwelling in _____" (Genesis 25:27)
15 "Ye therefore do greatly _____" (Mark 12:27)
21 "_____ the holy day" (Nehemiah 10:31)
22 Timothy and alfalfa
25 "And they shall _____ their swords into plowshares" (Isaiah 2:4)
26 Brontë's Jane

194

27 "A chariot with a _____ of horses" (Isaiah 21:9 NIV)
28 River dike
29 "How long will it be _____ thou be quiet?" (Jeremiah 47:6)
30 "From _____ even to Beersheba" (1 Kings 4:25)
33 "How _____, LORD?" (Psalm 79:5)
34 *Eight* in Milano (Ital.)
35 "Be of _____ cheer, Paul" (Acts 23:11)
37 Henry V nickname
38 "What _____ eased?" (Job 16:6) (2 words)
39 "For a light of the _____" (Isaiah 42:6)
41 Kelly or Autry
42 Chinese dynasty
43 "And slander celestial _____" (Jude 1:8 NIV)

44 "As _____ the thing they loved" (Hosea 9:10 NIV) (2 words)
45 Jewish ascetic
46 "Upon the ledges there was _____ above" (1 Kings 7:29) (2 words)
47 Detroit dud
48 "No man is an _____, intire" (Donne)
51 "When anyone went to a wine _____" (Haggai 2:16 NIV)
52 Harrow rival
53 "Terrible as an _____ with banners" (Song of Solomon 6:4)
54 Roman despot
55 "For I am a sinful _____ Lord" (Luke 5:8) (2 words)
56 "Forth from the garden of _____" (Genesis 3:23)

# PUZZLE 95

## ACROSS

1 Book of destruction of Jerusalem, five chapters long (abbr.)
4 Make clean
8 No (arch.)
11 "Lod, and _____, the valley of craftsmen" (Nehemiah 11:35)
12 A son of Jacob (Genesis 35:26)
14 Get older
15 Paul greeted this man as "mine own son" (abbr.)
16 "The night is far _____, the day is at hand" (Romans 13:12)
17 "All the Chaldeans, Pekod, and _____, and Koa" (Ezekiel 23:23)
18 Became acquainted
20 Caleb's daughter (Judges 1:12)
23 Large sea mammal
26 "Neither shall ye _____ enchantment, nor observe times" (Leviticus 19:26)
27 "The pool of _____ by the king's garden" (Nehemiah 3:15)
30 "The Cretians are alway _____" (Titus 1:12)
32 This man prophesied to the Jews in Babylon (abbr.)
33 Titanium (sym.)
34 To place
35 "He may _____ the tip of his finger" (Luke 16:24)
37 Anger
39 A measurement for oil (Leviticus 14:10)
40 "_____, five cities" (1 Chronicles 4:32)
42 The oldest copy was found among the Dead Sea Scrolls (abbr.)
43 First book in the Pentateuch (abbr.)
44 King of Bashan (Deuteronomy 3:11)
45 Single
46 Walk
48 "Now there came a _____ over all the land" (Acts 7:11)
50 Unhappy

51 "Jonah was gone down into the _____ of the ship" (Jonah 1:5)
53 Belonging to Bathsheba's first husband (poss.)
55 Relatives
58 "Punish the men that are settled on their _____" (Zephaniah 1:12)
61 Er's son (1 Chronicles 4:21)
64 Oath
66 "Helez the Paltite, _____" (2 Samuel 23:26)
67 "Not to _____ thee" (Ruth 1:16)
68 Partook
69 Deep hole
70 "Now the serpent was more subtil _____ any beast" (Genesis 3:1)
71 This NT book was likely written after AD 70, but no one knows (abbr.)

## DOWN

1 Abraham's nephew
2 "Eshtemoh, and _____," (Joshua 15:50)
3 "Beholdest thou the _____ that is in thy brother's eye" (Matthew 7:3)
4 "God saw that it _____ good" (Genesis 1:21)
5 "And the sucking child shall play on the hole of the _____" (Isaiah 11:8)
6 A son of Bani (Ezra 10:29)
7 "Come they not _____, even of your lusts" (James 4:1)
8 Book between Micah and Habakkuk (abbr.)
9 Time past
10 Exclamation of affirmation
13 Right hand (abbr.)
17 "Thou shalt break the _____ thereof" (Ezekiel 23:34)
19 "_____ wings of a great eagle" (Revelation 12:14)
21 Set of clothing
22 Solomon's great-grandson (1 Kings 15:8)

*by N. Teri Grottke*

24 "That which _____ been"
   (Ecclesiastes 6:10)
25 Son of Abdiel (1 Chronicles 5:15)
27 Stitch
28 "The fourth to _____"
   (1 Chronicles 25:11)
29 Smallest
30 Appendage
31 A river "before Egypt" (Joshua 13:3)
34 "Came to Joel the _____" (Joel 1:1)
36 "That _____ after the dust of the
   earth" (Amos 2:7)
38 Paul's hometown
39 Commanded militarily
40 Shammah's father (2 Samuel 23:11)
41 Leaders against him were Sanballat
   and Tobiah (abbr.)
43 Menahem's father (2 Kings 15:14)
44 Strange
47 "The barley was in the _____, and
   the flax was bolled" (Exodus 9:31)

49 Pose a question
51 Bed covering
52 Milcah's brother (Genesis 11:29)
54 "Destroy _____ kings and people"
   (Ezra 6:12)
56 "Of Hena, and _____?"
   (2 Kings 19:13)
57 "_____ that man, and have no
   company with him"
   (2 Thessalonians 3:14)
58 "The _____ of truth shall be
   established for ever"
   (Proverbs 12:19)
59 A son of Gad (Genesis 46:16)
60 Consume food
62 Area near Babylon (2 Kings 17:24)
63 Zephaniah's son (Zechariah 6:14)
65 Spider's art

# PUZZLE 96 — NATIONS IN THE PROMISED LAND

*I will. . .destroy all the people to whom thou shalt come.*
EXODUS 23:27

## ACROSS

1 "Now the _____ shall live by faith" (Hebrews 10:38)
5 Book after Micah
10 "And there _____ certain man at Lystra" (Acts 14:8) (2 words)
14 "No _____ will pitch his tent there" (Isaiah 13:20 NIV)
15 Enraged
16 A tenth of an ephah (Exodus 16:36)
17 A **NATION** Israel encountered in the Promised Land (Exodus 23:23)
19 "That nothing be _____" (John 6:12)
20 "_____ woe is past" (Revelation 9:12)
21 _____ Moines, Iowa
22 "Which trieth our _____" (1 Thessalonians 2:4)
24 Wallet fillers
26 "Or if he shall ask an _____" (Luke 11:12)
29 Sprint rival
30 "He _____ to Moses" (Romans 9:15 NIV)
31 Growl
32 Bright tropical fish
35 Rocky hill
37 VIP transport
39 An age
40 "Come again?"
43 Another **NATION** from Exodus 23:23
45 "And Jacob _____ pottage" (Genesis 25:29)
46 "It _____; be not afraid" (Matthew 14:27) (2 words)
47 "As if he blessed an _____" (Isaiah 66:3)
48 "He planteth an _____" (Isaiah 44:14)
50 "The apostles and the elders _____ consider this" (Acts 15:6 NIV) (2 words)
52 "I have _____ him to the LORD" (1 Samuel 1:28)
54 Dog's comments
58 KLM rival, once
59 Boston _____ Party

60 "By _____ rebuke I dry up the sea" (Isaiah 50:2 NIV)
61 "Our houses to _____" (Lamentations 5:2)
64 Spread hay
66 "The wilderness of ___ " (Exodus 16:1)
67 "Record this _____" (Ezekiel 24:2 NIV)
68 Another **NATION** from Exodus 23:23
72 Got an A
73 "Behold, _____ was opened" (Revelation 4:1) (2 words)
74 Unit of heredity
75 "A _____ of meat from the king" (2 Samuel 11:8)
76 "The fortified _____ ruin" (Isaiah 25:2 NIV) (2 words)
77 Not evens

## DOWN

1 "Now _____ well was there" (John 4:6)
2 Muse of astronomy
3 With rationality
4 Schedule abbreviation
5 "And _____ parts to dwell" (Nehemiah 11:1)
6 "That wicked men have _____ among you" (Deuteronomy 13:13 NIV)
7 Pass the _____ (take a collection)
8 Colorado native
9 "And he wanders into its _____" (Job 18:8 NIV)
10 "Let us _____ ourselves with loves" (Proverbs 7:18)
11 Another **NATION** from Exodus 23:23
12 "But _____ the spirits to see" (1 John 4:1 NIV)
13 "Which used curious _____" (Acts 19:19)
18 Commercials
23 Decorate in relief
25 WWII craft (abbr.)
27 "Departed into _____" (Matthew 4:12)

*by David K. Shortess*

28 Clamp together tightly, as teeth
31 Network
33 "Is there any thing _____ hard for me?" (Jeremiah 32:27)
34 "_____ it came to pass" (Luke 2:1)
36 Akron resident
38 "And giveth _____ to her household" (Proverbs 31:15)
40 "For they all saw _____ "(Mark 6:50)
41 "But when ye pray, _____ not vain repetitions" (Matthew 6:7)
42 Another **NATION** from Exodus 23:23
44 Unit of electrical potential
49 Canaan's father (Genesis 9:18)
51 Scotch fabrics
53 "O _____ not desired" (Zephaniah 2:1)
55 "And the land _____ from war" (Joshua 11:23)

56 "A _____ loveth at all times" (Proverbs 17:17)
57 "Have their _____ exercised to discern" (Hebrews 5:14)
60 Wood-cutting tool (var.)
61 Enos's grandfather (Luke 3:38)
62 "And thou shalt put it on a blue _____" (Exodus 28:37)
63 "He _____ on the ground" (John 9:6)
65 "And of _____ the priest, the scribe" (Nehemiah 12:26)
69 Former name of Tokyo
70 "And a _____ of new timber" (Ezra 6:4)
71 "Because _____ to the Father" (John 16:16) (2 words)

# PUZZLE 97

**ACROSS**

1 Child's favorite seat
4 Baby sheep
8 "Sharper than any twoedged _____" (Hebrews 4:12)
13 Zaccur's father (Nehemiah 3:2)
15 Carry out directions
16 Gomer's husband (Hosea 1:2–3)
17 Worry
18 Transgression
19 "Man named _____" (Acts 9:33)
20 "The mouth _____ meat" (Job 34:3)
22 This man convicted people for their non-Jewish wives (abbr.)
23 Paul founded their church, among others, and stayed three years (abbr.)
24 "What _____ ye to weep" (Acts 21:13)
25 Unload cargo (arch.)
28 To free
29 Petroleum product
30 Bird from the ark sent out three times
34 This OT book describes aspects of priesthood (abbr.)
36 "He bade them teach the children of Judah the _____ of the bow" (2 Samuel 1:18)
39 "Of Keros, the children of _____" (Nehemiah 7:47)
41 Color of blood
42 Before (arch.)
43 Sprint
44 Minor prophet who questioned God (abbr.)
45 Pass away
46 Possesses
47 Purim marks this queen's success (abbr.)
48 Abdiel's son (1 Chronicles 5:15)
49 Motel
50 "_____ the waters" (Exodus 15:25)
52 "Dip the _____ of his finger in water" (Luke 16:24)
54 "And _____ greedily after the error of Balaam" (Jude 1:11)
56 Opposite of *farther*

59 "Jotham, _____" (Hosea 1:1)
61 "Against Jerusalem, _____" (Ezekiel 26:2)
64 Untruth
65 "And also the name of the city shall be _____" (Ezekiel 39:16)
68 "Gather up the fragments that _____" (John 6:12)
70 Commanded militarily
71 Land measurement
72 "Shilshah, and Ithran, and _____" (1 Chronicles 7:37)
73 Gaddi's father (Numbers 13:11)
74 "_____, O Israel: The LORD our God is one LORD" (Deuteronomy 6:4)
75 Jehoshaphat's chief captain of Judah (2 Chronicles 17:14)
76 A child of Ezer (Genesis 36:27)
77 And _____ lay at his feet until the morning" (Ruth 3:14)

**DOWN**

1 "_____ up your eyes" (John 4:35)
2 Moses' father (Exodus 6:20)
3 "Thou _____ man and beast" (Psalm 36:6)
4 Opposite of *found*
5 A son of Aaron (Exodus 6:23)
6 "The sons of God saw the daughters of _____ that they were fair" (Genesis 6:2)
7 Near
8 "_____ to take fire" (Isaiah 30:14)
9 Opposite of *lost*
10 "As he saith also in _____" (Romans 9:25)
11 Harvest
12 Race
14 Ribai's son (2 Samuel 23:29)
19 Shaphan's father (2 Kings 22:3)
21 "For how can I _____ to see the evil that shall come unto my people?" (Esther 8:6)
22 Elijah's successor
26 Nobelium (sym.)
27 An altar (Joshua 22:34)

*by N. Teri Grottke*

31 "Are ye subject to _____"
(Colossians 2:20)

32 Blood vessel

33 First garden

34 Samson slew 1,000 Philistines here
(Judges 15:14–15)

35 "Shuthelah: of _____"
(Numbers 26:36)

37 "He shall _____ thee"
(Psalm 55:22)

38 Whole

40 Dathan's cohort in rebellion
(Numbers 16:1–3)

51 Suffix (inert gas)

53 Physical education (abbr.)

55 "And Abishua, and Naaman, and
_____" (1 Chronicles 8:4)

57 A son of Elam (Ezra 10:26)

58 Zorobabel's son (Luke 3:27)

60 Pharez's twin brother
(Genesis 38:27–30)

61 Anak's father (Joshua 15:13)

62 Pay attention to

63 So be it

66 Patriarch of a family of returned
exiles (Ezra 2:15)

67 In this place

69 A son of Jether (1 Chronicles 7:38)

70 Matthew, Mark, _____, John
(abbr.)

73 Its major cities are Cape Town and
Johannesburg (abbr.)

## ACROSS

1 To move in any direction by turning over and over
5 "For the remission of _____" (Acts 2:38)
9 Pork
12 Joram's son (Matthew 1:8)
14 Genuine
15 "_____, which were dukes" (Joshua 13:21)
16 "Slew a lion in a pit in a ___ ___ day" (1 Chronicles 11:22)
17 "Strangers of _____" (Acts 2:10)
18 Open
19 "Fourth part of an _____ of beaten oil" (Numbers 28:5)
20 Ahira's father (Numbers 10:27)
22 Simple
23 "I _____ that thou art a gracious God" (Jonah 4:2)
24 Actors play a _____
26 "_____ a right spirit within me" (Psalm 51:10)
28 "_____ said unto the king" (2 Samuel 13:35)
31 "Her mother in law _____ her" (Ruth 3:6)
32 "Mine eyes shall be _____ the faithful" (Psalm 101:6)
33 Youngster
35 Rim
36 "They _____ upon the camels" (Genesis 24:61)
38 "I am the _____ of Sharon" (Song of Solomon 2:1)
39 "Neither shall ye touch it, lest ye _____" (Genesis 3:3)
40 There was a marriage in _____ of Galilee" (John 2:1)
41 Type of fabric
42 Ratite
44 "He cast four _____" (Exodus 38:5)
45 Drink
46 "So that the earth _____ again" (1 Samuel 4:5)
47 "Nemuel, and Jamin, _____," (1 Chronicles 4:24)

50 "They _____ every one his mantle" (Job 2:12)
51 "Make thee an _____ of gopher wood" (Genesis 6:14)
54 King of the Amalekites (1 Samuel 15:8)
55 This man asked for a double portion of Elijah's spirit (abbr.)
57 "To the battle at _____" (Numbers 21:33)
59 "In _____ and caves of the earth" (Hebrews 11:38)
60 "God shall _____ away all tears from their eyes" (Revelation 21:4)
61 "Flee thou to _____" (Genesis 27:43)
62 Pose a question
63 "The land is as the garden of _____" (Joel 2:3)
64 Thirty-six inches

## DOWN

1 "Naaman, Ehi, and _____" (Genesis 46:21)
2 "Of _____, the family of the Oznites" (Numbers 26:16)
3 "As a roaring _____" (1 Peter 5:8)
4 Statute
5 Dried grain stalks
6 Ferrum
7 Used in counting (abbr.)
8 Espy
9 "The gods of Sepharvaim, _____, and Ivah?" (2 Kings 18:34)
10 "Kish the son of _____" (2 Chronicles 29:12)
11 "The wilderness of _____" (1 Samuel 23:24)
13 "From the tower of _____" (Ezekiel 29:10)
15 "When the judges _____" (Ruth 1:1)
21 "A _____ commandment I give unto you" (John 13:34)
22 Scheme
23 "That at the name of Jesus every _____ should bow" (Philippians 2:10)
24 Cord

by Tonya Vilhauer

25 "Children of Lod, Hadid, and
_____" (Ezra 2:33)
26 Waves used in broadcasting
27 "The sharp sword with two _____"
(Revelation 2:12)
28 "_____ was comforted"
(Genesis 38:12)
29 Beside
30 "The two pillars, one sea, and the
_____" (2 Kings 25:16)
31 Resting place
34 Cave
36 "There is a sound of abundance of
_____" (1 Kings 18:41)
37 "He died unto sin _____"
(Romans 6:10)
38 "Sealed it with the king's _____"
(Esther 8:10)
40 Baby's bed
41 "The blood upon the _____"
(Exodus 12:23)

43 Small branches
44 "They _____ in the dry places like
a river" (Psalm 105:41)
46 "_____ between Nineveh and
Calah" (Genesis 10:12)
47 Shammai's brother
(1 Chronicles 2:32)
48 "Hath been hid from _____"
(Colossians 1:26)
49 Grade
50 Mellow
51 "They gave them the city of _____"
(Joshua 21:11)
52 Behind
53 "Be ye _____ one to another"
(Ephesians 4:32)
55 Sheep
56 Cover
58 "That I might rest in the _____ of
trouble" (Habakkuk 3:16)

# PUZZLE 99

## ACROSS

1 City of the priests (1 Samuel 22:19)
4 A son of David (1 Chronicles 3:7)
9 Capable
12 Boat paddle
13 A river of Damascus (2 Kings 5:12)
14 Daniel had a vision by this river (Daniel 8:2)
15 "So they _____ it up" (Micah 7:3)
17 A grandson of Asher (Genesis 46:17)
18 Not any
19 "Then David put garrisons in _____" (1 Chronicles 18:6)
22 This is attached to the shoulder
23 Elderly
24 "The parts of _____" (Acts 2:10)
27 Her household reported contentions in the Corinthian church
30 "As he saith also in _____" (Romans 9:25)
31 A city of Judah (Joshua 15:52)
33 Twenty-first letter of the Greek alphabet
36 "Sons of _____" (1 Chronicles 7:12)
37 Saw
38 "Ye may be _____ also with exceeding joy" (1 Peter 4:13)
39 Type of tree
40 "Then they that _____ received his word were baptized" (Acts 2:41)
41 Revile
42 Bring together
43 Mineral potash (Proverbs 25:20)
44 A son of Jether (1 Chronicles 7:38)
45 A parson or Holy _____
46 "_____ the governor listeth" (James 3:4)
53 A king of Midian (Numbers 31:8)
54 "Plain from _____" (Deuteronomy 2:8)
55 "Tower of _____" (Genesis 35:21)
57 A son of Ulla (1 Chronicles 7:39)
58 A son of Seir the Horite (Genesis 36:20)
59 A son of Gad (Genesis 46:16)
60 "They fled before the _____ of Ai" (Joshua 7:4)
61 "Their _____ in wait on the west of the city" (Joshua 8:13)
62 Scarlet

## DOWN

1 Currently
2 Hand-driven boat propellers
3 Donkey sound
4 Hodiah's brother (1 Chronicles 4:19)
5 Ruth's son (Ruth 4:13–17)
6 "Ramah and _____" (Ezra 2:26)
7 "Suburbs, and _____" (1 Chronicles 6:73)
8 "Habor, and _____" (1 Chronicles 5:26)
9 Audibly
10 "Baked it in _____" (Numbers 11:8)
11 Bind
14 Brother of a parent
16 "Watch unto _____" (1 Peter 4:7)
20 "Helez the Paltite, _____" (2 Samuel 23:26)
21 "Not _____ angry" (Titus 1:7)
24 "Than one _____" (Mark 8:14)
25 Rephaiah's father (1 Chronicles 4:42)
26 Name of the well that the Lord told Moses about (Numbers 21:16)
27 Scold
28 Back of foot
29 "The elect _____" (2 John 1:1)
31 Nagge's son (Luke 3:25)
32 Past tense of *spit*
33 "Thee in this _____" (2 Kings 9:26)
34 Delilah cut Samson's
35 Lazy
38 Mourn
40 Small flying insect
42 Bathsheba's first husband (2 Samuel 11:3)
43 Greek form of *Noah* (Luke 17:26)
44 A son of Abishur (1 Chronicles 2:29)

*by N. Teri Grottke*

45 "Some of _____ disciples"
   (John 3:25)
46 "And _____ destroyed of the
   destroyer" (1 Corinthians 10:10)
47 This will be cast into the lake of fire
48 Jesus cried this on the cross
   (Mark 15:34)
49 Charge
50 Night sky illuminator
51 "Mahli, and _____"
   (1 Chronicles 23:23)
52 Not easily found
53 Male sheep
56 To free

# PUZZLE 100 — BIBLICAL BROTHERS

*A man of many companions may come to ruin,*
*but there is a friend who sticks closer than a brother.*
PROVERBS 18:24 NIV

## ACROSS

1 "Ourselves a _____ for you to follow" (2 Thessalonians 3:9 NIV)
6 "The wrath of the _____" (Revelation 6:16)
10 "And shall put it upon a _____" (Numbers 4:10)
13 Met offering
14 "To preach the word in _____" (Acts 16:6)
15 "_____ an Ithrite" (2 Samuel 23:38)
16 **BIBLICAL BROTHERS** found in Matthew 4 (3 words)
19 A grandson of Adam (Genesis 4:25–26)
20 "Commanded to _____ peoples" (Daniel 3:4 NIV)
21 "Wherefore _____ Sarah laugh" (Genesis 18:13)
22 Sun Yat-_____ (Chinese leader)
23 _____ Cruces, NM
24 Singer Martha
25 _____ Victor (abbr.)
28 **BIBLICAL BROTHERS** found in Matthew 17 (3 words)
31 British noblemen
34 Juan's aunt
35 "Suddenly _____ instant" (Isaiah 30:13) (2 words)
36 "Why _____ so fearful?" (Mark 4:40) (2 words)
37 "Followed the _____" (Genesis 24:61)
38 "How right they are to _____ you!" (Song of Solomon 1:4 NIV)
39 Wonderful!
40 "And none _____ deliver" (Micah 5:8)
41 Bells and whistles
42 **BIBLICAL BROTHERS** found in Genesis 25 (3 words)
45 The start and end of a Wisconsin city
46 *Summer* in Paris (Fr.)
47 "And bored a hole in the _____ of it" (2 Kings 12:9)
48 "If a man _____, shall he live again?" (Job 14:14)
51 PC alternative
52 *Own* in Scotland (Scot.)

53 "And counteth the _____" (Luke 14:28)
54 **BIBLICAL BROTHERS** found in Genesis 5 (3 words)
58 "But the name of the wicked shall _____" (Proverbs 10:7)
59 "For I have _____ blameless life" (Psalm 26:1 NIV) (2 words)
60 Wood-shaping tool
61 "And _____ it up" (Revelation 10:10)
62 "From the _____ of the tongue" (Job 5:21 NIV)
63 "The men of the _____ Nebo, fifty and two" (Nehemiah 7:33)

## DOWN

1 Jethro's son-in-law (Exodus 3:1)
2 "Wail, _____ tree" (Zechariah 11:2 NIV) (2 words)
3 "He has a _____" (Matthew 11:18 NIV)
4 Greek god of love
5 Ethernet, for example (abbr.)
6 Having woolly hairs
7 "The Gentiles to live _____ the Jews?" (Galatians 2:14) (2 words)
8 May be a POW
9 Head- or neckwear (var.)
10 "Like a _____, without cause" (Lamentations 3:52)
11 "Blessed _____ the meek" (Matthew 5:5)
12 "Or if the _____ flesh turn again" (Leviticus 13:16)
17 "The written account of _____ line" (Genesis 5:1 NIV)
18 "And Rachel _____, and was buried" (Genesis 35:19)
23 Freeway part
24 "Wind without _____" (Proverbs 25:14)
25 Helicopter part
26 "_____ is deceptive, and beauty" (Proverbs 31:30 NIV)
27 Boleyn, et al.

*by David K. Shortess*

28 "Shout with _____ God, all the earth!" (Psalm 66:1 NIV) (2 words)
29 "Behold, I _____ at the door, and knock" (Revelation 3:20)
30 Fifth son of Nebo (Ezra 10:43)
31 Guitar kin
32 "And towers in the wooded _____" (2 Chronicles 27:4 NIV)
33 "And his head _____ unto the clouds" (Job 20:6)
37 "His neck with a flowing _____?" (Job 39:19 NIV)
38 "There is _____ here" (John 6:9) (2 words)
40 Cry of disapproval
41 "Sin of Sodom, that was overthrown _____ moment" (Lamentations 4:6) (3 words)
43 "And, behold, a _____ is in thine own eye?" (Matthew 7:4)
44 Ravens fed him (1 Kings 17:1–6)
48 "Know what thy right hand _____" (Matthew 6:3)
49 "Now the parable is this: The seed _____ word of God" (Luke 8:11) (2 words)
50 Libnah, and _____, and Ashan" (Joshua 15:42)
51 "And with what measure ye _____, it shall be measured" (Matthew 7:2)
52 "If anyone _____ anything to them" (Revelation 22:18 NIV)
53 Chit's companion
54 *Mrs.* in Madrid (abbr.)
55 "My heart was _____ within me" (Psalm 39:3)
56 Teachers' organization (abbr.)
57 Arafat's organization (abbr.)

207

# PUZZLE 101

## ACROSS

1 This is attached to the shoulder
4 A temple gate (2 Kings 11:6)
7 Patriarch of a family of returned exiles (Ezra 2:57)
10 "The sons of Carmi; _____" (1 Chronicles 2:7)
12 Very (arch.)
13 Goat baby
14 "Suddenly there _____ from heaven a great light" (Acts 22:6)
15 Furthest part
16 Beach surface
17 Kept from detection
18 Belteshazzar (Daniel 1:7)
20 "He had cast _____ the waters" (Exodus 15:25)
21 "Which before these days _____ an uproar" (Acts 21:38)
23 Naaman's brother (Numbers 26:40)
25 Exclamation of affirmation
26 A son of Pashur (Ezra 10:22)
31 Peace
34 David's eldest brother (1 Samuel 17:13)
35 Make a mistake
36 "Alammelech, and _____" (Joshua 19:26)
37 A duke of Edom (1 Chronicles 1:51)
38 A brother of Bethuel (Genesis 22:22)
39 "_____ of cedar beams" (1 Kings 6:36)
40 Esarhaddon was king here (Ezra 4:2)
41 A son of Ephraim (Numbers 26:35)
42 Agreed
44 Are (arch.)
45 Fuss
46 "Which come to you in _____ clothing" (Matthew 7:15)
49 Generations
52 "_____, that was about his head" (John 20:7)
55 Capable
57 Lease
58 A son of Merari (1 Chronicles 24:27)
59 Her household reported contentions in the Corinthian church
61 This book was likely written during Jehoram's reign in Judah (abbr.)
62 "Cain. . .dwelt in the land of Nod, on the east of _____" (Genesis 4:16)
63 "Country; upon _____" (Jeremiah 48:21)
64 A son of Jacob
65 Opposite of *night*
66 Sprint

## DOWN

1 Eliud's father (Matthew 1:14)
2 She left Peter at the door (Acts 12:13–14)
3 Adam was the first
4 Gaddiel's father (Numbers 13:10)
5 "Pharisees began to _____ him vehemently" (Luke 11:53)
6 He came with Zerubbabel (Ezra 2:2)
7 A child of Ezer (Genesis 36:27)
8 "For ye tithe _____ and rue and all manner of herbs" (Luke 11:42)
9 Zechariah's father (Ezra 5:1)
10 Type of tree (Isaiah 44:14)
11 Rescue
12 Caused to go to a destination
16 Riverbank (Exodus 2:5)
19 Solomon's great-grandson (1 Kings 15:8)
22 Colored
24 Steal
26 Achim's son (Matthew 1:14)
27 "If we say that we have not sinned, we make him a _____" (1 John 1:10 NIV)
28 Border went to here from Remmonmethoar (Joshua 19:13)
29 Steward of Zimri's house in Tirzah (1 Kings 16)
30 Strong metal

by N. Teri Grottke

31 "Through faith also _____ herself received strength to conceive seed" (Hebrews 11:11)
32 Naum's son (Luke 3:25)
33 "I will put my _____ into their mind" (Hebrews 8:10)
34 Otherwise
37 Astonished (arch.)
38 Detest
40 "Garments, _____ stood" (Zechariah 3:3)
41 Ditch
43 Opposite of *west*
44 Abdiel's son (1 Chronicles 5:15)
46 Epidermis
47 A son of Reuben (Exodus 6:14)
48 Partner of fork and knife
49 "Of _____, the family of the Arodites" (Numbers 26:17)

50 A priestly city of Benjamin (Joshua 21:17)
51 Ahira's father (Numbers 1:15)
53 Adoniram's father (1 Kings 4:6)
54 "Will a lion roar in the forest, when he hath no _____?" (Amos 3:4)
56 "Hundred and _____ years old" (Joshua 24:29)
60 "Ye shall point out for you mount _____" (Numbers 34:7)

# WORD SEARCH

# PUZZLE 1 —
# INSTRUMENTS OF MUSICK

CORNETS.
CYMBALS
DULCIMER
FIR WOOD
FLUTE·
HARP
HORN
INSTRUMENTS
MUSICK
ORGAN
PIPE
PSALTERY

SACKBUT
SHOUT
SINGING
SONG
SOUND
STRINGED
TABRETS
TIMBRELS
TRUMPETS
VIOL
VOICE

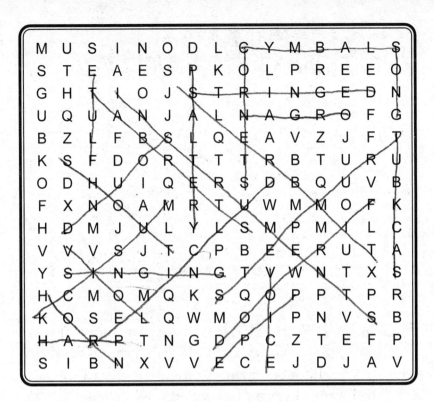

*by David Austin*

## BONUS TRIVIA

Which prophet asked if a leopard
could change his spots?

*Luke 1:42–45*

And she spake out with a loud voice, and said, Blessed art thou among women, and blessed is the fruit of thy womb. And whence is this to me, that the mother of my Lord should come to me? For, lo, as soon as the voice of thy salutation sounded in mine ears, the babe leaped in my womb for joy. And blessed is she that believed: for there shall be a performance of those things which were told her from the Lord.

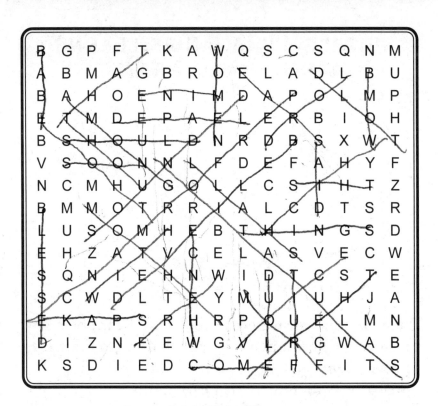

*by John Hudson Tiner*

## Bonus Trivia

Who said, "Weeds were
wrapped about my head"?

# PUZZLE 3 — ANANIAS LEARNS ABOUT PAUL'S PRAYER

### Acts 9:13–16

Then Ananias answered, Lord, I have heard by many of this man, how much evil he hath done to thy saints at Jerusalem: and here he hath authority from the chief priests to bind all that call on thy name. But the Lord said unto him, Go thy way: for he is a chosen vessel unto me, to bear my name before the Gentiles, and kings, and the children of Israel: for I will shew him how great things he must suffer for my name's sake.

```
G H K Z L S B A U L M B K X V
W I E P E E N O D N A I I K B
U J V F J C A W P D N A O Q D
M T A B E F O R E G Y N B L F
X E H W E H S R S V M A R O G
M G L E S S E V Q I U N A R W
L G H A N W I E J T S I E D D
L Y E E S N N H H H T A B M S
I L S N A U E O T I T S K R F
W O A T T R R B I N D E R E H
R F F C S I D E Y G F D I F N
S R L E T E L R J S I H P F Z
Z P M Y D N I E F A C S W U O
A A U M U C H R S A I N T S Z
N N E S O H C S P U P G Q P Q
```

*by John Hudson Tiner*

# BONUS TRIVIA

Who kept the ark of the covenant for
David and was blessed because of it?

# PUZZLE 4 — PSALM OF CHRIST

## *Psalm 22*

ASSEMBLY

BONES

CAST LOTS

CLEAVETH

CONFOUNDED

CRIED

DEATH

DELIVER

DESPISED

DOGS

DRIED UP

FORSAKEN

HEART

INCLOSED

MELTED

MY FEET

MY GARMENTS

MY GOD

MY HANDS

OUT OF JOINT

PIERCED

POTSHERD

POURED OUT

REPROACH

STARE

STRENGTH

TONGUE

TRUSTED

VESTURE

WATER

WICKED

WORM

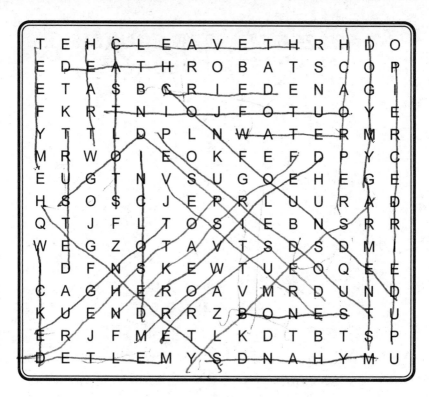

*by David Austin*

## Bonus Trivia

What transportation disaster befell the
apostle Paul as he was traveling to
Rome to stand trial before Caesar?

*Shipwreck. (Acts 27:21–44)*

*Acts 4:29–30*

And now, **Lord, behold their threatenings**: and **grant unto** thy **servants**, that **with** all **boldness they** may **speak** thy **word,** by **stretching forth thine hand** to **heal**; and **that signs** and **wonders** may be **done** by the **name** of thy **holy child Jesus.**

```
D  S  I  W  S  Q  L  A  O  M  D  X  E  S  K
H  T  P  V  C  R  P  U  O  J  U  R  N  L  L
V  J  T  K  T  S  K  N  A  N  Q  P  O  R  L
M  Q  H  H  U  N  A  M  E  B  M  L  D  W  Y
A  W  F  S  N  G  M  N  Y  Z  A  K  I  P  U
L  S  E  B  J  I  S  Z  O  E  S  T  O  R  L
X  J  Y  E  S  S  W  E  H  T  H  I  N  E  W
C  G  Y  H  S  G  S  G  R  A  N  T  Z  I  L
H  T  R  O  F  R  E  E  J  V  N  U  T  P  S
I  A  L  L  E  D  T  G  N  E  A  D  H  P  Y
L  Q  U  D  Z  C  R  C  T  D  T  N  A  G  L
D  O  N  H  H  G  I  H  J  H  L  S  T  E  E
T  O  R  I  K  A  E  P  S  Y  L  O  H  S  V
W  Z  N  D  H  Y  H  W  F  G  E  I  B  M  R
S  G  N  I  N  E  T  A  E  R  H  T  N  M  O
```

*by John Hudson Tiner*

# BONUS TRIVIA

What priestly garment did David use to ask
God whether he should pursue the Amalekites,
who had kidnapped two of his wives?

**John 6:26–27**

**Jesus answered them** and **said,** Verily, **verily,** I say unto you, Ye **seek** me, not because ye saw the **miracles,** but **because** ye did eat of the **loaves,** and were **filled. La-bour** not for the meat which **perisheth,** but for **that meat** which **endureth** unto **everlasting life, which** the Son of man **shall give unto** you: for him **hath** God the **Father sealed**.

```
E  Z  L  Y  R  M  G  R  V  X  S  M  Q  Z  P
Q  V  A  L  A  B  O  U  R  Y  V  U  U  S  L
T  E  E  I  T  Z  K  S  Q  Y  P  S  S  B  S
R  Y  P  R  G  O  L  X  E  E  J  A  Y  E  P
A  Y  D  E  L  L  I  F  R  S  N  Y  L  N  J
O  N  F  V  A  A  C  I  A  M  U  C  M  D  I
T  Z  S  H  I  P  S  I  M  A  A  A  C  U  D
N  H  S  W  B  H  D  T  L  R  G  O  C  R  P
U  G  A  A  E  A  U  I  I  L  O  A  V  E  S
I  T  W  T  P  R  D  M  F  N  Y  J  L  T  B
R  E  H  T  A  F  E  R  E  A  G  J  A  H  J
Y  X  I  E  G  U  L  D  S  Y  W  E  F  T  V
L  L  C  B  M  J  A  E  D  C  M  H  V  S  I
C  D  H  T  A  H  E  D  W  L  P  J  Y  I  K
P  Q  E  K  T  K  S  E  B  J  Y  N  G  I  G
```

*by John Hudson Tiner*

## BONUS TRIVIA

What troublesome desire did
Paul say is "common to man"?

AMALEKITE

AMORITE

ARDITE

ARELITE

ARODITE

ASHBELITE

BACHRITE

BERIITE

CANAANITE

DINAITE

ELAMITE

GESHURITE

HEBRONITE

IZEHARITE

KADMONITE

KENITE

KENIZZITE

KOHATHITE

MIDIANITE

MOABITE

PERIZZITE

RECHABITE

TARPELITE

ZEMARITE

```
I  T  A  H  E  C  T  B  A  C  H  R  I  T  E
A  R  O  D  I  T  E  T  I  R  O  M  A  T  S
E  I  Z  E  H  A  R  I  T  E  T  R  M  A  E
T  E  T  I  R  A  M  E  Z  H  P  D  S  K  L
I  W  E  T  I  D  R  A  E  E  K  H  E  E  K
M  G  B  H  O  J  U  B  L  E  B  Q  J  A  E
A  G  E  S  H  U  R  I  T  E  E  F  D  B  N
L  Z  R  F  Q  O  T  I  L  T  K  M  A  V  I
E  Z  I  J  N  E  N  I  I  I  O  I  F  A  Z
T  K  I  I  D  A  T  Z  T  N  K  B  T  R  Z
I  T  T  U  I  E  Z  O  I  A  E  D  I  E  I
B  E  E  D  Q  I  E  T  I  A  N  I  D  L  T
A  Q  I  V  R  F  E  X  A  N  I  W  M  I  E
O  M  O  E  H  M  K  O  H  A  T  H  I  T  E
M  J  P  E  T  I  B  A  H  C  E  R  L  E  M
```

*by David Austin*

# BONUS TRIVIA

What substance appeared on Gideon's fleece
one night—but not the next—to convince
him he was working in God's will?

**2 Kings 20:2–3**

**Then** he **turned** his **face** to the **wall**, and **prayed unto** the LORD, **saying**, I **beseech** thee, O LORD, **remember** now how I have **walked before thee** in **truth** and **with** a **perfect heart**, and **have done that which** is **good** in thy **sight**. And **Hezekiah wept sore**.

```
E  R  O  S  H  B  M  H  Y  G  F  T  G  P  E
V  D  E  T  P  V  E  Q  S  Q  B  A  J  O  W
H  G  E  M  P  Z  H  S  Y  X  F  K  L  V  I
C  N  L  N  E  Z  E  F  E  W  D  W  A  B  A
I  I  D  K  R  M  S  A  X  E  A  G  U  K  S
H  Y  I  N  F  U  B  C  D  L  C  N  U  Q  I
W  A  L  K  E  D  T  E  L  V  T  H  K  Z  E
H  S  A  U  C  H  Y  E  R  O  F  E  B  N  X
H  T  U  R  T  A  T  O  V  V  R  G  O  O  D
E  H  E  A  R  T  K  Z  L  A  M  D  C  Z  W
A  T  I  P  H  A  H  V  E  B  H  E  I  G  S
F  O  W  G  Y  H  P  E  K  Z  Y  F  T  E  Q
K  L  I  R  O  T  V  D  E  N  X  U  S  R  V
O  S  T  P  E  W  Q  D  B  A  T  U  W  M  W
Y  J  H  V  N  L  I  I  Y  Q  F  I  B  D  O
```

*by John Hudson Tiner*

# BONUS TRIVIA

What son of David cut his long hair
whenever it became too heavy for him?

BEAUTY

BUCKLER

FAITHFUL

FAVOUR

GLADNESS

GLORY

HELP

HOLY

HONOUR

HOPE

INHERITANCE

INTEGRITY

JOY

JUDGMENT

LIFE

LIGHT

LOVINGKINDNESS

MAJESTY

MARVELLOUS

MERCY

PEACE

PORTION

POWER

PRAISE

PURE

REFUGE

RIGHTEOUS

ROCK

SALVATION

STRENGTH

TRUTH

WAY

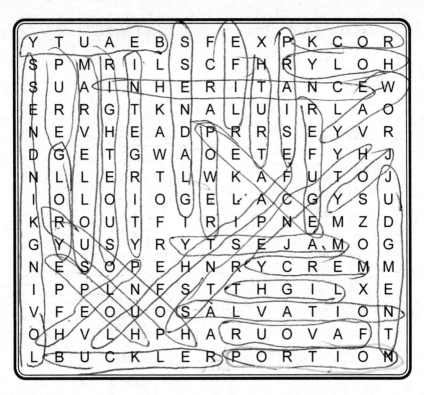

*by N. Teri Grottke*

# BONUS TRIVIA

What body fluid was part of the curse
that came by Adam and Eve's sin?

## PUZZLE 10 — FRIENDS AND ACQUAINTANCES OF JESUS

ANDREW
BARTHOLOMEW
BARTIMAEUS
CLEOPAS
ELIJAH
JAIRUS
JAMES
JOANNA
JOHN
JOHN THE BAPTIST
JUDAS
LAZARUS
MARTHA
MARY
MARY MAGDALENE
MATTHEW
MOSES
NATHANAEL
NICODEMUS
PAUL
PETER
PHILIP
SIMON ZELOTES
THOMAS
ZACCHAEUS

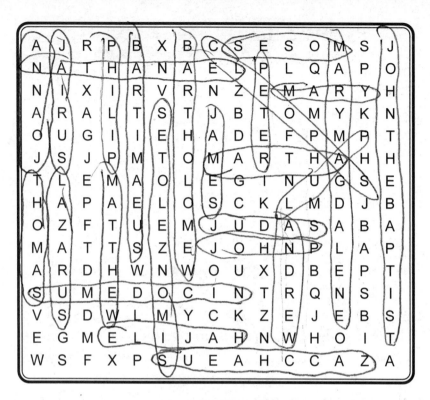

*by Paul Kent*

## Bonus Trivia

What synagogue official saw
his twelve-year-old daughter
raised to life by Jesus?

## John 17:1–3

These **words spake** Jesus, and **lifted** up his **eyes** to **heaven**, and **said**, **Father**, the **hour** is **come**; glorify thy Son, that thy Son **also** may **glorify** thee: as thou hast given him **power over** all **flesh**, that he **should** give eternal life to as **many** as thou hast **given** him. And **this** is **life eternal, that they might know thee** the **only true** God, and **Jesus Christ, whom thou hast sent.**

```
T D B W Y N R E K A P S Z I Y
U T H E E M R E W O P D E G H
P O U C H R I S T J R R L Y J
M R H D T D E H E E E O X S E
T D G T F L E S H V R W T H M
G A I E G A U T O I Q N T O V
S P V S V S A E F I L M A U G
I E E E T F A Y H I P A H L C
E C N H M T H I S F L N T D J
C U G T O O G R D S M Y R E W
R I S I N U C W O N K C D T S
M A P J L X R C M S B Y D N T
H G E X Y Z O B F T U S B D J
O E L G Q U Z B E C Q I E Q L
D J Q D M I X X V T F H T W V
```

*by John Hudson Tiner*

# Bonus Trivia

What king unwittingly signed a
decree that caused his friend, Daniel,
to be thrown into a den of lions?

### John 17:7–10

Now they have known that all **things whatsoever** thou hast given me are of thee. For I have given **unto** them the **words** which thou **gavest** me; and they have **received** them, and have **known surely** that I **came** out **from thee**, and they **have believed that** thou **didst send** me. I pray for them: I **pray** not for the **world**, but for them **which thou hast given** me; for **they** are thine. And all mine are thine, and **thine** are **mine**; and I am **glorified** in **them**.

```
T C N P D N T G B T S D I D A
W D Q N N S V B U H H E T S D
T H E M E J E G U I T I F C J
M S M V I L G P N N W O N K Q
K Q A O I E N L T G T H Q E K
A G Y E R E V E O S T A H W K
B B V V V F C W O R L D F V M
T E N I M A X E X Q I Y H U V
D V G S M F W O R D S F C Y C
D S P E N J U N N F F A I L Q
E W C P E T O F Y D U K H E R
S Z Z E R H H A S T E Q W R D
R S M B A A T R Z X F W D U V
S T Y V Y T Y B H M P Z W S E
F Y E H T Y K K L V D T E A Q
```

*by John Hudson Tiner*

## Bonus Trivia

What tiny seed did Jesus liken
the kingdom of heaven to?

*John 17:24–26*

Father, I will that they **also**, **whom** thou hast given me, be with me where I am; that **they** may **behold** my **glory**, **which** thou hast **given** me: for thou **lovedst** me **before** the **foundation** of the world. O **righteous Father**, the **world hath** not known thee: but I have known **thee**, and **these** have **known** that thou hast **sent** me. And I **have declared unto** them thy **name**, and **will** declare it: **that** the love **wherewith thou hast** loved me may be in them, and I in **them**.

```
O  B  U  D  T  B  R  G  W  T  A  H  T  N  P
I  C  K  X  O  H  C  I  H  W  H  B  X  O  N
J  Z  N  K  T  U  E  E  G  J  W  M  V  I  C
Y  R  O  L  G  D  E  Y  T  H  U  O  H  T  V
I  T  W  O  D  Y  E  V  E  A  T  O  E  A  C
M  J  N  V  S  X  M  R  U  V  R  E  R  D  K
G  I  V  E  N  L  E  M  A  E  D  D  O  N  E
R  H  M  D  S  W  A  W  I  L  L  X  F  U  V
Z  A  A  S  I  W  M  X  O  L  C  U  E  O  S
N  F  A  T  H  E  R  H  A  S  T  E  B  F  J
X  H  H  O  H  C  E  J  K  P  S  F  D  K  B
A  D  M  T  C  B  H  T  N  E  C  B  L  X  O
R  J  H  N  I  D  B  W  H  I  X  Q  R  A  G
J  C  J  U  U  O  O  T  X  P  J  R  O  U  P
Q  D  U  L  T  C  G  K  E  C  J  W  W  B  N
```

*by John Hudson Tiner*

# Bonus Trivia

What prophet did King Saul have a
medium at Endor call up from the dead?

*Ecclesiastes 3:1–8*

To every thing there is a **season**, and a **time** to <u>every purpose</u> **under** the **heaven**: a time <u>to be born</u>, and a time <u>to die</u>; a time <u>to plant</u>, and a time to **pluck** up that which is planted; a time to **kill**, and a time to **heal**; a time to <u>break down</u>, and a time to <u>build up</u>; a time to **weep**, and a time to **laugh**; a time to **mourn**, and a time to **dance**; a time to <u>cast away</u> stones, and a time to **gather** stones **together**; a time to **embrace**, and a time to **refrain** from embracing; a time to **get**, and a time to **lose**; a time to **keep**, and a time to cast away; a time to **rend**, and a time to **sew**; a time to keep **silence**, and a time to **speak**; a time to **love**, and a time to **hate**; a time of **war**, and a time of **peace**.

```
L O S I C E P A Q R B U L P A
G D K P E A C E N O N A S E M
E A E G H O S T O D I E S O L
T N T P E J O T E U A Q U S J
F C E H V B E R A S H R P Z F
Q E B R E A K D O W N E A K V
K Z T B R R J N F K A D A I E
T B O U Y E T T U K O Y S L T
D R P I P I F O Q Q W I V L A
N E L L U L F R G X L A U G H
A N A D R W U M A E O O R H M
J D N U P L M C N I T L V V W
V J T P O P B C K U N H S E W
Y T X M S H E A V E N Q E K Q
P T I M E M B R A C E P P R R
```

*by David Austin*

# Bonus Trivia

What "mighty hunter" built Nineveh
shortly after Noah's time?

**Romans 11:33–36**

O the **depth** of the **riches both** of the **wisdom** and **knowledge** of God! how **unsearchable** are his **judgments,** and his **ways past finding** out! For who hath **known** the **mind** of the **Lord**? or who hath **been** his **counsellor**? Or who **hath first given** to him, and it **shall** be **recompensed unto** him **again**? For of him, and **through** him, and to him, are all **things**: to **whom** be **glory** for **ever. Amen.**

```
R E C O M P E N S E D P A J H
B L G W A Y S F H F G H M R O
C B L D S G N I H T J B E H L
A A T A E N A W I U O T N U D
M H H Z H L T I D H G B V R X
A C R L C S W G N S W U Y B L
B R O A I X M O K G D R G Q F
H A U U R E V E N R M I H P T
N E G D N N T I O K V Q A M L
X S H T T S D L W E H S T J K
V N S K R N E M N S T R H M T
C U D I I E M L I C P T W O M
F G F F Q E V F L N E J X H P
B F Y H O B A H M O D S I W I
P K D J Y S J G L O R Y O P F
```

*by John Hudson Tiner*

## BONUS TRIVIA

What Jewish ruler was told by Jesus,
"Ye must be born again"?

AMAZIAH

ASA

AZARIAH

CHILDREN

COMMANDMENTS

DAVID

DILIGENTLY

GOOD LAND

GO WELL

HEALETH

HEAR

HEARKEN

HEZEKIAH

IN THE EYES

JEHOSHAPHAT

JOSIAH

JOTHAM

KEEP

OBSERVE

POSSESS

REIGN

SON OF AHAZ

STATUTES

UZZIAH

VOICE

```
O E J O T H A M R E T U L J C
T V O S Z M S T A T U T E S H
H R S C V E A Q U A I H D E U
K E I H O E N G G H O O A J Z
U S A I I M L Q O S J R V F Z
B B H L C Z M L H O K D I Z I
F O R D E Q A A E E D I A A A
V Z E R J T P H N W F L K D H
T H I E S H H K A D O I A E B
T A G N A S E U O F M G Z N D
I I N T H E E Y E S O E Q Q D
V Z F X P E A S W M K N N O H
M A Z A R I A H S I J T O T L
M M L V V J P R A O B L U S S
Y A T X M Q K H Q P P Y P R S
```

*by David Austin*

# BONUS TRIVIA

What occupation did the apostle Paul
have in addition to his missionary duties?

*Matthew 6:9–13*

**After** this **manner therefore pray** ye: Our **Father which** art in heaven, **Hallowed** be thy **name.** Thy kingdom **come,** Thy **will** be **done** in **earth,** as it is in **heaven.** Give us **this** day our **daily bread.** And forgive us our **debts,** as we **forgive** our **debtors.** And **lead** us not **into temptation,** but **deliver** us **from** evil: For **thine** is the **kingdom,** and the **power,** and the **glory,** for **ever. Amen.**

```
V C D A K Z G H K G A Z Z Y I
S I H T U F I P W L Z L F R E
W H E A V E N K M A N N E R N
S D A E L D V E I A F R O M O
F N V H Q L A I R E T F A W D
P E O C I R O E G E E D J D M
R Q D I T C D W R R W I L L O
Q G K H T D E E E B O O I Y D
E Y L W C A B H B D F F P E G
Q A W O S I T V L T P N L E N
B M M T R L O P L Q S I N D I
U E W N N Y R Q M Y V I W X K
V N T I A O S I R E H T A F O
X T X R M I M P R T T W X O M
O O P Q E N Z Y I F G P S Z P
```

*by John Hudson Tiner*

# BONUS TRIVIA

In what New Testament book
do we find this title for Christ:
"author and finisher of our faith"?

*Hebrews. (Hebrews 12:2)*

## *Acts 4:10–12*

Be it **known** unto you all, and to all the **people** of **Israel**, that by the name of **Jesus Christ** of **Nazareth**, whom ye **crucified**, **whom** God **raised from** the **dead**, **even** by him **doth** this man **stand** here **before** you **whole**. This is the **stone** which was set at **nought** of you **builders**, which is **become** the **head** of the **corner**. **Neither** is there **salvation** in any other: for there is **none other name under** heaven **given among** men, **whereby** we **must** be **saved**.

```
M  D  J  T  H  L  V  E  X  J  D  D  T  B  V
H  O  B  E  F  O  R  E  R  E  G  Q  U  E  K
O  T  V  L  S  K  K  N  V  R  N  I  N  C  G
Q  H  F  P  N  U  A  A  E  S  O  B  D  O  R
M  X  T  O  A  M  S  H  A  V  M  B  E  M  R
T  M  W  E  E  H  T  L  T  W  A  L  R  E  L
X  N  U  P  R  O  V  Q  H  H  Z  E  H  B  N
T  B  I  S  R  A  E  L  G  E  N  T  H  H  G
K  S  U  D  T  H  Z  S  U  R  I  E  T  N  K
K  T  T  I  E  C  T  A  O  E  V  E  N  V  Z
Q  D  O  A  L  O  N  C  N  B  L  M  C  O  H
T  N  D  E  N  D  A  E  D  Y  M  O  H  W  N
G  I  V  E  N  D  E  S  I  A  R  R  H  E  N
D  E  I  F  I  C  U  R  C  B  C  F  V  W  X
K  S  X  H  X  M  O  T  S  I  R  H  C  B  J
```

*by John Hudson Tiner*

## Bonus Trivia

What elderly prophetess met Mary,
Joseph, and the baby Jesus at the temple and
thanked God for the redemption to come?

# PUZZLE 19 — ON MARS' HILL

*Acts 17:22–23*

Then **Paul stood** in the **midst** of **Mars' hill**, and **said**, Ye men of **Athens**, I **perceive that** in all **things** ye are too **superstitious**. For as I **passed** by, and **beheld your devotions**, I **found** an **altar** <u>with this</u> inscription, To THE UNKNOWN GOD. **Whom therefore** ye **ignorantly worship**, him **declare I unto** you.

```
P N E R S M S I S D I I F D D
B W U X U O T F E R A L C E D
O O Y U O H O V Y T R H U S E
Y N I L I W O R S H I P A S X
I K Q Y T T D F I P M L J A Q
Y N M K I N S N E H T A A P D
V U S O T V A R M A S P R U Y
G B N C S S O R R U A E J S F
V S H Z R F D L O U I R M D Z
I X J K E I J I L N D C L K Q
F Q Q R P Q P T M I G E O U L
W O E G U W I T H T H I S S V
M H U D S Y A A I E I V C J U
T H I N G S K H B O G E I L Q
P Z L A D T T T O T N U U B H
```

*by John Hudson Tiner*

# BONUS TRIVIA

What prophet foretold the outpouring
of God's Spirit at Pentecost?

# PUZZLE 20 — PAUL'S PRAYER FOR THE EPHESIANS

*Ephesians 3:14–19*

For **this cause** I bow my **knees unto** the **Father** of our **Lord Jesus** Christ, of **whom** the **whole family** in **heaven** and **earth** is **named**, that he **would grant** you, **according** to the **riches** of his **glory**, to be **strengthened with might** by his **Spirit** in the **inner** man; that **Christ** may **dwell** in **your hearts** by **faith**; **that** ye, **being rooted** and **grounded** in **love**, may be able to comprehend with all saints what is the breadth, and length, and depth, and height; and to know the love of Christ, which passeth knowledge, that ye might be filled with all the fulness of God.

```
E  G  N  I  E  B  I  J  N  F  F  A  I  T  H
U  L  R  Z  D  T  H  I  S  Q  C  E  I  R  N
L  R  O  O  T  E  D  E  Y  C  P  S  V  E  S
S  G  X  H  U  Y  E  L  O  U  E  U  V  O  N
L  T  L  D  W  N  S  R  S  T  R  A  E  H  L
L  R  R  O  K  M  D  P  E  E  E  C  R  L  P
E  W  U  E  R  I  V  E  N  N  H  H  O  T  W
W  L  Q  O  N  Y  L  N  D  A  T  F  J  V  H
D  F  T  G  Y  G  I  S  M  I  Q  A  W  L  O
Z  O  T  N  U  B  T  E  W  S  Z  M  F  M  M
W  U  S  E  A  D  D  H  J  S  P  I  R  I  T
X  V  T  S  I  R  H  C  E  I  F  L  B  G  K
M  O  U  H  J  O  G  I  S  N  G  Y  N  H  R
H  A  O  S  A  L  A  R  U  F  E  S  I  T  P
B  P  O  L  H  T  C  J  S  H  M  D  P  B  E
```

*by John Hudson Tiner*

## BONUS TRIVIA

\What Greek letter did Jesus pair
with "Alpha" to describe Himself?

### Romans 15:30–33

Now I **beseech** you, **brethren**, for the **Lord Jesus Christ's sake**, and for the **love** of the **Spirit**, that ye **strive together** with me in **your prayers** to God for me; that I may be **delivered from them** that do not **believe** in **Judaea**; and that my **service which** I **have** for **Jerusalem** may be **accepted** of the **saints**; **that** I may **come unto** you with joy by the **will** of God, and may with you be **refreshed**. Now the God of **peace** be **with** you all. **Amen**.

```
A  S  B  Q  J  N  V  T  L  O  L  H  V  D  X
N  T  U  L  H  E  V  A  H  O  M  L  T  H  Y
U  E  Q  S  C  S  R  E  Y  A  R  P  I  I  H
I  H  K  D  E  A  I  U  Z  X  O  D  R  W  W
N  I  W  A  E  J  K  A  S  E  R  V  I  C  E
A  Y  L  A  S  H  E  C  T  A  H  T  P  Z  M
W  O  D  M  E  J  S  C  R  U  L  Q  S  B  J
Y  U  O  E  B  S  D  E  L  I  V  E  R  E  D
J  R  D  N  A  S  H  P  R  Z  F  E  M  P  E
C  H  R  I  S  T  S  T  H  F  T  K  E  R  E
N  K  N  T  E  R  U  E  W  H  E  A  G  V  O
O  T  M  G  Y  I  O  D  R  H  C  R  O  H  J
S  C  O  M  E  V  T  E  V  E  I  L  E  B  L
F  T  R  O  A  E  N  V  U  E  N  C  N  H  X
Y  L  F  Y  Z  F  U  G  D  J  N  T  H  E  M
```

*by John Hudson Tiner*

# BONUS TRIVIA

What baking product was banned from
Israelite homes for an entire week
during the Passover celebration?

## Malachi 3:7–10

Even from the **days** of your **fathers** ye are **gone away** from **mine ordinances**, and have not kept them. **Return unto** me, and I will return unto you, **saith** the LORD of hosts. But ye said, **Wherein** shall we return? Will a **man rob God**? Yet ye **have robbed** me. But ye say, Wherein have we robbed thee? In tithes and **offerings**. Ye are cursed with a curse: for ye have robbed me, even this **whole nation**. Bring ye **all** the **tithes into** the **storehouse**, that there may be meat in mine house, and **prove** me **now** herewith, saith the LORD of hosts, if I will not **open** you the **windows** of **heaven**, and **pour** you out a **blessing**, that there shall not be room enough to receive it.

```
L I G N F D B L E S S I N G S
L O N H U E R A T M A A O L W
E F Y M T O P O U R T I W E A
R H A O I P R J L I U O T N I
Q N W T T E E D O S J G F H B
Z F A Q H N T N I G O D A A W
V Z J O E E U F M N K U D V I
T B U N S U R I E I A W N E N
O S D I Q Q N S H R H N V T D
E F X A W E M O H E M J C L O
M L V D E B B O R F A W V E W
J P B U A Y T E X F H V M Q S
K Q P P L Y I P R O V E E R S
Q W M P L N S N L O V B T N N
G Z T E F P S E I B B X V V C
```

*by David Austin*

# BONUS TRIVIA

What did Jesus do on a Sabbath day
that so infuriated the Pharisees they
began plotting to kill Him?

ASTROLOGERS

BALAAM

BARJESUS

CHARMER

CURIOUS ARTS

DIVINATION

EGYPT

ELYMAS

ENCHANTMENT

ENDOR

FAMILIAR SPIRIT

JEZEBEL

MAGICIANS

NECROMANCER

PHARAOH

PROGNOSTICATORS

SIMON OF
   SAMARIA

SONS OF SCEVA

SOOTHSAYING

STARGAZERS

WITCHCRAFT

WIZARD

```
S R O T A C I T S O N G O R P
T I S O N S O F S C E V A C T
R J M G N I Y A S H T O O S F
A T E O D I V I N A T I O N A
S S N Z N E C R O M A N C E R
U T T E O D R A Z I W G N C
O B A R M B F A R O E Y B D H
I Y L R O T E S H E P H A O C
R S Y T G L N L A T M X L R T
U S U E S A O A Y M N R A E I
C R L S E A Z G H M A R A U W
P H A R A O H E E C A R M H H
S U S E J R A B R R N S I N C
A M A G I C I A N S S E R A E
F A M I L I A R S P I R I T I
```

*by Paul Kent*

## BONUS TRIVIA

What prophet summoned fire from heaven
to destroy fifty-one soldiers carrying King
Ahaziah's command to "Come down"?

*Acts 2:22–23*

Ye men of **Israel, hear these words; Jesus** of **Naza-reth**, a man **approved** of God **among** you by **miracles** and **wonders** and **signs, which** God did by him in the **midst** of you, as ye **yourselves also** know: him, **being delivered** by the **determinate counsel** and **foreknowl-edge** of God, ye have **taken**, and by **wicked hands have crucified** and **slain**.

```
X  J  J  V  M  M  M  I  R  A  C  L  E  S  D
Z  T  V  I  V  L  Y  X  I  C  R  K  R  W  F
V  Z  D  W  M  Y  S  A  G  W  U  T  F  O  G
U  S  R  E  D  N  O  W  H  N  C  J  L  R  A
T  H  O  L  E  S  N  U  O  C  I  B  B  D  I
U  D  D  Q  T  H  E  A  R  Y  F  E  E  S  I
Z  E  T  E  S  W  A  H  V  S  I  T  B  O  Z
E  V  A  H  R  I  T  Z  I  Q  E  R  S  S  N
K  O  W  E  S  E  G  U  T  R  D  L  D  E  I
T  R  B  H  R  U  V  N  M  E  A  N  V  D  A
A  P  R  A  I  A  S  I  S  R  A  E  L  E  L
K  P  Z  C  M  C  N  E  L  H  I  C  O  K  S
E  A  Z  O  K  A  H  O  J  E  G  Y  T  C  A
N  L  N  Z  T  T  I  A  O  P  D  C  H  I  J
E  G  D  E  L  W  O  N  K  E  R  O  F  W  R
```

*by John Hudson Tiner*

# BONUS TRIVIA

What fellow government official—
formerly an enemy—became Pontius
Pilate's friend during Jesus' trial?

### Revelation 1:4–6

**John** to the seven **churches** which are in **Asia: Grace** be unto you, and **peace**, from him which is, and which was, and which is to **come**; and from the **seven Spirits which** are **before** his **throne**; and from **Jesus Christ**, who is the **faithful witness**, and the **first begotten** of the **dead**, and the **prince** of the kings of the **earth**. Unto him that **loved** us, and **washed** us **from** our **sins** in his own **blood**, and hath **made** us **kings** and **priests** unto God and his **Father**; to him be **glory** and **dominion** for ever and **ever**. **Amen**.

```
G X E M O C K B I Y R O L G E
J N T S I R H C E F K F N R F
O U J J P T M U H G X H Z A C
N M M E R O O S R R O S I C O
A S I A S P R I N C E T W E A
U D E Q D U F N R V H H T N M
U O U W E E S S E F S E T E E
J O H N C S T N U Y S G S A N
J L D A F N S L U H P Z N O F
O B E F O R E S W B I Y I I H
B P H E E L I J E H R N R S K
J D S E N O R H T N I S S P L
M Q A I V V P Q E M T C B U L
Y C W E E E N B O I S I H X M
C S D M D D R D V M M T W W B
```

*by John Hudson Tiner*

# Bonus Trivia

Whose loss, according
to the book of Romans,
meant "riches" for the Gentiles?

(ZI—L:II suvuoy) ·s, jəvisi

### *Luke 19:1–10*

And **Jesus entered** and **passed** through **Jericho**. And, behold, there was a **man named Zacchaeus**, which was the chief **among** the **publicans**, and he was **rich**. And he **sought** to see Jesus who he was; and could not for the **press**, because he was **little** of **stature**. And he ran before, and **climbed** up into a **sycomore tree** to see him: for he was to **pass** that **way**. And when Jesus came to the place, he looked up, and saw him, and said unto him, Zacchaeus, make **haste**, and come down; for to day I must **abide** at thy **house**. And he made haste, and came down, and received him **joyfully**. And when they saw it, they all **murmured**, saying, That he was gone to be guest with a man that is a **sinner**. And Zacchaeus stood, and said unto the **Lord: Behold**, Lord, the **half** of my **goods** I **give** to the **poor**; and if I have taken any thing from any man by **false accusation**, I restore him **fourfold**. And Jesus said unto him, This day is **salvation** come to this house, forsomuch as he also is a **son** of Abraham. For the Son of man is **come** to **seek** and to **save** that which was **lost**.

```
S  S  A  P  G  J  O  Y  F  U  L  L  Y  G  N
S  Y  C  O  M  O  R  E  S  Z  D  R  O  L  O
H  A  L  F  Y  N  O  I  T  A  V  L  A  S  I
O  H  C  I  R  A  N  D  R  C  P  E  P  Y  T
U  M  V  W  E  N  W  O  S  C  P  N  U  D  A
S  T  U  S  E  L  O  B  N  H  R  T  B  L  S
E  O  L  R  I  P  N  K  A  A  E  E  L  O  U
K  A  U  T  M  O  J  E  M  E  S  R  I  F  C
F  C  T  G  S  U  S  E  J  U  S  E  C  R  C
D  L  I  P  H  A  R  S  R  S  T  D  A  U  A
E  I  E  A  C  T  V  E  V  I  G  I  N  O  E
M  M  T  S  P  O  E  E  D  I  C  N  S  F  D
A  B  S  S  L  R  M  L  V  G  C  H  O  L  I
N  E  A  E  T  O  B  E  H  O  L  D  O  M  B
H  D  H  D  S  S  T  A  T  U  R  E  V  G  A
```

*by N. Teri Grottke*

## BONUS TRIVIA

What did the psalmist say God's words,
or promises, are sweeter than?

Honey. (Psalm 119:103)

*Genesis 9:8–10, 13*

And God **spake unto Noah,** and to his **sons** with him, **saying,** And I, **behold,** I **establish** my covenant with you, and with **your seed after** you; and with every **living creature** that is with you, of the **fowl,** of the **cattle,** and of every beast of the earth **with** you; **from** all **that** go out of the ark, to **every beast** of the earth. . . . I do set my bow in the **cloud,** and it **shall** be for a **token** of a **covenant between** me and the **earth.**

```
K W D J R C B T H A T S R L Y
U A L V X E U S P A K E G W Y
C C O I T C I N H H E C O A
K R H W Y L L C T F T D U F D
E J E L B I Z I A O W R M R L
O E B A R B W F K L T M A E U
N C T E T S A E B I O W V E X
U S S N U N J K J D P J T A
E X L U A Y R E V E G U N T G
Z D G Y Y N O E S N S W U X D
V U W H I S E R I K O D S· T V
M O R F N H N V D F M A A R W
M L T E G A I O O H D Z H K P
T C A T T L E Y S C K P Q L R
G H S C I L A Y D M Q U V Z U
```

*by John Hudson Tiner*

# BONUS TRIVIA

What kind of bird did God
miraculously provide for the Israelites,
who had grown tired of manna?

*Quail (Exodus 16:11–13)*

AARON

BLOOD

BREAD

DELIVERED

DESTROY

DESTROYER

EGYPT

EXECUTE

FEAST

FIRSTBORN

GENERATIONS

HOUSES

JUDGMENT

MEMORIAL

MOSES

OBSERVE

ORDINANCE

OVER

PASS

PHARAOH

PLAGUE

SEVEN DAYS

SMITE

UNLEAVENED

```
S F P H A R A O H T U H E N K
E G Y P T M B A M R T L E Y E
V L W G K S E E R U E G M H O
E J U Q E J F M N O B Z O F O
N Q A R V N D L O Z N J S V F
D R V K D D E S T R O Y E R T
A E O B T A L R E U I R S O O
Y F D B V P I I A S Q A R B Q
S V E E T A V F Y T U D L R X
A W N A M S E O O H I O M E J
L E M L S S R V V N O O H A J
D P S M I T E I A D L U N D I
T X M Q S K D N F Q P P R S S
Q W M E X E C U T E U G A L P
J U D G M E N T P N V B T B G
```

*by David Austin*

# BONUS TRIVIA

What captain in Deborah's army is listed
in Hebrews as a hero of faith, among those
who "quenched the violence of fire"?

*Barak. (Judges 4:14–15; Hebrews 11:32–34)*

## *Revelation 15:2–3*

And I saw as it **were** a sea of glass **mingled with fire:** and **them** that had **gotten** the **victory** over the **beast,** and over his **image,** and over his **mark,** and **over** the **number** of his **name, stand** on the sea of **glass, having** the **harps** of God. And **they sing** the song of **Moses** the **servant** of God, and the **song** of the **Lamb,** say-**ing, Great** and **marvellous** are thy **works, Lord** God **Almighty; just** and **true** are thy **ways, thou King** of **saints.**

```
Z C X J W R J G K R M V T G M
M Z D T S T W K R S T N I A S
T N M H H R O G A E N H R W E
J V H O F U A D M H A V I N G
F A U O V E R K E R E T E S A
V J F B C P E A P L H H E V M
B G W K T D B S L B G R K E I
Y S I A J S M O D M V N H J N
V N F G Y Z U D U A I T I E C
G N I Y A S N J N L C G T M G
L S R B E A S T W K T T H P T
A Y E H T R D E A O O D G T X
S J T S M R E H F G R J N G Y
S I N G O W D W E E Y K O O X
K G L L E M A N F P D A S U E
```

*by John Hudson Tiner*

# BONUS TRIVIA

What king of Israel was known
for his furious chariot driving?

Jehu (2 Kings 9:20)

269

*Daniel 6:21–23*

Then **said** Daniel **unto** the king, O king, **live** for **ever**. My God hath **sent** his **angel**, and **hath shut** the **lions' mouths**, that they have not hurt me: **forasmuch** as before him **innocency** was found in me; and **also before thee**, O king, **have** I **done** no hurt. **Then** was the **king exceeding glad** for him, and **commanded that they should** take Daniel up out of the den. So **Daniel** was **taken** up out of the den, and no **manner** of **hurt** was **found upon** him, **because** he **believed** in his God.

```
D N H T G S T D H A B O H M L
F E A C A K P N G Y B S D A D
L H D L U O H S E G S L K N T
T H E N U M B G W S L A U I C
L E I N A D S L H H E Y I M S
W Y T E O M R A U T G N D D U
I O G O X P M D R U N S Z Q K
I O Z I Y C U O T O A X B D S
I B E F O R E H C M F T E S H
V T W M A N N E R I D V C T U
E T H E E N O D L E N A R T
W E T K E C B U I I G H U Q F
E V A H Y V G V L O N R S O D
M T C U E A E E T N I G E G F
L R L V N Y B R N S K N L J C
```

*by John Hudson Tiner*

# BONUS TRIVIA

What position of authority
did Pontius Pilate hold?

### Deuteronomy 14:4–18

BAT
CAMEL
CHAMOIS
CONEY
CORMORANT
CUCKOW
DEER
EAGLE
GLEDE
GOAT
HARE
HART
HAWK
HERON
KITE
LAPWING

NIGHT HAWK
OSPRAY
OSSIFRAGE
OWL
OX
PELICAN
PYGARG
RAVEN
ROEBUCK
SHEEP
STORK
SWAN
SWINE
VULTURE
WILD GOAT
WILD OX

```
H W T A S H E S C O N E Y K C
T S I T M W E D T U W D H I K
L P E L I C A N W K C L E T E
E G H A D H O N O J U K R E Q
J F K P E G A R F I S S O Z R
F Q A W V Z O W M J Y F N W K
D E T I B T U A K O A O D N W
I Q L N Q V U L T U R E V I F
X P Y G A R G R A W P A L G C
M H O O A L A H O E S D N H A
H A R T E E M V E E O J A T M
T R L D M L V H E X B M V H E
P E E T B U S B Y N O U T A L
X M Q K Q P P A R I S Q C W W
M P N V K R O T S W I N E K B
```

*by David Austin*

# BONUS TRIVIA

What daughter of Bethuel
was wife of the patriarch Isaac?

*Exodus 24–30*

ALTAR

ARK

BLOOD

BREASTPLATE

BREECHES

COAT

COVENANT

EPHOD

FIRE

GARMENTS

GIRDLE

HOLY

INCENSE

LAMPSTAND

LAVER

LINEN

MERCY

MITRE

OIL

PLACE

SEAT

SHEWBREAD

TABLE

VAIL

WINGS

```
E  T  A  E  S  X  B  K  X  O  I  R  B  L  B
O  S  E  X  L  Q  D  G  P  N  E  R  J  U  G
I  N  R  Y  Z  I  G  P  C  V  E  L  B  A  T
L  W  I  C  T  C  L  E  A  E  L  I  A  V  C
L  Z  F  R  E  A  N  L  C  A  Q  V  Z  A  K
M  I  E  E  U  S  Y  H  R  T  A  O  C  S  E
L  O  N  M  E  L  E  K  F  I  K  N  P  P  V
R  A  T  E  O  S  A  B  R  O  L  Q  H  K  S
M  Q  M  H  N  U  R  A  T  L  A  O  S  M  O
D  P  N  P  K  B  N  G  I  R  D  L  E  F  S
I  Y  C  R  S  D  A  E  R  B  W  E  H  S  G
B  L  O  O  D  T  T  N  A  N  E  V  O  C  N
Z  Q  Q  B  R  E  A  S  T  P  L  A  T  E  I
A  E  C  A  L  P  J  N  N  R  A  I  L  G  W
G  A  R  M  E  N  T  S  D  V  M  I  T  R  E
```

*by N. Teri Grottke*

# BONUS TRIVIA

What man, described in Acts as
"full of faith and of the Holy Ghost,"
was one of seven chosen to relieve
the apostles of waiting on tables?

| | |
|---|---|
| ATONEMENT | PEACE |
| BURNT | PEOPLE'S |
| CONSECRATION | PRAISE |
| DRINK | PRAYERS |
| FIRE | RANSOM |
| FIRSTFRUITS | SACRIFICE |
| GIFTS | SANCTUARY |
| HEAVE | SAVOUR |
| INCENSE | SIN |
| LORD'S | SWEET |
| MEAT | TRESPASS |
| MEMORIAL | VOLUNTARY |
| OBLATION | WAVE |

```
W A V E G T L A I R O M E M E
P A T O S I G R A N S O M R V
T R G E A N F D R I N K N U A
Y A A F E R E T N I F O K O E
R S E I I W B C S W I G S V H
A S Y M S R S F N T A S T A N
U A R H F E E G A I S T I S F
T P A J S A C R E N B R U N W
C S T P E A C E U P R A R Y S
N E N T N E M E N O T A F L E
A R U V S T V O L U T O T B L
S T L N E C I F I R C A S U P
Z W O S R E Y A R P C G R R O
T C V G A S D R O L X M I N E
S O B L A T I O N C F K F T P
```

*by N. Teri Grottke*

# BONUS TRIVIA

What leprous army commander,
told to wash in the Jordan for healing,
preferred to wash in the Abana or
Pharpar rivers of his homeland?

AGATE

AMETHYST

BADGERS

BERYL

BLUE

BRACELETS

BRASS

CARBUNCLES

DIAMOND

EMERALD

GOATS

GOLD

HAIR

JASPER

JEWELS

LIGURE

LINEN

OIL

ONYX

PURPLE

RAMS

RED

RINGS

SAPPHIRE

SARDIUS

SCARLET

SHITTIM

SILVER

SKINS

SPICES

STONES

TABLETS

TOPAZ

WOOD

```
D I A M O N D W O O D D Q H B
S S T E L E C A R B L N L M A
T S S L J L E R I A H I V M D
A G U I S S X R R E O Z I C G
O N I N I K P E U Q L T N A E
G I D E L B M I R G T P D R R
T R R N V E Y E C I I L R B S
S M A R E R D E H E O L F U E
Y P S S R Y U S T G S J S N P
H J R T I L D A M Z O S K C B
T E N E H D G A A N E L I L R
E W B L P A E P Y N H K N E A
M E L B P D O X O S W U S S S
A L U A A T E T J A S P E R S
I S E T S S S Y S C A R L E T
```

*by N. Teri Grottke*

## Bonus Trivia

What great-grandson of Ruth became
the most prominent king of Israel?

BIRD

BREAD

BREAST

BULLOCKS

CALF

CAUL

CORN

COW

EWE

FAT

FLOUR

FRANKINCENSE

FRUITS

GOAT

HEAD

INWARDS

ISAAC

JESUS

KID

KIDNEYS

LAMB

LEGS

OIL

OILED

PIGEONS

RAM

RIGHT

RIPE

RUMP

SHEEP

SHOULDER

TURTLEDOVE

UNLEAVENED

WAFER

WINE

```
T  L  K  E  S  K  C  O  L  L  U  B  E  P  O
U  H  O  Y  N  A  R  E  D  L  U  O  H  S  I
N  S  G  E  L  W  B  X  L  F  S  A  H  H  L
L  F  G  I  F  S  O  T  T  N  E  F  C  Y  E
E  L  M  O  R  A  Y  C  O  V  R  E  R  Q  D
A  A  A  S  A  Q  T  E  O  A  C  A  A  S  I
V  M  R  H  C  T  G  D  N  N  N  R  I  X  E
E  B  W  E  H  I  E  K  R  D  R  A  B  X  N
N  R  F  E  P  L  I  O  I  U  I  S  G  P  I
E  E  K  P  T  N  C  N  O  J  W  K  S  M  W
D  A  T  R  C  T  W  L  D  A  E  H  T  U  D
R  S  U  E  F  A  F  R  F  A  R  S  I  R  A
I  T  N  L  R  C  I  E  M  Z  K  N  U  W  E
B  S  A  D  N  P  R  S  W  R  I  V  R  S  R
E  C  S  I  E  I  P  C  I  E  D  Z  F  G  B
```

*by N. Teri Grottke*

# BONUS TRIVIA

What devout man held the baby
Jesus when Mary and Joseph
presented Him at the temple?

BAALIM

BROKEN

BURNETH

BURNT

CALF

CARVED

COMMANDED

CUT DOWN

DESPISED

DEVILS

EARTH

GODS

GRAVEN

HEAVEN

IDOL

IMAGE

INCENSE

MANY

MOLTEN

OFFERED

ONE

OTHER

SACRIFICE

STRANGE

```
C M A N Y B T I A L E S U E S
T O S T R A N G E T E I D O N
W L N O D C K E R A M E G H O
O T K E E U O Q J A R F B Z F
E E A N V V H M G Z V T J F K
N N S D R E T E M B S E H T U
O E F L A C D D I A Q Q N V F
X A W V C M E O C T N R U B O
H M E J L O S R C M L D V V T
J N P B U F I D B U R N E T H
Y T X M Q F P K O A T Q P D E
P R S Q I E S W M G A D P N R
V B T C D R E N G Z T L O E F
P S E I O E D E V I L S I W B
X V V C L D J E L L V W O M N
```

*by David Austin*

# BONUS TRIVIA

What king of Assyria insulted God
to King Hezekiah of Judah—
and paid for it with his life?

Sennacherib (2 Kings 19:5-13, 35-37)

# PUZZLE 37 — MOSES' FORTY-DAY PRAYER

*Deuteronomy 9:26–27*

I **prayed therefore** unto the LORD, and **said,** O **Lord GOD, destroy** not thy people and **thine inheritance,** which thou hast **redeemed through** thy **greatness, which thou hast brought forth** out of **Egypt with** a **mighty hand. Remember** thy **servants, Abraham, Isaac,** and **Jacob; look** not **unto** the **stubbornness** of **this people,** nor to their **wickedness,** nor to **their** sin.

```
C A A S I M H A S T R R M T T
S P V S S T N A V R E S S H O
D S I E P H I R P D B G I I U
E C E N A D D I E M M N Y S B
A B P N H N K E K A E Z T P S
J W D R D E M H Y H M B H S T
I H O O W E R T T A E F E M Q
H I L B D S K I D R R N R I F
Z C H B S V W C T B T P E G M
T H G U O R B P I A L B F H H
D E S T R O Y X E W N T O T Q
L E A S D Q J R P O U C R Y O
D T H R O U G H D T P O E B Z
G B O C A J O B S N F L H P R
J L O O K M S L C U C V E T W
```

*by John Hudson Tiner*

## BONUS TRIVIA

What man, a Horonite, opposed
Nehemiah and the Jews rebuilding
the walls of Jerusalem?

# PUZZLE 38 — CURSINGS AND BLESSINGS

*Leviticus 26*

ABHOR

AGUE

BEASTS

BURNING

CHASTISE

CONSUME

DESOLATE

DUE

ENEMIES

EYES

FLEE

FRUIT

FRUITFUL

FULL

FURY

HEART

INCREASE

LAND

NEW

OLD

PEACE

PESTILENCE

PLAGUES

RAIN

RESPECT

ROB

SAFELY

SEASON

SLAIN

SORROW

STORE

SWORD

TERROR

VAIN

VINTAGE

WILD

YIELD

```
V E M D T S M C H A S T I S E
Q I U E T C D B U R N I N G R
S E N O C R E I Z S W W B F O
O F R C O N N P L A B H O R R
R E R W R S E A S O N G W U R
R O S U V E I L C E Y M Y I E
O A L K I N A Q I I R L Y T T
W K T D N T H S E T E S R Z A
N I A V T W F L E F S P U S L
B Y N I A R D U A M E E F E O
P N E W G G D S L N C E P I S
E T R A E H U B D O D S Y M E
A A F L E E O E V F U L L E D
C D L I W R S E U G A L P N S
E I E M U S N O C S T S A E B
```

*by N. Teri Grottke*

## BONUS TRIVIA

How many days had Jesus fasted
in the desert when Satan tempted
Him to turn stones into bread?

*Forty. (Matthew 4:1–4)*

*James 5:13–16*

Is any among you **afflicted**? let him pray. Is any **merry**? let him **sing psalms**. Is any sick **among** you? let him **call** for the **elders** of the **church**; and let **them** pray **over** him, **anointing** him **with** oil in the **name** of the Lord: and the prayer of **faith** shall **save** the **sick**, and the **Lord** shall **raise** him up; and if he **have committed sins, they shall** be **forgiven** him. **Confess your faults** one to another, and pray one for **another**, that ye may be **healed**. The **effectual fervent prayer** of a **righteous** man **availeth much**.

```
A  L  Y  U  C  O  N  F  E  S  S  M  P  V  M
V  F  B  P  A  O  H  N  R  S  S  A  T  D  W
A  R  F  P  M  H  M  A  E  U  N  F  L  V  M
I  U  A  L  T  B  C  M  V  O  O  A  N  T  L
L  R  Z  I  I  W  U  R  I  E  U  Y  C  H  L
E  Z  A  S  S  C  N  N  U  T  D  B  J  E  A
T  F  H  P  H  E  T  E  C  H  T  R  K  M  H
H  T  I  W  R  I  G  E  V  G  C  E  O  A  S
Z  G  H  D  N  A  F  K  D  I  N  N  D  L  U
D  C  S  G  T  F  Y  R  D  R  G  I  F  W  P
K  H  T  N  E  V  R  E  F  T  M  R  S  Q  S
C  A  L  L  W  N  L  W  R  E  H  T  O  N  A
I  E  U  J  S  A  V  E  R  S  E  E  I  F  L
S  U  A  L  E  M  V  R  E  V  O  S  Y  N  M
W  R  F  H  X  E  Y  L  S  E  L  D  E  R  S
```

*by John Hudson Tiner*

# BONUS TRIVIA

Whose tomb was marked by a
pillar erected by her husband, Jacob?

*Acts 1:23–25*

And they **appointed** two, **Joseph called Barsabas,** who
was **surnamed Justus,** and **Matthias.** And **they prayed,**
and **said,** Thou, **Lord,** which **knowest** the **hearts** of all
men, **shew whether** of **these** two **thou hast chosen,**
that he may **take part** of **this ministry** and **apostle-
ship, from which Judas** by **transgression fell, that** he
**might** go to his own **place.**

| | | | | | | | | | | | | | | |
|---|---|---|---|---|---|---|---|---|---|---|---|---|---|---|
| P | A | R | T | T | T | A | H | T | V | L | O | R | D | Y |
| T | S | C | A | L | L | E | D | W | H | H | D | N | E | X |
| T | U | F | K | P | S | S | H | R | R | E | Q | I | Y | I |
| M | R | S | E | S | P | I | A | E | F | A | Y | D | A | M |
| B | N | A | T | L | C | O | H | B | U | R | B | P | R | S |
| U | A | I | N | H | L | T | I | T | A | T | O | O | P | W |
| L | M | H | T | S | E | W | O | N | K | S | J | M | J | Q |
| A | E | T | C | H | G | S | Y | G | T | U | R | G | O | G |
| J | D | T | W | E | N | R | E | L | D | E | C | A | L | P |
| Z | U | A | R | W | T | E | E | A | N | T | D | H | B | S |
| Q | P | M | S | S | T | S | S | S | U | T | S | U | J | A |
| A | D | V | I | S | H | W | J | O | S | E | P | H | O | S |
| C | W | N | A | I | G | I | H | K | H | I | M | S | X | Z |
| D | I | H | P | I | I | T | C | Z | Y | C | O | Y | E | T |
| M | M | U | V | T | M | Q | X | E | J | L | M | N | X | R |

*by John Hudson Tiner*

# BONUS TRIVIA

What type of tree immediately withered
when Jesus cursed it—an event Jesus used
to teach His disciples about faith?

# PUZZLE 41 — VIRTUOUS WOMAN

*Proverbs 31:10–31*

BLESSED
BRINGETH
BUYETH
CLOTHING
CONSIDERETH
EXCELLEST
FOOD
GOOD
HEART
HER
HONOUR
HOUSEHOLD
KINDNESS
LINEN
MAKETH
MERCHANDISE

PERCEIVETH
PLANTETH
PURPLE
REJOICE
RUBIES
SCARLET
SELLETH
SILK
SPINDLE
STRENGTH
VINEYARD
VIRTUOUS
WILLINGLY
WISDOM
WORKETH

```
S  W  I  S  D  O  M  R  M  O  E  A  L  H  E
P  S  V  C  H  A  E  S  E  B  U  Y  E  T  H
I  T  I  C  K  H  M  X  R  R  U  B  I  E  S
N  E  R  E  O  P  E  R  C  E  I  V  E  T  H
D  S  T  R  E  N  G  T  H  E  D  K  W  N  W
L  H  U  L  F  W  S  K  A  K  L  I  E  A  O
E  S  O  D  E  O  G  I  N  H  L  L  D  L  R
C  E  U  O  E  V  O  N  D  L  O  L  E  P  K
I  L  S  O  H  S  I  D  I  E  O  N  O  S  E
O  L  O  G  J  P  S  N  S  H  R  U  O  Q  T
J  E  J  T  U  F  G  E  E  I  L  E  B  U  H
E  T  Z  R  H  L  F  S  L  Y  L  I  T  Q  R
R  H  P  A  Y  I  U  S  A  B  A  K  N  H  V
Z  L  J  E  F  O  N  K  S  C  A  R  L  E  T
E  D  T  H  H  T  E  G  N  I  R  B  D  B  N
```

*by David Austin*

## BONUS TRIVIA

What mount saw the deaths of
King Saul and his sons in battle?

Gilboa. (1 Samuel 31:8)

*Luke 10:38–42*

Now it came to pass, as they went, that he entered into a certain village: and a certain woman named **Martha** received him into her house. And she had a **sister** called **Mary,** which also **sat** at Jesus' **feet,** and **heard** his **word**. But Martha was **cumbered** about **much serving,** and came to him, and said, Lord, dost thou not care that my sister hath left me to **serve alone?** **bid** her therefore that she **help** me. And **Jesus answered** and said unto her, Martha, Martha, thou **art careful** and **troubled about many things:** but **one thing** is **needful:** and Mary hath **chosen** that **good part,** which shall not be taken away from her.

R T R P C P B T R O U B L E D
J H T F Z C I H E L P V I M M
K I R S E R V E O Q H L S A U
T N A M W Z O K L J S C E B C
F G P B S A T W A I U U R O H
J C A R E F U L S M W Y V U W
N E S O H C V T B S Y X I T E
H L D X J A E E U I F Q N U G
E N O L A R R S W E S B G M O
M U B I D E E U E D G O V P I
A Y O M D J C T Y R N W O G M
R M D E R E W S N A I O O B R
T A C L F C T D A E H E N R U
H R S I V B R A M H T T J E D
A Y G O O D A Q L U F D E E N

*by N. Teri Grottke*

# BONUS TRIVIA

What city was the birthplace
of the apostle Paul?

# PUZZLE 43 — HALL OF FAITH

*Hebrews 11:4–37*

ABEL

ABRAHAM

AFFLICTED

BARAK

DAVID

DESTITUTE

ENOCH

GEDEON

IMPRISONMENT

ISAAC

JACOB

JEPHTHAE

JOSEPH

MOCKINGS

MOSES

NOAH

OTHERS

RAHAB

SAMSON

SAMUEL

SARA

SAWN

SCOURGINGS

SLAIN

STONED

THE PROPHETS

TORMENTED

```
P  B  Q  R  E  S  A  T  K  I  B  E  P  R  L
B  S  W  K  M  O  S  E  S  E  T  N  E  G  O
H  A  O  I  E  J  C  U  Q  H  J  F  O  T  B
Z  M  R  J  M  T  O  J  E  P  H  T  H  A  E
F  S  O  A  Q  P  U  P  O  A  B  E  L  B  H
A  O  T  C  K  V  R  T  Z  S  R  J  F  R  K
D  N  O  O  K  O  G  I  I  S  E  A  T  A  B
T  U  R  B  P  I  I  D  S  T  A  P  H  H  O
D  I  M  H  Q  Q  N  E  E  O  S  W  H  A  V
N  O  E  D  E  G  G  G  N  N  N  E  N  M  B
I  T  N  F  X  A  S  W  S  O  O  M  D  M  O
S  E  T  M  J  A  F  F  L  I  C  T  E  D  L
A  L  E  U  M  A  S  S  A  R  A  H  S  N  M
A  L  D  A  V  I  D  V  I  V  J  P  B  U  T
C  Y  T  X  M  Q  K  Q  N  P  P  R  S  Q  W
```

*by David Austin*

# BONUS TRIVIA

---

What man, attempting to steady the
ark of the covenant on its cart,
was struck dead for touching it?

*1 Kings 18:27, 37*

And it **came** to **pass** at **noon**, that **Elijah mocked them**, and **said**, Cry **aloud**: for he is a god; **either** he is **talking**, or he is **pursuing**, or he is in a **journey**, or **peradventure** he **sleepeth**, and **must** be **awaked**. . . . Hear me, O Lord, hear me, that **this people** may **know** that thou art the Lord God, and **that thou hast turned their heart back again**.

```
J  M  B  D  E  K  A  W  A  X  K  C  Q  M  O
H  W  E  B  R  N  T  G  B  Y  C  S  W  F  F
A  T  O  H  U  O  H  D  A  T  A  H  T  F  J
J  B  E  O  T  W  M  U  E  I  B  U  O  H  T
I  V  B  P  N  X  Q  O  D  M  N  M  H  S  C
L  O  R  D  E  U  E  L  P  O  E  P  U  D  A
E  M  J  R  V  E  T  A  N  C  L  M  A  K  M
Y  C  P  I  D  L  L  X  O  K  Y  W  A  S  K
M  G  G  U  A  J  G  S  O  E  N  T  H  C  S
H  Q  T  U  R  N  E  D  N  D  A  E  D  R  B
G  B  N  I  E  S  S  R  X  L  A  D  R  W  K
N  Y  I  R  P  M  U  S  K  R  K  I  G  Z  L
Q  M  O  J  H  O  E  I  T  H  E  R  S  B  D
V  I  X  E  J  H  N  H  N  H  A  S  T  Q  D
K  K  M  M  J  G  F  T  T  G  Q  H  F  E  R
```

*by John Hudson Tiner*

# Bonus Trivia

What town in Judea was
the birthplace of Jesus?

**Acts 11:5–7**

I was in the **city** of **Joppa praying**: and in a **trance** I saw a **vision**, **A certain vessel descend**, as it had **been** a **great sheet, let down from heaven** by four **corners**; and it **came even** to me: upon the which **when** I had **fastened mine eyes**, I **considered**, and saw **fourfooted** beasts of the **earth**, and **wild beasts**, and **creeping things**, and **fowls** of the air. And I **heard** a **voice saying** unto me, **Arise, Peter; slay** and eat.

```
D F C E M A C I T S D I D V V
G E O V A O Q H S L E T D L A
E G N U Q R N A A W G O W R X
S N S E R E T D Y N W S I E O
W Y I R T F T H I N G S L L A
C H D M R S O Y N D E Z D A K
E J E V E N A O G D R C E M Y
C O R N E R S F T N R A Y C J
I P E L P Y T I C E H S E A Q
O P D H C W Y L E C D T S H R
V A U H V R E P R S T S E E N
Q M N O I S I V T E H A T E Z
F O W L S N R E A D V E E X E
Q R Y E G O A P I E P B E R L
X F V W X C E C N A R T T T G
```

*by John Hudson Tiner*

# BONUS TRIVIA

What is the first Bible book in
which a rainbow is mentioned?

# PUZZLE 46 — HABAKKUK'S PRAYER OF PRAISE

*Habakkuk 3:1-3*

A **prayer** of **Habakkuk** the **prophet** upon **Shigion-oth**. O LORD, I **have heard** thy **speech**, and was **afraid**: O LORD, **revive** thy **work** in the midst of the years, in the **midst** of the **years make known**; in **wrath remember mercy.** God **came** from **Teman**, and the **Holy** One **from mount Paran. Selah**. His **glory covered** the **heavens**, and the **earth** was **full** of his **praise.**

```
A E G X D M P K Z H R V K O W
A X N P A U E M A C T R A M Q
D I A R F A I L N S J G Y C S
E S I A R P E N D W S L C R Y
X N E Y Y S H I G I O N O T H
D G A E H T M A M H D N E O A
X Y A R E M E M B E R A K Z V
E R W R A T H H R A R V I Z E
S O Z H R P E E P T K C G W X
X L B C D A V L H O D K Y O F
G G T E V O I X B E R P U R A
S N D E C Y V L R L O P O K H
S W N P M S E K A M L M T Y O
W S W S O A R L I H L U W Z U
F O B M O U N T Z D E A F K Y
```

*by John Hudson Tiner*

## BONUS TRIVIA

In what city did silversmiths—fearing
the effect of Paul's preaching on their
idol-making business—stir up a riot?

**Micah 4:2–3**

Come, and let us go up to the **mountain** of the LORD, and to the **house** of the **God** of Jacob; and he **will teach** us of **his ways,** and we will **walk** in his **paths:** for the law shall go forth of **Zion,** and the word of the LORD from **Jerusalem**. And he shall **judge** among many people, and **rebuke** strong **nations afar** off; and they shall beat their **swords into plowshares,** and their **spears** into **pruninghooks:** nation shall not lift up a sword against nation, **neither shall** they **learn war any more.**

```
W  A  L  M  S  I  T  R  U  D  R  O  E  M  F
K  L  W  G  W  A  L  K  K  E  H  E  O  J  G
H  O  Z  P  O  S  J  U  Q  I  S  U  A  U  J
F  B  I  L  R  D  H  Z  S  P  N  C  F  D  Q
A  V  O  O  D  U  W  T  E  T  O  T  Z  G  J
F  R  N  W  S  K  N  A  A  B  I  D  O  E  T
D  B  I  S  T  U  R  I  Y  P  T  O  W  D  I
Q  L  Q  H  V  S  N  F  N  S  A  F  A  R  X
L  L  E  A  R  N  A  W  M  G  N  O  R  H  M
J  L  R  R  M  L  N  E  I  T  H  E  R  V  V
J  P  J  E  R  U  S  A  L  E  M  O  B  U  Y
T  X  M  S  B  Q  K  L  Q  A  O  P  O  P  R
S  Q  W  M  P  U  A  N  Y  C  R  N  V  K  B
T  N  G  Z  T  H  K  E  F  H  E  P  S  I  S
B  X  V  V  S  C  J  E  S  U  O  H  E  T  L
```

*by David Austin*

## BONUS TRIVIA

What sparkling substance does
the writer of Proverbs compare
to the poison of a viper?

*Luke 1:46–50*

And **Mary said,** My **soul doth magnify** the **Lord,** and my **spirit** hath **rejoiced** in God my **Saviour.** For he hath **regarded** the low **estate** of his **handmaiden:** for, **behold,** from **henceforth** all generations **shall call** me **blessed.** For he that is **mighty hath done** to me **great things;** and **holy** is his **name.** And his **mercy** is on **them that fear** him **from** generation to **generation.**

```
V  K  M  I  I  N  E  D  I  A  M  D  N  A  H
W  R  R  L  L  B  L  E  S  S  E  D  O  E  H
G  A  H  X  D  T  H  A  T  D  V  D  N  T  B
B  E  M  A  N  E  I  F  R  A  F  C  A  W  H
D  O  N  E  K  D  C  A  C  B  E  H  O  L  D
V  T  M  E  N  J  G  I  G  F  Z  R  F  C  R
M  N  Y  E  R  E  L  R  O  M  S  T  G  Y  O
O  E  T  M  R  A  M  R  A  J  A  D  V  O  L
R  L  H  C  U  C  T  R  Y  M  E  J  Q  O  M
F  N  G  T  O  H  Y  I  S  A  I  R  S  D  I
P  T  I  R  I  P  S  U  O  G  G  G  R  K  B
L  U  M  N  V  M  H  T  U  N  N  A  Z  V  D
J  L  O  F  A  P  A  L  L  I  E  F  M  N  V
E  T  A  T  S  E  L  L  H  F  E  X  V  Q  F
V  K  U  C  D  M  L  T  S  Y  L  O  H  H  I
```

*by John Hudson Tiner*

# BONUS TRIVIA

How many leprous men came to Jesus
requesting a mass healing—for which
only one returned to praise God?

Ten. (Luke 17:11–19)

# PUZZLE 49 — PRAYER FOR SPIRITUAL WISDOM

## Ephesians 1:16–19

**Cease** not to give **thanks** for you, **making mention** of you in my **prayers; that** the God of our **Lord Jesus Christ,** the **Father** of glory, may **give** unto you the **spirit** of **wisdom** and **revelation** in the **knowledge** of him: the **eyes** of **your understanding being enlightened;** that ye may know what is the **hope** of his **calling,** and what the **riches** of the **glory** of his **inheritance** in the **saints,** and **what** is the **exceeding greatness** of his power to **us-ward** who **believe, according** to the **working** of his **mighty power.**

```
G  R  E  A  T  N  E  S  S  P  O  W  E  R  G
G  N  I  D  R  O  C  C  A  L  H  N  S  N  M
N  X  I  J  E  S  U  S  X  A  L  R  I  G  A
I  Y  R  D  D  Y  K  C  T  I  E  E  I  Q  K
D  R  I  R  N  R  T  N  G  Y  B  V  E  R  I
E  O  O  N  X  A  I  H  A  G  E  E  V  U  N
E  L  S  B  H  S  T  R  G  H  M  L  E  O  G
C  G  W  T  P  E  P  S  U  I  T  A  I  Y  S
X  H  D  I  N  I  R  E  R  O  M  T  L  D  V
E  R  R  E  S  I  U  I  Y  E  N  I  E  R  F
T  I  D  I  L  D  A  E  T  E  D  O  B  A  V
T  C  P  Y  S  W  O  S  M  A  S  N  T  W  F
U  H  O  P  E  T  O  M  Q  A  N  H  U  S  T
Q  E  C  A  L  L  I  N  G  C  E  C  H  U  Y
E  S  A  E  C  G  N  I  K  R  O  W  E  O  X
```

*by John Hudson Tiner*

# BONUS TRIVIA

What suffering Old Testament
saint complained that God would
"terrifiest" him with visions?

*Matthew 13:2–4*

And **great multitudes were gathered together** unto him, so **that** he went **into** a **ship**, and sat; and the **whole** multitude **stood** on the **shore**. And he **spake many things unto** them in **parables, saying**, Behold, a **sower went forth** to sow; and **when** he **sowed, some seeds fell** by the way **side**, and the **fowls came** and **devoured them** up.

```
T  S  U  G  L  L  E  F  S  M  A  N  Y  D  P
P  A  N  N  X  M  H  R  U  E  C  G  P  T  U
R  I  D  I  Q  T  E  L  E  E  E  A  N  W  L
H  I  G  Y  H  W  T  H  L  W  R  D  P  H  D
U  R  E  A  O  I  F  O  T  A  O  I  S  E  U
B  W  T  S  T  O  O  D  B  F  H  F  R  N  B
C  R  Q  U  G  H  V  L  O  F  S  U  P  F  I
R  B  D  L  T  A  E  R  G  Y  O  T  N  U  M
S  E  T  D  E  S  T  R  N  V  T  W  H  N  S
S  K  H  D  E  H  F  P  E  K  N  E  L  D  H
P  W  I  T  N  W  I  D  P  D  I  N  Q  S  W
A  S  N  B  E  H  O  L  D  E  X  T  I  K  C
K  N  G  D  S  G  H  S  O  M  E  R  S  K  D
E  L  S  O  E  L  O  H  W  A  H  Z  W  T  U
C  R  A  H  G  E  U  T  J  C  M  P  Z  M  F
```

*by John Hudson Tiner*

# BONUS TRIVIA

What apostle had a vision of animals
being let down from heaven in a
sheet—and realized God had
offered salvation to the Gentiles?

*Matthew 5:3–9*

**Blessed** are the **poor** in **spirit**: for **theirs** is the **kingdom** of **heaven**. Blessed are they **that mourn**: for they shall be **comforted**. Blessed are the **meek**: for they shall **inherit** the **earth**. Blessed are they **which** do **hunger** and **thirst after righteousness**: for they shall be **filled**. Blessed are the **merciful**: for they shall **obtain mercy**. Blessed are the **pure** in **heart**: for they shall see God. Blessed are the **peacemakers**: for **they shall** be **called** the **children** of God.

```
R  V  I  B  W  D  D  U  O  F  M  O  O  K  L
E  F  E  B  L  E  S  S  E  D  B  L  L  Q  C
G  I  K  M  T  U  T  C  I  T  E  P  O  O  R
N  L  O  R  B  H  F  H  A  G  A  L  M  K  N
U  L  A  P  U  R  E  I  S  A  M  F  L  M  P
H  E  A  V  E  N  N  L  C  Z  O  M  T  A  B
H  D  Y  B  W  A  T  D  Q  R  O  W  U  E  C
M  A  H  R  D  S  C  R  T  D  E  N  U  E  R
E  O  C  T  R  E  M  E  G  L  L  M  Y  I  X
R  G  U  I  R  Y  D  N  M  L  S  C  E  W  O
C  Y  H  R  A  A  I  C  I  A  U  Q  H  D  Q
Y  T  U  E  N  K  E  E  M  H  K  I  T  J  M
K  T  A  H  T  R  Y  G  G  S  C  E  Z  V  Z
S  S  E  N  S  U  O  E  T  H  G  I  R  V  C
J  S  R  I  E  H  T  G  T  I  R  I  P  S  W
```

*by John Hudson Tiner*

# BONUS TRIVIA

What precious metal, according
to Proverbs, cannot compare
to the value of wisdom?

*John 19:26–28*

**When** Jesus **therefore** saw his mother, and the disciple **standing** by, **whom** he **loved,** he saith unto his mother, **Woman,** behold thy son! **Then** saith he to the disciple, **Behold** thy **mother!** And **from** that **hour** that **disciple took** her **unto** his own **home. After this,** Jesus know-**ing** that all **things were** now **accomplished, that** the **scripture might** be **fulfilled, saith,** I **thirst.**

```
F M S Z H J W T R Z W A M S E
K O I P R T E M O H C H L G B
Y Z N G W A E R W C Z N E N Y
W E R E H H K N O W I N G I K
R S R E H T O M O F K K Z H S
E J C V K W P M D F E O M T Z
C D I R F L A E R U Y R A R K
N L U O I N L O R L G N E E O
J O W S E P M E Z F D W H H O
H H H G I L T S R I H T J J T
Y E T C A F H U N L O V E D P
D B S I A V E G R L R A S I R
B I X Z A U N T O E L W U F G
D B T Q R S I H T D R B S V T
Q K O B V P K K Y N B C R Q S
```

*by John Hudson Tiner*

# BONUS TRIVIA

What second wife of Elkanah
provoked his other wife, Hannah,
over her barrenness?

# PUZZLE 53 — SPEAKING ON A PLAIN

## Luke 6:17, 20–21

And he came **down with them**, and **stood** in the **plain**, and the **company** of his disciples, and a **great multitude** of **people** out of all **Judaea** and **Jerusalem**, and **from** the sea **coast** of **Tyre** and **Sidon**, **which came** to **hear** him, and to be **healed** of **their diseases**. . . and he **lifted** up his **eyes** on his **disciples**, and **said**, Blessed be ye **poor**: for **yours** is the **kingdom** of God. Blessed are ye that **hunger** now: for ye shall be **filled**. **Blessed** are ye **that weep** now: for ye **shall laugh**.

```
T O T S O M K H F B D Z T N Z
J M E H T D G D E L A E H J R
C Q U A E U G O P E O P L E L
J L M L A I N O G S S M E S M
S A L L T P R T E S J R I E L
G I S Q O I M S A E A D U J W
F R S O D O T S R D O H Z O Y
T Y R E D I I U D N P U N T Y
A E Y G S H S W D G Z N B F H
H S N L W A E C T E R G S R C
T I A I L M E L I F T E D O I
K V P E A C E S D P T R A M H
X S M C Y L H T I W L S A T W
R D O W N E P T A D T E L E I
Y K C L R H S T S H X V S H H
```

*by John Hudson Tiner*

## Bonus Trivia

What did the apostle Paul, writing to the Thessalonians, say that those who refused to work should be kept from doing?

*John 4:11–14*

The **woman saith** unto him, Sir, thou hast **nothing** to **draw** with, and the **well** is **deep**: from **whence** then hast thou that **living** water? Art thou **greater** than our **father Jacob**, which gave us the well, and drank thereof himself, and his **children**, and his **cattle**? **Jesus answered** and said unto her, **Whosoever drinketh** of this water shall **thirst again**: But whosoever drinketh of the water that I shall give him shall **never** thirst; but the **water** that I shall give him shall be in him a well of water **springing** up into **everlasting life**.

G R E H W E L L B E V E R J E
N A E A T L B O S P E E W U S
D E T E G O C J T U Q S O J F
B E R Z V A F H S Q A U M V Z
R J E D J E I P F K D S A T B
T C R P L R R N U W H E N C E
O A A D S I I L F H Q J Q V G
W D X T N A H W A O M O H M N
L R M G T L V C T S V J P B I
G I I Y T L X M H O T L Q K H
A N S W E R E D E E M I P R T
G K I A Q W M P R V N F N V O
T E N V I G Z T N E V E R G N
F T P S I T I B G R E A T E R
X H V V C L H J E L L V W O B

*by David Austin*

# BONUS TRIVIA

What word did the writer of Ecclesiastes
use to describe the sleep of a laborer?

*Sweet. (Ecclesiastes 5:12)*

ABUNDANCE

BOUNTIFULLY

DEFENCE

DOUBLE

FARTHING

FOUND

HOUSE

LEND

LITTLE

MAMMON

MONEY

MUCH

NEIGHBOUR

POOR

PORTION

REAP

RICH

SATISFIED

SHEKEL

SILVER

SOWETH

SPARINGLY

STOLEN

STUFF

THIEF

TREASURY

USURER

USURY

VANITY

WISDOM

```
N E F R U E J F O U N D T O G
M H O U S E E V D M S T U F F
K T U B L P A L A A L U A P W
K E S B O N E M B E I R R A G
H W U O I U M U T S T O L E N
P O R T I O N R A H T S O R R
D S Y J N D E T I D L H U Q J
F B Z F A A I N I E E E I Q A
V Z J N S S G M R F F K K E D
T B C U F M H M O E U E T U F
O E R I D O B I U N V L E N D
Q Y E Q V D O F X C E L L R A
W D M O H S U M J E H Y I Y L
M Y L G N I R A P S L C V S V
J P B U Y W T X M Q H K Q P P
```

*by David Austin*

# BONUS TRIVIA

What Old Testament woman was buried
in a cave in the field of Machpelah?

### Psalm 86:1–5

A **Prayer** of **David**.

Bow **down thine** ear, O Lord, **hear** me: for I am **poor** and **needy. Preserve** my soul; for I am **holy**: O thou my God, **save** thy servant that **trusteth** in thee. Be **merciful** unto me, O Lord: for I cry unto thee **daily. Rejoice** the soul of thy **servant**: for unto thee, O Lord, do I **lift** up my **soul**. For **thou, Lord**, art **good**, and **ready** to **forgive**; and **plenteous** in **mercy unto** all **them that call upon thee.**

```
O  E  F  Y  I  W  S  D  G  N  P  U  D  R  L
T  H  O  U  D  O  O  G  S  K  D  T  Q  Z  I
N  E  O  T  U  P  O  N  U  W  P  Z  D  B  F
U  G  H  L  C  D  R  P  M  H  D  E  I  I  T
R  E  A  D  Y  P  C  E  M  L  K  R  V  N  F
E  D  E  L  P  G  V  P  S  M  M  R  A  A  P
E  N  I  H  T  O  W  U  B  E  E  V  D  E  S
R  A  C  D  T  M  O  V  J  J  R  E  C  T  H
D  T  R  O  R  E  C  R  O  E  C  V  J  J  O
T  O  H  W  T  H  T  I  S  G  I  I  E  I  W
L  V  L  N  M  T  C  S  L  W  F  G  J  N  X
Y  D  E  E  N  E  Z  L  U  L  U  R  S  D  W
G  L  R  M  P  R  A  Y  E  R  L  O  H  L  K
P  C  P  N  V  C  R  T  A  H  T  F  M  P  E
Y  J  P  G  F  Z  Q  S  E  G  G  M  B  G  C
```

*by John Hudson Tiner*

# BONUS TRIVIA

What melting substance did the
psalmist say his heart had turned to?

*Luke 11:1–4; Matthew 6:9–13*

| | |
|---|---|
| ART | GLORY |
| BREAD | HALLOWED |
| COME | HEAVEN |
| DAILY | INDEBTED |
| DAY | KINGDOM |
| DEBTORS | LEAD |
| DEBTS | NAME |
| DELIVER | ONE |
| DISCIPLES | OUR |
| DONE | POWER |
| EARTH | PRAY |
| EVER | SAY |
| EVERY | SINS |
| EVIL | TEACH |
| FATHER | TEMPTATION |
| FOREVER | THY |
| FORGIVE | WHICH |
| GIVE | WILL |

```
D E V E R Y L I A D Q E M O C
P B R E H T A F F H C I H W T
D R R S H S O L C I S T B E D
T Y A E D C I U I F F Y D M F
S E Z Y A S A N R V R A E B W
H E M T K D R E S N E D T D W
R H L P H I H O T L E R Z E R
R E Y P T Y N T T I A V H T E
D E V Y I A E G R B Q B A B V
A O W E R C T E D A E B L E E
J W N O R O S I V O E D L D H
S I A E P O L I O I M U O N G
A L E M A N F G D N G C W I B
Y L M E S R E V I L E D E R Y
T O F O R G I V E M O Z D K E
```

*by N. Teri Grottke*

## BONUS TRIVIA

What nationality, hated by Jews,
provided the "good guy" character in
Jesus' parable of a man beaten by robbers?

# PUZZLE 58 —
# THE PRAYER OF JABEZ

## *1 Chronicles 4:9–10*

And **Jabez** was **more honourable** than his **brethren**: and his **mother called** his **name** Jabez, **saying, Because** I **bare** him with **sorrow**. And Jabez called on the **God** of **Israel**, saying, Oh that thou **wouldest bless** me **indeed**, and **enlarge** my **coast**, and that **thine hand might** be with me, and that thou wouldest **keep** me from **evil**, that it may not **grieve** me! And God **granted** him that which he **requested**.

```
A G D B G I N D E E D B C M U
S O R R O W S X V N P G O I T
P T W I D O C R Y A K T A G W
C H K C E L W U A M H H S H O
H I D A D V J M V E N C T T U
Q N E L P B E A R O L U N O L
F E G L J I G F B A R E E L D
B Z K E E P M O R E G D S E E
R R X D V S F N E N Z E T G S
E K N Q I V Q E I S J T M R T
T A H E L A F Y Z D U N I A G
H O N O U R A B L E N A C L T
R E Q U E S T E D J R R C N H
E M J W Y L P I A X B G Q E S
N Y I O K B L E S S M Z L R B
```

*by Paul Kent*

## BONUS TRIVIA

What modern-day nation, with its
capital at New Delhi, marked the
eastern extent of King Xerxes's nation?

ADVERSARY

AHAZ

ALL HIS DAYS

ANGER

ATHALIAH

BROKEN

COME TO
  NOUGHT

DESTROYER

DESTRUCTION

DREADFUL

ENEMY

HAMAN

INIQUITY

PAIN

PROVOKE

PUNISHMENT

SIGHT

SNARED

SORROWS

TRAVAILETH

WICKED MAN

WICKED WOMAN

WICKED WORKS

WOE

WROUGHT

```
F E B R U A H S N A R E D E S
C N R T S A H W O E S R T N S
M E O C N Y R A S R E V D A I
W M K G O O A W Z A D E E M G
I Y E O U M O D D E S D P D H
C R N G V R E F S T K U A E T
K L H W R O U T R I N K I K R
E T E O L R O O I H G N C A
D H S O J U Y P S N U L Q I V
W J F B C E Z H F Q O A L W A
O V Z T R J M F K D T U B A I
M W I C K E D W O R K S G T L
A O U I N I Q U I T Y O D H E
N I A T H A L I A H A M A N T
Q Q V F X A W M O H M J L M H
```

*by David Austin*

# BONUS TRIVIA

Saul of Tarsus consented to the
death of which Christian martyr?

*Stephen. (Acts 7:58–59; 8:1)*

# PUZZLE 60 — PRAYERS OF WORSHIP IN HEAVEN

*Revelation 11:16–17*

And the **four** and **twenty elders,** which sat **before** God on their **seats, fell upon their faces,** and **worshipped** God, **saying,** We **give** thee **thanks,** O LORD God **Almighty, which** art, and **wast,** and art to **come; because thou** hast **taken** to **thee** thy **great power,** and **hast reigned.**

```
D H K A N I T S R D N I X F H
V S A Y I N G Q E R S T A E S
K K W L O Z A P I D W V S X U
Q U O U M M P K G E E S B P O
U P G W M I Y Q N F R K O G H
L V E A H J G T E E O N K R T
X O T S A H Y H D L F A C E S
N I R L U K T L T L E H I A U
A O L D W A E Q H Y B T R T F
W I R G K G C C L I H Q S R G
C O M E V R I E H T F A H F G
X B N E W H U V B R W G J Z A
I T Z P W O D O E E H T B R D
H R D R N U P C F B I E J A T
C N J M K G O A S W W Z M Q M
```

*by John Hudson Tiner*

## BONUS TRIVIA

What great prophet heard God say, "Man looketh on the outward appearance, but the Lord looketh on the heart"?

### John 3:4–7

**Nicodemus saith** unto him, How can a man be born **when** he is old? can he enter the **second time** into his **mother's womb,** and be born? **Jesus answered,** Verily, **verily,** I say unto thee, **Except** a man be born of **water** and of the Spirit, he **cannot enter into** the **kingdom** of God. That which is born of the flesh is **flesh;** and that **which** is born of the **Spirit** is spirit. **Marvel** not **that** I **said unto thee,** Ye **must** be **born again.**

| | | | | | | | | | | | | | | |
|---|---|---|---|---|---|---|---|---|---|---|---|---|---|---|
| D | P | L | B | S | B | W | R | K | R | W | B | H | F | N |
| S | U | F | G | T | I | R | I | P | S | T | H | F | X | I |
| N | R | O | B | C | A | N | N | O | T | P | L | E | T | D |
| Z | V | E | V | E | G | U | P | R | E | E | H | T | N | I |
| E | B | F | H | D | H | R | E | T | S | C | P | O | C | A |
| H | E | H | O | T | H | C | A | H | I | X | C | M | Y | S |
| S | U | M | E | D | O | C | I | N | L | E | V | R | A | M |
| Z | G | K | I | T | A | M | Q | H | S | A | I | T | H | F |
| S | Q | U | N | T | O | G | F | U | W | W | V | R | S | Q |
| T | H | I | G | H | X | N | A | O | X | A | E | S | U | Q |
| J | P | Z | S | A | H | P | M | I | L | T | R | R | S | V |
| F | M | U | S | T | O | B | N | B | N | E | I | A | E | Q |
| D | E | K | S | I | Q | O | D | E | G | R | L | M | J | D |
| B | Q | B | L | M | N | M | S | G | G | W | Y | N | P | V |
| N | L | K | F | Z | T | S | B | Q | N | W | L | U | N | Q |

*by John Hudson Tiner*

# BONUS TRIVIA

What wayward prophet was thrown overboard by pagan sailors frightened by a violent storm at sea?

## Ecclesiastes 2–11

| | |
|---|---|
| ABUNDANCE | LOVETH |
| CHILDHOOD | NEIGHBOUR |
| CONSIDERED | PEOPLE |
| DEVICE | REJOICE |
| ENJOY | REWARD |
| ENVIED | RICHES |
| EQUITY | RIGHTEOUS |
| FINDETH | SATISFIED |
| FOOL | SILVER |
| HAND OF GOD | SPIRIT |
| HEART | UNDER THE SUN |
| JOYFULLY | VANITY |
| KNOWLEDGE | VEXATION |
| LABOUR | WISDOM |
| LAUGHTER | WISE |
| LIFE | YOUTH |

```
W  I  S  D  O  M  A  F  I  N  D  E  T  H  G
Q  S  G  P  E  O  P  L  E  L  O  V  E  T  H
R  R  I  U  S  A  T  I  S  F  I  E  D  I  M
E  K  U  L  A  U  G  H  T  E  R  X  E  R  S
C  K  P  O  V  H  E  A  R  T  R  A  S  I  E
H  O  N  U  B  E  E  E  I  A  I  T  J  P  H
I  M  N  O  I  A  R  N  B  O  G  I  O  S  C
L  K  U  S  W  C  L  U  V  Z  H  O  Y  V  I
D  R  P  E  I  L  N  R  Z  I  T  N  F  A  R
H  C  L  U  N  D  E  R  T  H  E  S  U  N  E
O  L  U  O  A  J  E  D  K  Q  O  D  L  I  W
O  I  W  N  O  Z  O  R  G  E  U  N  L  T  A
D  F  C  I  O  F  T  Y  E  E  S  A  Y  Y  R
D  E  C  U  S  G  H  A  N  D  O  F  G  O  D
D  E  V  I  C  E  Q  U  I  T  Y  O  U  T  H
```

*by David Austin*

# BONUS TRIVIA

What was Jesus doing in a boat
immediately before calming a
storm that terrified His disciples?

# PUZZLE 63 — PRAYER FOR SAFEKEEPING

*Psalm 141:2–4*

Let my **prayer** be set **forth** before **thee** as **incense**; and the **lifting** up of my **hands** as the **evening sacrifice**. Set a **watch**, O Lord, **before** my **mouth**; **keep** the **door** of my **lips**. **Incline** not my **heart** to any **evil thing**, to **practise wicked works with** men **that** work **iniquity**: and let me not eat of **their dainties**.

| L | T | H | A | T | H | T | H | S | D | X | H | T | I | W |
|---|---|---|---|---|---|---|---|---|---|---|---|---|---|---|
| W | P | T | Y | T | O | R | O | A | R | E | K | E | G | J |
| R | K | R | U | T | S | M | I | C | A | I | E | D | D | T |
| F | D | O | A | O | I | N | E | R | O | F | E | B | R | C |
| X | M | F | Q | C | T | U | T | I | W | A | P | H | T | F |
| Q | F | R | P | I | T | L | Q | F | A | M | P | P | T | H |
| Y | N | S | E | W | O | I | L | I | P | S | E | K | Z | A |
| V | I | S | J | R | G | F | S | C | N | Z | L | H | W | N |
| W | U | T | D | K | N | T | S | E | W | I | C | K | E | D |
| V | A | L | H | X | I | I | S | P | E | T | E | V | W | S |
| C | T | H | P | E | N | N | E | K | A | G | H | U | W | J |
| X | H | B | M | Z | E | G | B | W | R | R | L | I | V | E |
| R | H | G | N | C | V | X | Z | E | E | O | S | M | N | H |
| Z | D | W | N | R | E | Y | A | R | P | O | W | W | R | G |
| O | R | I | N | C | L | I | N | E | P | D | G | X | H | G |

*by John Hudson Tiner*

## BONUS TRIVIA

What conspiring son of King
David caused his father to flee
for his life from Jerusalem?

*Absalom. (2 Samuel 15:13–37)*

*1 Samuel 1:9–2:21*

ASKED
BARREN
BLESSED
CALLED
CHILD
FAVOUR
HANDMAID
HANNAH
HUSBAND
MOTHER
PETITION
POURED

PRAYED
PRIEST
REMEMBER
SAMUEL
SON
SOUL
VISITED
VOWED
WEPT
WIFE
YEARLY

```
H A M F E D C A C E F I W S T
M I F R M W Y E B A R R E N E
E G P R I E S T V L L P P H O
J U Q O A O J O F O E L T B Z
F Q A R U V U Z V T W S E J F
K D L L T R B T I U A E S D O
D Y I Q Q V E T S F S X D E A
W S H M O H I D I M K J L Y D
M L A A V O M O T H E R D A V
J P N M N B U Y E T D N X R M
Q K N Q U D P P D R A S O P Q
W M A P R E M E M B E R N S V
B T H N G Z L A S T E F P S I
B X V V C J E U I L L V W O B
M H F S U P H N J D L I H C K
```

*by David Austin*

# BONUS TRIVIA

On which of the six days of
creation did God create light?

*1 Samuel 1:11*

And she **vowed** a vow, and **said,** O LORD of **hosts,** if **thou** wilt **indeed look** on the **affliction** of thine handmaid, and **remember** me, and not **forget** thine handmaid, but **wilt** give unto **thine handmaid** a man **child, then** I **will give** him **unto** the LORD all the **days** of his **life,** and **there shall** no **razor come upon** his **head.**

```
N W S R M O R U L G N D Z W U
U O A W L C O M E I F E J M B
D L I H C H Z V D V I W H S A
Y L D T T B A O T E R E H T Q
T N F L C V R W T G E T K S H
Y K P T H I N E I N Q D H A T
O S S H A L L D M L U D N Z Z
D M X P O I O F R E L D P I X
H Q Q R P C G O F Z M F S L X
E V D A E H B A K A L B U T C
X Z B W Y B L S I S S P E V Q
J W Z B L H S D Y T O G F R B
B R C U A P Y A I S R A I Z X
P E Z I S O D T N O P U L J Y
W M K Z O F C R F H R W M F L
```

*by John Hudson Tiner*

## BONUS TRIVIA

What Old Testament prophet,
who called himself "a child," wore
a wooden yoke as an object lesson?

Jeremiah. (Jeremiah 1:6; 27:1–2; 28:12–14)

*1 Samuel 2:1–3*

And **Hannah prayed**, and **said**, My **heart rejoiceth** in the Lord, mine **horn** is **exalted** in the Lord: my mouth is **enlarged over mine enemies**; **because** I rejoice in thy **salvation**. There is none **holy** as the Lord: for there is **none beside thee**: **neither** is **there** any **rock like** our God. **Talk** no **more** so **exceeding proudly**; let not **arrogancy come** out of **your mouth**: for the Lord is a God of **knowledge**, and by him **actions** are **weighed**.

```
T  H  T  N  E  S  U  A  C  E  B  O  R  O  X
C  T  S  A  R  X  D  P  Z  N  R  V  H  Y  B
S  E  X  A  L  T  E  D  R  L  E  E  H  T  V
C  C  X  N  I  K  U  H  E  A  V  R  H  P  Y
N  I  R  C  K  D  E  G  R  R  Y  A  O  T  L
H  O  L  Y  E  A  D  R  X  G  A  E  E  M  D
H  J  I  Z  R  E  O  E  H  E  C  B  D  M  U
R  E  E  T  L  G  D  N  A  D  T  A  Y  M  O
R  R  M  W  A  E  M  I  N  E  I  T  H  E  R
R  Y  O  N  H  V  K  M  N  R  O  C  K  B  P
C  N  C  G  S  T  L  R  A  G  N  G  E  K  A
K  Y  I  W  O  O  U  A  H  P  S  S  R  S  Z
H  E  K  G  R  O  A  O  S  E  I  M  E  N  E
W  L  V  D  Y  G  X  L  M  D  R  B  K  T  T
F  X  N  W  J  U  C  G  E  N  O  N  V  C  L
```

*by John Hudson Tiner*

# BONUS TRIVIA

How old was the boy Jesus when
He amazed people in the temple
with His spiritual insights?

Twelve. (Luke 2:41–52)

343

ACCEPTABLE

AFFLICT

ANOINT

ASHES

ASSEMBLY

BOW DOWN

BREAK EVERY YOKE

CHOSEN

DAYS

ESTHER

FAST

GREATEST

HEARD

HIGH

KING

LEAST

MAIDENS

MORDECAI

NIGHT

NINEVEH

PEOPLE

PROCLAIMED

SACKCLOTH

SANCTIFY

SOLEMN

THREE

VOICE

WASH

WHEN YE FAST

```
D A S R L E Q E M A I D E N S
B P G E S H V M E A R S Y A D
O R R O W B O M O R D E C A I
W O E G E T I E H G H K P O A
D C A A J S C U Q E C T J F N
O L T F K A E H B L A Z F A O
W A E F I E Q A O C S R S V I
N I S L N L V T C S H S D S N
Z M T I G W H E N Y E F A S T
J E H C F I P I R M S N A S K
D D E T G T N T B Y C B O S T
U O R H A E D L I T Y L Q Q T
V F X B V A Y W I P E O P L E
M O L E H M J F L M M L K V V
J E H S A W Y P N I G H T E B
```

*by David Austin*

# Bonus Trivia

What young king removed all the
mediums and spiritists from Judah,
as required in the book of the law
found by his priest, Hilkiah?

CHEERFUL
CONSIDER
EVERY
FEASTS
GLADNESS
GOOD
HARP
JOY
LORD
MORNING
NEW MOONS
PEACE

PIPE
PRAISE
REGARD
SABBATHS
STAND
TABRET
THANK
TIDINGS
TRUTH
VIOL
WINE

```
L  O  R  D  N  O  P  A  R  E  V  R  Y  T  M
E  V  E  V  E  R  Y  O  J  Q  E  L  I  O  J
G  H  G  O  T  J  P  Y  Q  E  J  F  B  S  Z
F  Q  A  A  H  R  V  Z  J  F  C  K  T  D  T
B  T  R  U  A  O  D  I  S  O  Q  A  Q  V  F
T  I  D  I  N  G  S  H  N  X  N  A  E  W  M
O  H  S  M  K  L  T  S  J  D  L  M  N  P  L
V  E  C  V  J  A  I  P  B  U  Y  T  I  X  M
F  Q  K  H  B  D  Q  P  P  G  M  R  W  S  Q
W  E  T  B  E  N  E  W  M  O  O  N  S  M  P
N  V  A  R  B  E  T  N  G  Z  R  O  T  E  F
P  S  B  S  A  S  R  I  B  P  N  V  D  X  V
V  C  R  J  T  S  E  F  R  L  I  L  V  W  O
B  M  E  H  F  S  S  A  U  O  N  P  U  P  N
J  K  T  R  U  T  H  Y  L  L  G  I  E  J  A
```

*by David Austin*

# Bonus Trivia

What instrument did the young
boy David play to soothe the
troubled spirit of King Saul?

# PUZZLE 69 — PRAYER OF CONFIDENCE

## *Psalm 17:6–9*

I **have called** upon thee, for thou **wilt** hear me, O God: **incline thine** ear unto me, and **hear** my **speech. Shew** thy **marvellous lovingkindness**, O **thou** that **savest** by thy **right hand** them **which** put **their trust** in thee from **those** that **rise** up **against them. Keep** me as the **apple** of the eye, **hide** me **under** the **shadow** of thy **wings**, from the **wicked that oppress** me, **from** my **deadly enemies**, who **compass** me **about.**

```
S H A D O W T S E V A S S S W
R S D N A H H S E L W G P Q R
K H E A R A E N N I N T C D D
J K K N A T I W E I Y G H T P
I W C Y D H R N W C A L L E D
X H I L T N E U C Q G G M V M
B I W B C M I T S L C L A A S
Q C G C I D T K H T I A R H S
M H C E E P S K G G U N V S A
T A S A S H E W E N I R E J P
M E D T U O B A D E I R L J M
Y L D L A G H E P S P V L U O
Y X C I W H R T E P F R O M C
I N M W H K T B O X L H U L A
R J W T T D Q O W J T E S P O
```

*by John Hudson Tiner*

# BONUS TRIVIA

What famous tree of Lebanon
was used by the psalmist as a
metaphor for the righteous?

## *Luke 9:1–6*

Then he called his twelve disciples together, and gave them **power** and **authority** over all **devils**, and to **cure diseases**. And he sent them to **preach** the **kingdom** of **God**, and to **heal** the **sick**. And he said unto them, **Take nothing** for your **journey**, neither **staves**, nor **scrip**, neither **bread**, neither **money**; neither have two **coats** apiece. And whatsoever **house** ye enter into, there **abide**, and thence depart. And whosoever will not receive you, when ye go out of that city, **shake off** the **very dust** from your **feet** for a **testimony against** them. And they departed, and went through the **towns**, preaching the **gospel**, and **healing** every where.

```
A G D V V E R Y E D I B A Z F
H F D U S T A V E S R E G N S
A Y N O M I T S E T L J Y J I
G A G Y E N O M A S E A F T C
C O U C O A T S E R H H E B K
M S D T K D E N U K E A X H E
M E Y N H J A C D A A E K Z E
E S E L F O E E L V P T X E G
T A N E E M R I R G I H A M Q
S E R P E P N I N B R C S O B
N S U S T G O N T C C A L D J
I I O O S N W O T Y S E I G F
A D J G R E S U O H H R V N F
G T D E T A P O W E R P E I O
A H L B J G N I H T O N D K T
```

*by N. Teri Grottke*

# BONUS TRIVIA

What Egyptian crops were destroyed by
the plague of hail called down by Moses?

*Acts 7:51–53*

Ye **stiffnecked** and **uncircumcised** in **heart** and **ears,** ye do **always resist** the **Holy Ghost**: as your fathers did, so do ye. Which of the **prophets** have not **your fathers persecuted**? and **they** have **slain them which showed before** of the **coming** of the **Just** One; of **whom** ye have **been** now the **betrayers** and **murderers**: who have **received** the law by the **disposition** of **angels,** and **have** not **kept** it.

```
G F U A I B F I I U N E E B P
T H O L Y Z X J D N V T P E K
S N O Z G N I M O C S S R T Z
U T O S H O W E D I T S R R T
J P I I T S G E S R E R Y A H
A M S F T O V E F C H E F Y E
L S K L F I R N U U P R P E Y
W H A V E N S T U M O E L R M
A G W C Z G E O H C R D S S B
Y A E W W D N C P I P R A Z E
S R E H T A F A K S H U F M C
M L I O B E F O R E I M W W N
E C A M I E B M A D D D D L O
H N W I R L K R U O Y W M N E
T K Z Y N Q T C Q F F W L N R
```

*by John Hudson Tiner*

# BONUS TRIVIA

What city was the site of
King Xerxes's royal citadel?

Shushan. (Esther 1:2)

353

# PUZZLE 72 — NAMES OF GOD

ABBA
ALMIGHTY GOD
ANCIENT OF DAYS
BREAD OF LIFE
COUNSELLOR
DELIVERER
EVERLASTING KING
FATHER
GOOD SHEPHERD
I AM
JEHOVAH

KING OF KINGS
LAMB
LAMB OF GOD
LIVING GOD
LORD OF LORDS
PRINCE OF PEACE
REDEEMER
ROCK OF ISRAEL
SAVIOUR
WONDERFUL

```
E  F  I  L  F  O  D  A  E  R  B  J  O  H  S
E  V  C  O  U  N  S  E  L  L  O  R  S  A  L
P  C  E  L  T  S  F  A  T  H  E  R  N  A  T
A  R  E  R  I  C  H  B  V  L  E  C  M  L  D
S  K  I  E  L  V  E  B  G  I  I  B  E  M  R
D  G  H  N  J  A  I  A  O  E  O  A  J  I  E
R  E  N  W  C  E  S  N  N  F  R  U  U  G  H
O  Q  L  I  O  E  H  T  G  S  J  F  R  H  P
L  B  Z  I  K  N  O  O  I  G  F  Q  A  T  E
F  M  Z  A  V  F  D  F  V  N  O  J  F  Y  H
O  A  D  M  D  E  O  E  P  A  G  D  T  G  S
D  L  T  A  U  K  R  G  R  E  H  K  O  O  D
R  D  Y  I  C  Q  Q  E  N  F  A  V  I  D  O
O  S  F  O  X  A  W  M  R  I  U  C  O  N  O
L  H  R  E  D  E  E  M  E  R  K  L  E  M  G
```

*by David Austin*

# BONUS TRIVIA

What physical characteristic initially
hindered Zacchaeus from seeing Jesus?

*2 Samuel 7:22–23*

**Wherefore** thou art great, O LORD God: for there is **none** like thee, **neither** is **there** any God **beside** thee, **according** to all that we **have heard** with our ears. And **what** one nation in the **earth** is like thy people, **even like Israel, whom** God **went** to redeem for a people to **himself,** and to **make** him a **name,** and to do for you **great things** and **terrible,** for thy **land, before** thy **people, which** thou **redeemedst** to thee from **Egypt, from** the **nations** and **their gods?**

```
Q  W  E  N  T  P  F  L  E  A  R  S  I  B  E
U  M  R  L  J  S  M  O  H  W  N  M  D  G  M
I  O  E  H  B  B  D  B  H  O  E  C  Y  B  A
Y  R  H  T  T  I  O  E  I  B  I  P  U  H  N
A  F  T  T  H  R  R  T  M  F  T  L  P  A  V
B  C  W  L  G  E  A  R  B  E  H  A  E  Z  B
U  W  C  D  F  N  I  E  E  V  E  N  F  E  M
B  E  F  O  R  E  S  R  X  T  R  D  L  B  K
M  E  R  V  R  O  Z  H  L  T  N  P  E  W  R
P  E  K  I  L  D  L  H  A  K  O  C  S  R  W
T  V  L  S  G  N  I  H  T  E  N  X  M  H  H
Q  A  X  O  T  R  W  N  P  B  E  S  I  D  E
E  H  D  W  U  L  E  W  G  R  T  C  H  K  A
N  S  B  V  R  F  Z  A  C  C  H  N  A  L  R
L  H  T  E  O  J  W  X  T  N  P  M  O  H  D
```

*by John Hudson Tiner*

## BONUS TRIVIA

What Philistine city's name is
still heard in the news today,
often with the word "strip"?

*1 Corinthians 13:1–5*

Though I **speak** with the **tongues** of **men** and of angels, and have not charity, I am **become** as **sounding brass**, or a **tinkling** cymbal. And though I have the **gift** of **prophecy**, and **understand** all **mysteries**, and all **knowledge**; and though I have all **faith**, so that I could **remove** mountains, and have not charity, I am **nothing**. And though I **bestow all** my **goods** to **feed** the **poor**, and though I **give** my **body** to be **burned**, and have not charity, it **profiteth** me nothing. **Charity suffereth long**, and is **kind**; charity **envieth** not; charity **vaunteth** not **itself**, is not **puffed** up, **doth** not behave itself unseemly, seeketh not her own, is not easily provoked, thinketh no evil. . . .

```
D B V A U N T E T H R O O P H
E A Z L Z Q K V S J M F O S T
F C V L D A K O E E G E D S I
F Y M B E E I M G H U O N A A
U C Y P G Q N E O I O G Y R F
P E S M M I D R I G V D N B O
Y H T E R E F F U S O E L O V
T P E F L E S T I B D E E F T
I O R U N D E R S T A N D Z D
R R I Y W M O S O U N D I N G
A P E S O Y N O T H I N G W L
H D S C T P R O F I T E T H O
C H E V S T I N K L I N G U N
M B H T E I V N E J H T O D G
U M J F B E G D E L W O N K H
```

*by N. Teri Grottke*

## BONUS TRIVIA

What town, along with Bethsaida, did not
repent when Jesus performed miracles there
and thus received a pronouncement of woe?

# PUZZLE 75 — LOVE CHAPTER, PART TWO

## *1 Corinthians 13:5–13*

. . .Doth not **behave** itself **unseemly, seeketh** not her **own,** is not **easily** provoked, **thinketh** no **evil**; rejoiceth not in iniquity, but **rejoiceth** in the **truth**; beareth all things, **believeth** all things, **hopeth** all things, **endureth** all things. **Charity** never **faileth**: but whether there be **prophecies**, they shall **fail**; whether there be tongues, they shall **cease**; whether there be knowledge, it shall **vanish** away. For we know in **part**, and we prophesy in part. But when that which is **perfect** is come, then that which is in part shall be done away. When I was a **child,** I **spake** as a child, I understood as a child, I **thought** as a child: but when I became a **man,** I put away **childish** things. For now we see **through** a **glass, darkly**; but then **face** to face: now I know in part; but then shall I know even as also I am **known**. And now abideth faith, **hope,** charity, these **three**; but the **greatest** of these is charity.

B E L I E V E T H H S I N A V
E T E P O H Y L I S A E M Y S
X H H T E R U D N E P P B L E
C I O T H G U O H T Q A H M I
H N W S H T H R O U G H K E C
I K N H T E C I O J E R V E E
L E G O E L T F K D Y I A S H
D T R P L Y I R B N L S E N P
I H E E I T P A A F E E T U O
S Y A T A I K Q F P K X C B R
H L T H F R T H R E E H E N P
V K E S S A L G T I T H F W A
N R S D W H M H J U A L R O P
V A T B E C A F R V H C E N T
P D L I H C N T E G F A P K U

*by N. Teri Grottke*

# BONUS TRIVIA

What annual celebration was instituted to commemorate the Jews' victory over their enemies in Queen Esther's time?

*Purim. (Esther 9:20–28)*

*Daniel 9:4–5*

And I **prayed unto** the LORD my God, and **made** my **confession**, and **said**, O **Lord**, the **great** and **dreadful** God, **keeping** the **covenant** and **mercy** to them that **love** him, and to **them that** keep his **commandments**; we have **sinned**, and have **committed iniquity**, and have **done wickedly**, and **have rebelled**, **even** by **departing** from thy **precepts** and **from** thy **judgments**.

```
J  M  D  W  P  R  E  C  E  P  T  S  Q  G  V
Q  V  Z  J  I  N  I  Q  U  I  T  Y  E  A  H
I  C  I  X  M  B  M  D  J  N  Z  V  N  W  N
T  O  U  T  H  A  T  U  E  K  O  L  D  F  S
N  V  O  C  F  L  D  M  U  L  U  E  O  P  G
M  E  H  T  O  G  D  E  Y  F  L  V  N  R  C
U  N  V  R  M  N  T  E  D  P  M  E  E  A  W
D  A  D  E  A  I  F  A  T  O  A  A  B  Y  Y
I  N  N  M  Y  T  E  E  S  T  T  Q  D  E  C
A  T  M  O  F  R  O  M  S  Q  I  E  O  D  R
S  O  H  P  D  A  S  V  U  S  N  M  V  R  E
C  F  G  N  I  P  E  E  K  N  I  E  M  A  M
X  R  Y  L  D  E  K  C  I  W  T  O  W  O  H
S  O  E  Q  N  D  G  S  A  P  F  O  N  W  C
D  T  Q  R  V  J  Q  Z  J  P  X  M  B  B  K
```

*by John Hudson Tiner*

# BONUS TRIVIA

What "prince of the devils" did Pharisees
accuse Jesus of using to cast out demons?

## Psalm 3:1–4

*A Psalm of David, when he fled from Absalom his son.*

Lord, how are they **increased** that **trouble** me! many are **they that rise** up **against** me. **Many** there be **which** say of my **soul, There** is no **help** for him in God. Selah. But **thou,** O Lord, art a **shield** for me; my **glory,** and the **lifter** up of **mine head.** I **cried unto** the Lord **with** my **voice,** and he **heard** me out of his **holy hill. Selah.**

```
Q  X  X  L  N  B  O  Y  C  I  N  C  Q  F  R
I  S  N  A  H  E  L  P  N  T  S  I  X  K  D
S  E  N  G  J  L  H  C  I  H  W  H  B  R  K
T  L  M  A  P  F  R  W  I  A  F  O  O  D  B
D  A  V  I  D  E  R  E  H  T  N  L  F  U  R
E  H  B  N  A  W  L  O  Y  I  K  Y  E  U  T
I  Y  H  S  I  D  H  B  M  L  L  C  P  D  R
R  M  E  T  A  M  S  H  U  U  I  L  D  K  D
C  D  H  H  A  L  E  O  U  O  H  T  M  C  V
Z  V  P  N  T  A  O  L  V  S  R  E  D  S  O
O  G  Y  H  R  S  T  M  S  E  T  T  X  S  L
H  E  A  D  B  P  N  A  T  S  E  N  I  M  Q
I  U  T  D  O  M  U  F  D  S  Q  Z  O  I  Z
G  U  B  S  Y  S  I  X  I  I  L  A  Z  P  L
Z  F  C  P  G  L  O  R  Y  V  T  H  Z  W  Q
```

*by John Hudson Tiner*

# BONUS TRIVIA

What type of tree surrounded a
man on a red horse in a vision
of the prophet Zechariah?

## *Isaiah 40:28–31*

Hast thou not **known**? hast thou not **heard**, that the **everlasting God**, the LORD, the **Creator** of the ends of the **earth, fainteth** not, neither is weary? there is no **searching** of his **understanding**. He **giveth power** to the faint; and to them that have no **might** he **increaseth** strength. Even the **youths** shall faint and be **weary**, and the **young men** shall utterly **fall**: but they that **wait** upon the LORD **shall renew** their **strength**; they shall mount up with **wings** as **eagles**; they shall **run**, and not be weary; and they shall **walk**, and **not faint**.

```
M O U I K S E F A I N T I Z C
R S G N I H C R A E S T Q U K
A D O C D O G L W I N G S L E
E W E R H E L H O J N G S U Q
N J F E B A R Z F Q N T W A V
Z J F A F R C S H I R W E K D
T L B S T T R U T E O D A T I
P O W E R H E S N A A Q R I H
Q R V T S F A G M X N R Y A T
W D O H M L T O I E H D D M Y
W N A J R H O L G V N M I O L
A L V E U E R V H N E J U N P
L B V U N Y N T T X U T M Q G
K E A G L E S E K Q H O H P P
R S Q W M P N V W S B T Y N G
```

*by David Austin*

# BONUS TRIVIA

What great king of Israel captured the
fortress of Zion from mocking Jebusites?

*David. (2 Samuel 5:6–8)*

BEZALEEL

CAPTURED

CHERUBIMS

DAVID

EKRON

ELI

EMERODS

FOUR RINGS

GLORY OF THE LORD

GOLD

HOPHNI

MERCY SEAT

MICE

OVERLAID

OXEN

PHILISTINES

PHINEHAS

SACRIFICING

SHEEP

SHITTIM WOOD

SOLOMON

STAVES

TEMPLE

TESTIMONY

WINGS

```
S G N I W P H I N E H A S Z A
L E L E E L A Z E B L T H W Q
A Y N O M I T S E T P I E C M
S M D P R J B R D C S P E N S
P X A Q H Y G A E B M I P T H
T H V S T F O U R R I N G S I
A O I O G V L F U C B O O D T
E P D L X M D P T A U R R O T
S H W O I E E R P H R K U R I
Y N A M X S N Q A M E E M E M
C I R O M N T V C I H L C M W
R T Y N Z W V I E C C P O E O
E E L P M E T O N E P D B R O
M S T A V E S O V E R L A I D
G N I C I F I R C A S W Q N K
```

*by Paul Kent*

# BONUS TRIVIA

What were Peter, James, and John
doing while Jesus was praying and
agonizing in Gethsemane?

*Luke 18:10–12*

Two men **went** up **into** the **temple** to pray; the one a Pharisee, and the other a publican. The **Pharisee stood** and **prayed thus with himself,** God, I **thank thee**, that I am not as **other** men are, **extortioners, unjust, adulterers,** or **even** as **this publican.** I **fast twice** in the **week,** I **give tithes** of all **that** I **possess.**

```
V  S  H  E  P  F  T  S  N  Q  N  T  A  H  T
P  M  R  N  N  L  W  H  J  T  F  S  F  D  M
E  H  G  E  E  A  I  V  D  E  Y  A  R  P  V
D  U  A  Z  N  V  C  Z  N  P  D  F  E  T  Q
D  X  D  R  N  O  E  I  S  U  W  F  H  H  R
L  R  N  I  I  A  I  E  L  Y  G  U  T  I  V
D  D  Y  O  N  S  H  T  S  B  S  F  O  S  E
D  Z  S  U  S  T  E  V  R  Y  U  W  H  V  F
R  L  S  R  I  R  O  E  H  O  W  P  I  Q  O
F  J  E  T  E  M  P  L  E  I  T  G  M  W  U
F  R  S  R  H  D  O  O  T  S  F  X  S  W  P
L  X  S  H  F  E  C  H  U  N  W  Z  E  R  V
B  Z  O  E  I  S  E  J  W  E  E  K  L  B  G
X  D  P  T  H  A  N  K  H  Q  Y  W  F  T  W
V  X  M  X  J  U  H  K  V  K  Z  Q  Q  Y  E
```

*by John Hudson Tiner*

# BONUS TRIVIA

What was the name of Ruth's
first husband, who died?

*Mahlon. (Ruth 4:10)*

371

*Luke 18:13–14*

And the **publican, standing afar** off, **would** not **lift** up so **much** as his **eyes unto heaven**, but **smote upon** his **breast, saying**, God be **merciful** to me a **sinner**. I **tell** you, **this** man **went down** to his **house justified rather than** the **other**: for **every** one that **exalteth** himself shall be **abased**; and he **that humbleth himself shall** be **exalted**.

```
D  B  X  M  L  F  D  M  M  D  R  K  S  R  P
A  S  U  A  O  L  V  E  E  Y  E  S  C  U  J
Z  M  T  B  B  W  U  M  I  Z  N  T  B  H  D
N  E  V  A  E  H  C  F  R  F  N  L  O  C  B
J  R  V  S  N  O  P  U  I  E  I  U  A  U  C
W  J  V  E  G  D  B  L  W  C  S  T  N  M  L
L  M  Z  D  R  C  I  D  A  E  R  M  S  S  T
L  T  G  S  A  Y  I  N  G  D  X  E  O  U  H
E  L  H  O  N  R  X  F  G  N  Z  X  M  T  J
T  E  A  A  E  X  A  L  T  E  D  A  E  Y  E
H  U  P  H  T  S  A  E  R  B  R  L  O  C  O
N  X  T  F  S  H  F  S  N  N  B  T  U  T  D
I  A  I  H  P  A  A  M  X  H  E  V  O  O
R  L  H  F  B  M  R  I  U  E  O  T  N  U  W
N  F  T  T  A  S  Y  H  R  J  T  H  I  S  N
```

*by John Hudson Tiner*

# BONUS TRIVIA

Who said, "Now, O Lord, take,
I beseech thee, my life from me; for it
is better for me to die than to live"?

### Psalm 102:1–4

*A Prayer of the **afflicted**, when he is **overwhelmed**, and **poureth** out his **complaint before** the LORD.*

Hear my **prayer**, O LORD, and let my cry **come** unto **thee**. **Hide** not thy **face from** me in the day when I am in **trouble; incline thine** ear **unto** me: in the day **when** I **call answer** me **speedily**. For my **days** are **consumed** like **smoke**, and my **bones** are **burned** as an **hearth**. My heart is **smitten**, and **withered like grass**; so **that** I **forget** to eat my **bread**.

```
F R O M C F W Q T R O U B L E
R B E F O R E T G V G Z R H H
E E M W N T H E E N C C E K Y
Y M O E S B X R H O E C A F G
A A C S U N W T M T C H D P O
R F A S M H A P B N E Y W V J
P R F Z E O L S U U C X D F B
G H S L D A K J R X A Y V O L
F T M Z I E U E N I L C N I F
D E H N R C R H E I L E K O S
D R T I M T T E D J S E R Y J
F U O B N R H E H F V G A H I
N O I L A E E A D T E D I H P
Z P V E F P N E T T I M S M L
A Q H T S R H J M A W W E N M
```

*by John Hudson Tiner*

## BONUS TRIVIA

What relative do the Proverbs say
a young man should call "wisdom"?

**Philippians 4:6–9**

Be careful for nothing; but in every thing by **prayer** and **supplication** with **thanksgiving** let your **requests** be **made known** unto God. And the **peace** of God, which **passeth** all **understanding**, shall keep your **hearts** and **minds** through <u>Christ Jesus</u>. Finally, brethren, **whatsoever things** are **true**, whatsoever things are **honest**, whatsoever things are **just**, whatsoever things are **pure**, whatsoever things are **lovely**, whatsoever things are of **good report**; if there be any **virtue**, and if there be any **praise**, think on these things. Those things, which ye have both **learned**, and **received**, and **heard**, and **seen** in me, do: and the God of peace shall be with you.

```
K  J  U  S  T  R  V  H  R  P  E  S  E  N  A
T  P  M  N  L  O  V  E  L  Y  E  M  D  K  L
W  U  R  K  D  I  C  A  E  E  I  G  H  O  J
U  R  E  A  R  E  Q  R  J  N  D  N  T  R  H
F  E  Q  T  I  W  R  D  D  P  O  B  H  E  O
Z  F  U  V  Q  S  H  S  R  I  O  A  A  P  N
N  E  E  S  V  Z  E  A  T  J  G  R  N  O  E
P  D  S  F  K  D  Y  A  T  A  T  T  K  R  S
B  A  T  T  U  E  C  O  M  S  N  D  S  T  T
I  Q  S  Q  R  I  V  F  X  A  O  D  G  A  W
M  O  H  S  L  E  A  R  N  E  D  E  I  M  J
T  L  M  P  E  C  A  E  P  L  V  E  V  N  V
J  R  P  P  B  T  H  I  N  G  S  U  I  E  G
Y  U  U  T  X  M  H  Q  K  N  O  W  N  K  R
S  U  S  E  J  T  S  I  R  H  C  Q  G  P  P
```

*by David Austin*

# BONUS TRIVIA

What king, the son of Solomon,
threatened to place his subjects
under a heavy yoke—and caused
many of the tribes of Israel to rebel?

Reboboam. (1 Kings 12:1–19)

## Jonah 2:1–3

Then **Jonah prayed** unto the LORD his God out of the **fish's** belly, and **said**, I cried by **reason** of **mine affliction** unto the LORD, and he heard me; out of the **belly** of **hell cried** I, and thou **heardest** my **voice**. For **thou hadst cast** me **into** the **deep,** in the **midst** of the **seas;** and the **floods compassed** me **about**: all thy **billows** and thy **waves** passed **over** me.

```
P  S  H  S  I  F  C  P  C  F  L  C  N  I  F
Y  L  L  E  B  C  L  Y  J  O  P  A  B  Y  O
A  T  M  C  A  E  H  V  F  D  E  R  K  H  P
F  F  U  C  C  R  I  E  D  I  E  S  E  T  H
R  Y  F  O  F  V  D  E  E  A  F  L  O  V  X
D  W  C  L  B  X  Y  E  S  S  L  F  Q  U  U
Q  J  A  Q  I  A  U  O  S  W  O  V  E  R  N
M  X  S  V  R  C  N  E  A  T  O  D  F  L  P
Q  I  T  P  E  C  T  X  P  M  D  L  R  V  U
N  R  K  E  D  S  H  I  M  Z  S  F  L  O  D
E  I  M  Q  D  V  C  J  O  N  A  H  H  I  L
S  U  M  I  N  T  O  N  C  N  A  T  X  C  B
U  S  M  H  N  U  B  E  F  D  L  C  K  E  A
E  K  X  P  E  E  D  H  S  A  E  S  C  E  L
W  B  M  A  V  V  B  T  X  O  T  T  O  Z  J
```

*by John Hudson Tiner*

# BONUS TRIVIA

How many of those "redeemed from
the earth" stood with the Lamb on
Mount Zion in John's Revelation?

**Mark 16:19–20**

So **then after** the Lord had **spoken unto** them, he was **received** up **into heaven**, and sat on the **right hand** of God. And **they went forth**, and **preached every where**, the **Lord working** with **them**, and **confirming** the **word with signs following**. Amen.

```
T H G I R U A X T R N R C W A
W F A E V E R Y X W E O A A Y
U K M V G A C Z L D N Q D J N
M R X W A F T E R F L P W L R
X I V P U H E O I R P O M I Z
R B S G E S W R I V R C X L F
T A H M N E M F G K E Z E P R
G Q T G J I I G I X A D W I W
M O I Z N E W N W X C N E S T
I S W G E D G O T L H W R N X
A D I W V S T U L O E R E J B
X B Y Q A H L N Q L D K H N Y
F M C E E T O T R E O N W P T
A M E N H T R O F P L F A O H
J X J P B T D S S F S W R H C
```

*by John Hudson Tiner*

## BONUS TRIVIA

What was the first name of the apostle
known as "the zealot" or "Zelotes"?

Simon. (Luke 6:12–16)

# PUZZLE 86 —
## DESCENDANTS OF DAVID

*Matthew 1:6–16*

| | |
|---|---|
| ABIA | JOSAPHAT |
| ABIUD | JORAM |
| ACHAZ | JOATHAM |
| ACHIM | JOSEPH |
| AMON | JOSIAS |
| ASA | MANASSES |
| AZOR | MATTHAN |
| ELEAZAR | OZIAS |
| ELIAKIM | ROBOAM |
| ELIUD | SADOC |
| EZEKIAS | SALATHIEL |
| JACOB | SOLOMON |
| JECHONIAS | ZOROBABEL |
| JESUS | |

```
R  C  P  J  E  S  C  M  E  L  I  U  D  S  T
S  T  M  E  D  K  J  Z  A  H  C  A  A  U  L
W  K  E  E  G  J  H  O  S  N  C  L  R  S  O
J  U  Q  J  O  F  E  B  A  H  A  Z  E  E  F
Q  A  V  S  Z  L  J  C  I  T  F  S  T  J  K
D  T  E  M  E  B  T  M  H  J  H  U  S  O  D
I  P  Q  A  L  Q  L  I  J  O  R  A  M  E  V
H  F  Z  T  I  X  E  A  Z  S  N  B  M  W  S
M  A  O  T  A  L  B  I  H  I  M  I  J  L  A
R  M  L  H  K  V  A  B  I  A  V  U  A  J  D
P  B  U  A  I  S  B  B  Y  S  T  D  X  S  O
M  Q  Z  N  M  J  O  S  A  P  H  A  T  K  C
Q  O  P  P  R  C  R  O  B  O  A  M  M  S  Q
R  W  M  P  A  N  O  M  O  L  O  S  N  O  V
B  T  N  J  G  E  Z  E  K  I  A  S  Z  T  N
```

*by David Austin*

# BONUS TRIVIA

Which king installed
waterworks in Jerusalem?

Hezekiah (2 Kings 20:20)

## Psalm 8:3–6

When I **consider** thy **heavens,** the work of thy **fingers,** the **moon** and the **stars, which** thou hast **ordained;** **what** is man, that thou art **mindful** of him? and the son of man, **that** thou **visitest** him? For thou hast made him a **little lower than** the **angels,** and hast **crowned** him **with glory** and **honour.** Thou **madest** him to **have dominion over** the **works** of thy **hands; thou hast** put all **things under** his **feet.**

```
Q C R O F H N N I H G W Y W G
L I T T L E O O E V A H C D Q
U B X Z E O V C R O W N E D X
F L J Z M E W H O Z H Q D I I
D D L H U X F E I N A D X S S
N I S L E G N A R S S Z H M O
I O O M G S R V R T T I B R W
M D I L G W R E I I V Y D R K
R U O N O H G N D S P A J E S
M R I R I N B S T N I S W V R
Y H K S I M U H S N U T H O C
T S C F O O O G E O C A E G X
A T M I H P A D D O F R N S N
H G K T H A N T A H T S U K T
W I T H V W W M M V V A Y W Y
```

*by John Hudson Tiner*

# BONUS TRIVIA

In what Roman province were
the seven churches located?

# PUZZLE 88 — DAVID PRAYS FOR REFUGE

*Psalm 142:5–7*

I **cried** unto **thee**, O LORD: I **said**, Thou art my **refuge** and my **portion** in the **land** of the **living**. **Attend unto** my cry; for I am **brought very** low: **deliver** me **from** my **persecutors**; for **they** are **stronger than** I. **Bring** my **soul** out of **prison, that** I may **praise** thy **name**: the **righteous shall compass** me **about**; for **thou shalt deal bountifully with** me.

```
K  D  Q  O  A  T  T  E  N  D  P  R  Y  P  P
Y  E  H  T  I  F  R  O  M  E  G  U  F  E  R
E  Z  G  N  I  V  I  L  R  D  E  D  C  M  A
D  V  U  U  D  T  Q  S  E  S  O  H  P  O  I
A  E  B  I  R  B  E  I  T  A  D  N  T  B  S
G  L  A  O  W  C  R  R  E  F  B  O  A  T  E
S  S  P  L  U  C  O  M  P  A  S  S  H  D  R
O  U  H  T  F  N  A  Z  B  T  D  I  T  R  O
V  J  O  A  G  N  T  O  W  B  R  R  X  C  H
Z  R  C  E  L  G  U  I  R  R  E  P  O  Z  V
S  U  R  X  T  T  I  F  O  V  Z  L  L  G
H  H  O  I  F  H  N  A  B  U  I  K  V  A  X
E  N  A  H  T  G  G  R  V  G  L  L  E  N  B
S  O  U  L  T  R  B  I  N  H  E  L  R  D  J
V  V  U  B  L  A  U  N  R  T  D  X  Y  U  S
```

*by John Hudson Tiner*

# BONUS TRIVIA

Whom did Paul instruct to counsel the
"rich in this world" to trust in the living
God rather than their "uncertain riches"?

# PUZZLE 89 — DAVID'S PRAYER OF REPENTANCE

### Psalm 51:1–3

*To the **chief Musician**, A **Psalm** of **David**,
when Nathan the **prophet came** unto him,
after he had **gone** in to <u>Bath-sheba</u>.*

**Have mercy upon** me, O God, according to thy **lovingkindness: according unto** the **multitude** of thy **tender mercies blot** out my **transgressions. Wash** me **thoroughly** from **mine iniquity,** and **cleanse** me **from** my sin. For I **acknowledge** my transgressions: and my sin is **ever before** me.

```
S  B  A  T  H  S  H  E  B  A  X  A  E  Y  U
N  S  O  R  Y  T  I  U  Q  I  N  I  G  J  R
Y  L  E  A  H  J  R  E  D  D  A  N  E  E  G
B  L  C  N  C  N  M  E  R  C  I  E  S  V  K
E  G  H  S  D  K  V  Y  V  D  C  V  N  A  W
C  W  I  G  C  N  N  F  R  E  I  L  A  H  D
I  A  E  R  U  T  I  O  A  X  S  M  E  D  L
C  K  F  E  P  O  C  K  W  V  U  N  L  M  A
G  W  M  S  R  C  R  P  G  L  M  N  C  N  O
N  A  A  S  A  O  R  O  T  N  E  E  T  G  D
C  L  M  I  N  E  F  I  H  A  I  D  R  O  T
M  E  K  O  D  X  T  E  D  T  F  V  G  C  Q
O  G  O  N  E  U  I  F  B  H  Q  T  O  E  Y
R  X  E  S  D  E  K  H  S  A  W  G  E  L  H
F  T  T  E  H  P  O  R  P  N  O  P  U  R  M
```

*by John Hudson Tiner*

## BONUS TRIVIA

What type of tree does the
love-smitten woman of the Song
of Solomon compare her man to?

# PUZZLE 90 — SUFFERING SERVANT

*Isaiah 53:5–7*

But he was **wounded** for our **transgressions**, he was **bruised** for our **iniquities**: the **chastisement** of our **peace** was **upon** him; and **with** his **stripes** we are **healed**. All we **like** sheep have **gone astray**; we **have turned every** one to his own way; and the LORD **hath laid** on him the **iniquity** of us all. He was **oppressed**, and he was **afflicted**, yet he **opened** not his mouth: he is **brought** as a **lamb** to the **slaughter**, and as a **sheep before** her **shearers** is **dumb**, so he **openeth** not his **mouth**.

```
O  S  H  E  A  R  E  R  S  Z  Y  D  D  Q  P
Q  P  E  E  H  S  B  R  N  A  R  M  I  E  J
S  R  E  A  T  O  R  O  O  F  E  L  A  M  B
H  E  C  N  F  U  O  S  I  F  V  C  L  I  P
P  T  I  H  E  Z  U  N  S  L  E  A  V  O  G
H  H  U  T  A  T  G  Z  S  I  U  B  P  U  D
V  G  W  O  I  S  H  Y  E  C  Z  P  V  R  E
C  U  H  I  M  U  T  D  R  T  R  D  O  K  K
B  A  D  Q  T  I  Q  I  G  E  E  L  I  N  V
I  L  E  N  U  H  G  I  S  D  E  L  A  E  H
B  S  S  Q  R  O  S  S  N  E  P  H  T  A  H
L  M  I  F  N  X  E  U  A  I  M  N  V  S  V
B  N  U  E  E  D  O  R  R  O  P  E  N  E  D
I  F  R  D  D  W  A  S  T  R  A  Y  N  N  T
K  P  B  K  L  H  D  K  S  E  P  I  R  T  S
```

*by John Hudson Tiner*

## Bonus Trivia

What kind of stone, according to the
apostle Paul, did God lay in Zion?

*Mark 14:35–36*

And he **went forward** a **little,** and **fell** on the **ground,** and **prayed that,** if it **were** possible, the **hour might pass** from him. And he **said,** Abba, **Father,** all **things** are **possible unto thee; take away this** cup **from** me: **nevertheless** not what I **will,** but **what thou wilt**.

```
Y  R  F  M  W  Q  B  Q  Q  E  L  W  I  L  L
V  C  D  O  E  M  R  S  P  E  I  S  I  C  K
V  G  M  B  R  J  R  A  R  Y  E  T  A  R  E
D  B  T  N  E  W  S  M  A  G  T  H  G  I  M
L  T  E  G  E  S  A  U  Y  L  C  M  T  A  D
S  S  E  L  E  H  T  R  E  V  E  N  A  S  S
U  P  E  K  B  C  S  P  D  J  S  D  H  F  C
O  J  T  T  L  I  W  D  A  E  G  D  W  R  R
X  L  L  D  H  R  S  X  J  V  N  T  U  O  F
D  X  L  T  C  N  L  S  C  U  I  O  H  M  Z
N  Q  E  O  S  U  B  C  O  T  H  A  T  A  Z
U  L  F  A  T  H  E  R  Y  P  T  H  W  S  L
N  K  O  Q  Z  N  G  R  K  G  Z  A  Z  I  M
T  T  U  K  N  V  U  O  H  T  Y  E  K  O  B
W  Q  W  V  F  B  Z  D  S  H  B  C  B  E  W
```

*by John Hudson Tiner*

# Bonus Trivia

What king of Israel solved a child
custody dispute by proposing that
the child be cut in half?

# PUZZLE 92 — VERBS FROM THE PROVERBS

ANSWERETH

DELIVER

DESPISETH

DESTROYETH

DWELL

EXALTETH

FINDETH

GATHERETH

GOETH

INCREASETH

LABOURETH

LEAVETH

LOVETH

MAKETH

PERCEIVE

PRESERVE

PURSUETH

RECEIVE

REFUSETH

REJOICETH

REWARDETH

SEEMETH

TRUST

TURNETH

UNDERSTAND

WALKETH

```
M  I  D  V  U  R  T  N  E  M  T  S  U  R  T
H  T  E  D  N  I  F  F  A  L  T  H  G  E  E
Y  H  L  W  L  D  W  K  E  A  E  T  O  C  R
E  V  I  E  C  R  E  P  H  B  O  E  I  E  J
U  D  V  L  Q  T  R  S  J  O  F  N  B  I  W
P  Z  E  L  H  E  D  F  T  U  C  R  Q  V  A
U  L  R  S  S  A  N  V  G  R  R  U  Z  E  L
R  E  J  E  P  F  A  A  E  E  O  T  K  X  K
S  A  R  D  G  I  T  A  W  T  T  Y  S  A  E
U  V  B  O  T  H  S  A  L  H  U  O  E  L  T
E  E  E  D  E  E  R  E  J  O  I  C  E  T  H
T  T  I  R  T  D  E  Q  T  Q  V  V  M  E  H
H  H  E  H  E  F  D  X  A  H  W  E  E  T  M
O  T  H  T  M  A  N  S  W  E  R  E  T  H  J
H  L  H  R  E  F  U  S  E  T  H  M  H  H  L
```

*by David Austin*

# Bonus Trivia

Which king failed to give glory
to God and was struck dead by
an angel and eaten by worms?

*Genesis 32:9–11*

And **Jacob** said, O God of my father **Abraham**, and God of my **father Isaac**, the LORD which **saidst** unto me, **Return** unto thy **country**, and to thy **kindred**, and I will **deal** well with thee: I am not **worthy** of the **least** of all the **mercies**, and of all the **truth**, which **thou** hast **shewed** unto thy **servant**; for with my **staff** I **passed over** this **Jordan**; and now I am **become** two **bands**. **Deliver** me, I **pray thee**, from the hand of my **brother**, from the **hand** of Esau: for I **fear** him, **lest** he **will** come and **smite** me, and the **mother** with the **children**.

```
L  M  F  A  P  S  B  C  H  L  R  F  N  E  L
D  N  B  R  O  T  H  E  R  R  E  D  R  E  U
E  E  A  W  C  I  S  H  E  A  V  A  V  G  P
A  Y  R  D  L  E  X  H  Q  K  O  R  S  J  G
C  B  B  D  R  E  T  U  R  N  W  E  D  T  C
O  P  R  V  N  O  J  E  N  S  I  V  N  C  Y
U  E  A  A  M  I  J  C  T  C  L  I  A  E  V
N  N  O  Y  H  F  K  A  R  N  L  L  B  E  U
T  B  S  H  J  A  F  E  T  L  A  E  D  S  R
R  E  H  T  A  F  M  L  G  T  S  D  I  A  S
Y  C  U  R  C  N  U  J  I  H  E  E  E  U  N
C  O  I  O  O  U  D  B  E  S  T  F  E  A  I
K  M  F  W  B  V  J  W  S  S  A  U  O  H  T
W  E  S  M  I  T  E  A  E  U  E  A  R  H  T
R  U  L  O  R  D  P  L  K  Y  R  J  C  T  Q
```

*by John Hudson Tiner*

## BONUS TRIVIA

Who ministered to Jesus
after Satan left him?

# PUZZLE 94 — HOW TO LIVE FOREVER

*1 John 2:14–15, 17*

I have written unto you, **fathers**, because ye have **known** him that is **from** the **beginning**. I have **written unto** you, **young** men, **because** ye are **strong**, and the **word** of God abideth in you, and ye **have overcome** the **wicked** one. Love not the world, **neither** the **things** that are in the world. If any man love the world, the **love** of the Father is not in him. . . . And the **world passeth away**, and the **lust thereof**: but he **that doeth** the **will** of God **abideth** for **ever**.

```
N  M  J  V  E  H  K  D  R  E  V  E  X  Z  Q
S  E  W  C  G  R  Q  E  R  T  V  G  T  Z  Q
J  O  I  T  U  O  V  K  N  O  W  N  X  L  J
B  V  M  T  H  T  C  C  L  A  W  A  Y  U  X
S  E  Q  O  H  I  P  I  H  T  E  D  I  B  A
O  R  G  O  A  E  N  W  T  H  E  R  E  O  F
V  C  E  I  P  G  R  G  E  J  X  E  Q  P  R
H  O  B  H  N  I  L  S  S  L  A  P  T  G  O
L  M  W  U  T  N  U  F  S  Y  U  F  A  B  M
H  E  O  T  Y  A  I  I  A  V  N  S  H  G  X
V  Y  E  H  C  Q  F  N  P  S  T  W  T  O  G
K  N  A  E  T  B  M  Y  G  N  O  R  T  S  P
Y  V  B  O  X  E  B  H  T  R  X  G  E  K  W
E  E  Z  V  K  A  O  L  L  I  W  Z  E  M  Z
H  H  R  T  F  Z  K  D  O  Z  C  G  F  N  J
```

*by John Hudson Tiner*

# BONUS TRIVIA

Who wrote that the purpose of
the law was to give "knowledge
of sin" and establish guilt?

# PUZZLE 95 — WISDOM OR WEALTH

## *2 Chronicles 1:7–12*

In that night did God **appear** unto **Solomon**, and said unto him, **Ask** what I shall **give thee**. And Solomon said unto God, Thou hast shewed great mercy unto David my father, and hast **made** me to **reign** in his stead. Now, O LORD God, let thy **promise** unto David my father be **established**: for thou hast made me king over a **people** like the dust of the earth in **multitude**. Give me now **wisdom** and **knowledge**, that I may go out and come in before this people: for who can **judge** this thy people, that is so great? And God said to Solomon, **Because** this was in thine **heart**, and thou hast not asked **riches**, **wealth**, or **honour**, nor the life of thine enemies, neither yet hast asked **long life**; but hast asked wisdom and knowledge for thyself, that thou mayest judge my people, over whom I have made thee king: wisdom and knowledge is **granted** unto thee; and I will give thee riches, and wealth, and honour, such as none of the **kings** have had that have been **before** thee, neither shall there any **after** thee have the like.

| V | O | S | H | K | A | S | C | M | E | T | L | U | L | R |
|---|---|---|---|---|---|---|---|---|---|---|---|---|---|---|
| L | A | B | E | E | M | A | D | E | T | I | J | O | J | U |
| Q | J | B | E | C | A | U | S | E | F | B | Z | F | Q | A |
| V | Z | E | J | S | F | R | K | O | T | D | T | K | B | T |
| U | J | F | K | O | T | D | T | I | L | N | N | Q | Q | V |
| R | U | O | N | O | H | A | F | M | X | O | A | P | A | W |
| M | D | R | O | W | P | H | B | U | W | M | M | R | M | J |
| L | G | E | P | P | E | M | L | L | V | O | V | O | G | J |
| P | E | R | E | T | F | A | E | T | I | D | B | M | N | U |
| Y | T | A | O | X | M | D | L | I | K | S | G | I | V | E |
| Q | R | K | P | Q | G | I | O | T | P | I | H | S | R | P |
| R | S | Q | L | E | F | W | N | U | H | W | N | E | M | P |
| N | V | B | E | E | T | N | G | D | G | E | I | G | D | Z |
| T | E | F | P | R | I | C | H | E | S | G | E | S | S | I |
| B | X | V | V | C | J | E | L | L | N | V | W | O | B | M |

*by David Austin*

# BONUS TRIVIA

Who was the surviving member
of King Saul's family to whom
David showed kindness?

*Mark 6:3–5*

Is not **this** the **carpenter**, the son of **Mary**, the **brother** of **James**, and **Joses**, and of **Juda**, and **Simon**? and are not his **sisters** here with us? And **they were offended** at him. But **Jesus said unto** them, A **prophet** is not **without honour**, but in his own **country**, and **among** his own kin, and in his own **house**. And he **could there** do no **mighty work**, **save that** he **laid** his **hands upon** a few **sick folk**, and **healed them**.

```
U  M  U  P  Q  G  Z  I  R  F  K  T  M  O  U
V  O  F  D  E  L  A  E  H  S  J  D  D  X  A
Y  B  F  E  C  N  T  P  H  E  E  S  A  E  T
R  R  W  F  O  N  R  R  T  S  S  D  I  A  S
T  J  A  M  E  S  H  O  N  O  U  R  H  G  N
N  U  I  P  V  N  J  P  T  J  S  T  N  S  G
U  S  R  M  A  S  D  H  P  G  K  D  S  N  M
O  A  E  E  S  M  I  E  Y  Q  J  I  N  W  X
C  C  K  S  H  S  O  T  D  C  S  B  K  A  A
S  O  I  G  U  T  U  M  Y  T  H  G  I  M  H
N  C  U  T  W  O  O  A  E  X  W  W  O  R  K
K  P  L  L  H  Y  H  R  B  O  T  N  U  F  A
L  X  A  T  D  E  S  Y  B  Z  G  H  O  T  P
V  U  I  R  P  H  R  Z  B  A  H  L  E  P  D
U  W  D  M  L  T  W  E  R  E  K  Z  A  M  U
```

*by John Hudson Tiner*

# Bonus Trivia

Who was the first apostle
chosen by Jesus?

*Andrew. (John 1:40–41)*

403

*Nehemiah 1:4–5*

And it **came** to **pass, when** I **heard these words**, that I sat **down** and **wept,** and **mourned certain days,** and **fasted,** and **prayed before** the God of heaven, and **said,** I **beseech thee,** O LORD God of **heaven,** the **great** and **terrible** God, that **keepeth covenant** and **mercy** for **them that love** him and **observe** his **commandments. . . .**

```
S T H E M H D M L V C L R L K
Y F E W D R O L D B A A E O D
A W H R X U W Q S S E H M N S
D E Y A R P N Q B S S E I E S
N F T N D I U D E T S A F V R
K D E N M P B H S W T R P A Y
H D H Y A E T L E R H D X E J
C O M M A N D M E N T S I H T
O B S E R V E C C A E A M P M
R X F L J M G V H W P F E W S
C E H H Q B E F O R E W A R S
C W C T I O A R W C E E H T G
Q C R S A I D A C V K Y S A N
Q T L A K S Z P O Y J W X H U
X Z W O B F C L I J R X I T D
```

*by John Hudson Tiner*

# BONUS TRIVIA

What animal tried to avoid
an angel three times?

### Psalm 140:4–7

**Keep** me, O Lord, from the **hands** of the **wicked**; **preserve** me **from** the **violent** man; who have **purposed** to **overthrow** my **goings**. The **proud** have hid a **snare** for me, and **cords**; they have **spread** a net by the **wayside**; **they have** set **gins** for me. **Selah.** I **said unto** the Lord, Thou art my God: **hear** the **voice** of my **supplications**, O Lord. O God the Lord, the **strength** of my **salvation, thou hast covered** my **head** in the day of **battle**.

| | | | | | | | | | | | | | | |
|---|---|---|---|---|---|---|---|---|---|---|---|---|---|---|
| F | T | Y | T | L | J | G | N | G | G | I | N | S | W | J |
| G | O | I | N | G | S | J | T | O | T | N | U | A | X | F |
| U | N | D | E | K | C | I | W | H | V | P | R | T | P | L |
| H | N | R | L | X | G | K | O | W | P | J | K | A | M | W |
| O | O | O | O | K | Q | U | U | L | R | P | E | U | V | M |
| X | V | L | I | Y | E | J | I | D | E | R | E | V | O | C |
| P | J | E | V | T | V | C | X | K | S | O | P | R | H | S |
| D | V | E | R | R | A | E | H | E | E | U | F | T | H | R |
| A | R | O | R | T | H | V | S | A | R | D | G | A | E | Y |
| E | C | H | I | A | H | E | L | P | V | N | N | L | T | P |
| R | G | O | A | C | N | R | O | A | E | D | T | H | P | B |
| P | N | C | R | L | E | S | O | R | S | T | E | T | D | H |
| S | A | I | D | D | E | X | T | W | A | Y | S | I | D | E |
| C | G | G | E | D | S | S | F | B | Q | A | M | U | K | A |
| P | F | X | V | E | E | P | R | M | H | J | F | J | P | D |

*by John Hudson Tiner*

# Bonus Trivia

Who was the sorcerer at Paphos who
was struck blind by Paul for his heresy?

### 2 Chronicles 6:40–42

Now, my God, let, I **beseech thee**, thine **eyes** be **open**, and let thine **ears** be **attent unto** the **prayer that** is **made** in **this** place. Now **therefore arise**, O LORD God, **into** thy **resting place, thou**, and the ark of thy **strength**: let thy **priests**, O LORD God, be **clothed with salvation**, and let thy **saints rejoice** in **goodness**. O LORD God, **turn** not **away** the **face** of **thine anointed**: remember the **mercies** of **David** thy **servant**.

```
N  W  I  L  U  R  E  S  T  I  N  G  R  G  Q
R  S  N  N  O  Q  T  H  I  S  N  Y  S  K  B
R  J  T  A  Z  R  E  J  O  I  C  E  A  N  I
E  O  O  R  R  R  D  C  G  B  I  T  I  W  J
B  S  T  S  E  I  R  P  A  C  T  P  N  N  A
M  N  F  F  V  N  S  M  R  E  R  R  T  I  T
E  V  O  A  K  E  G  E  N  G  T  A  S  U  N
M  R  D  I  G  P  M  T  Q  O  N  Y  F  O  B
E  D  E  H  T  O  L  C  H  O  A  E  N  H  A
R  C  T  N  T  A  H  T  I  D  V  R  C  T  N
F  I  A  H  I  P  V  N  S  N  R  E  A  R  S
W  A  P  L  E  H  T  L  I  E  E  K  U  I  Y
P  B  C  Y  P  E  T  Y  A  S  S  T  X  D  L
F  H  E  E  D  A  M  R  E  S  H  D  H  K  V
Q  S  T  U  E  P  J  B  E  U  S  K  K  R  V
```

*by John Hudson Tiner*

# BONUS TRIVIA

What is the name of the river east of the
Jordan where Jacob wrestled with God?

*Luke 15:11–32*

BELLY
CERTAIN
CITIZEN
COUNTRY
DIVIDED
FAIN
FALLETH
FAR
FATHER
FEED
FIELDS
FILLED
GATHERED
GIVE
GOODS
HUSKS

JOURNEY
LIVING
MIGHTY
PORTION
RIOTOUS
SONS
SPENT
SUBSTANCE
SWINE
TOGETHER
TOOK
TWO
WANT
WASTED
YOUNGER

```
J P Y P E C N A T S B U S W F
O G O O T I G Y R D Z E R D A
U O U R P T Y T D E M A L B I
R O N T F I T H L D F S D L N
N D G I W Z O G R I R U E J Y
E S E O N E O I Z V J O R H R
Y Z R N R N K M Q I T T E A E
E S D L E I F C W D G O H O H
N U I A S X O A E N M I T E T
I O U K O U S L I F L R A V E
W L S S N T L V G A A L G I G
S U O T E I I S P E N T A G O
H N R D F L F A L L E T H F T
S Y S T N A W I F D E E F E F
C E R T A I N R O W T N R B R
```

*by N. Teri Grottke*

# BONUS TRIVIA

Who grieved at the death of her brother
and appealed to Jesus for help?

*2 Samuel 22:47–49*

The LORD **liveth**; and **blessed** be my rock; and **exalted** be the God of the **rock** of my **salvation**. It is God that **avengeth** me, and that bringeth **down** the **people under** me. And that **bringeth** me **forth** from **mine enemies**: thou **also** hast **lifted** me up on **high above them that rose** up **against** me: **thou hast delivered** me **from** the **violent** man.

```
G P M A J H A S T B R O B F X
F J D C X L Q P C B O H M N E
U D D G S L L N C Q T H O U I
D E S O R M K I M D A N R F Z
U N G T W M P C O B H S F H F
R A G A I N S T O B T H T U D
P I B S V D D V R R G R S U E
Q V A V J E E I V I O L E N T
H E T D S E N R H F Z N I D F
S X H S R G D G E N M A M E I
M A E V E O D V E V D I E R L
O L M T S A L V A T I O N H D
B T H T E V I L C D H L E E Y
H E L P O E P G S L S F E S Y
C D F H M E G M V S O M V D F
```

*by John Hudson Tiner*

# BONUS TRIVIA

The second temple, completed by returned
exiles, is known by what name?

Zerubbabel's. (Zechariah 4:9)

# CROSSWORD ANSWERS

PUZZLE 1

PUZZLE 2

PUZZLE 3

PUZZLE 4

PUZZLE 5

PUZZLE 6

**PUZZLE 7**

**PUZZLE 8**

**PUZZLE 9**

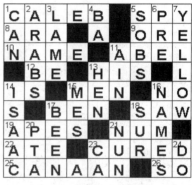

**PUZZLE 10**

**PUZZLE 11**

**PUZZLE 12**

415

**PUZZLE 13**

**PUZZLE 14**

**PUZZLE 15**

**PUZZLE 16**

**PUZZLE 17**

**PUZZLE 18**

**PUZZLE 19**

**PUZZLE 20**

**PUZZLE 21**

**PUZZLE 22**

**PUZZLE 23**

**PUZZLE 24**

**PUZZLE 25**

**PUZZLE 26**

**PUZZLE 27**

**PUZZLE 28**

**PUZZLE 29**

**PUZZLE 30**

**PUZZLE 31**

**PUZZLE 32**

**PUZZLE 33**

**PUZZLE 34**

**PUZZLE 35**

**PUZZLE 36**

419

PUZZLE 37

PUZZLE 38

PUZZLE 39

PUZZLE 40

PUZZLE 41

PUZZLE 42

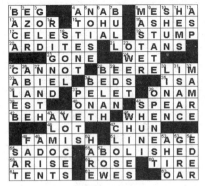

Puzzle 43

Puzzle 44

Puzzle 45

Puzzle 46

Puzzle 47

Puzzle 48

**PUZZLE 49**

**PUZZLE 50**

**PUZZLE 51**

**PUZZLE 52**

**PUZZLE 53**

**PUZZLE 54**

PUZZLE 55

PUZZLE 56

PUZZLE 57

PUZZLE 58

PUZZLE 59

PUZZLE 60

**PUZZLE 61**

```
K I N D S   C U P S   A B B A
I S A A C   A N A H   D O E R
S H U N A M M I T E   J A D A
H I M   L I E T H   B U N A H
      B E L L Y   E A R E D
C H   U S E     U T T E R
R E L Y   C A L A H   G A T
A R A   R A H A M   E R R
G E N   H U R A M   E S A U
    G H O S T   U E L   M E
  B U I L T   B E S A I
R E A D Y   F E V E R   S A W
U R G E   M A G I S T R A T E
L E E S   A M A L   H O R E B
E A S T   N E T S   Y E A R S
```

**PUZZLE 62**

```
V I S I T       H E A P S
I S H T O B   R   H A S R A H
A R I S A I   E   E N T I R E
L A M   H E L P I N G   S E M
S E E R   R E A I A   S I N A
    L A E L   D I M   R E N T
  S H A U L   R   R I N G S
      S C U M   R A G S
R E C O R D   R   T H E I R S
A L O N E   G A T   T   M A W
M A R   O A T H S   S A V E
A S P S   S H E E T   A G E E
H A S U P H A   R A I M E N T
  H E A R E R   E R R O R S
    S H O A       E A S Y
```

**PUZZLE 63**

```
M A R T   S H E E P   A B E L
E L A H   P A L L U   M E N E
L I V E   A V O I D   A N O N
E K E R   N E T H E R M O S T
A E N O N     H U N T
    F O E S     S H O B A B
U S E   S C A B     U R G E
C O N F E C T I O N A R I E S
A D D I     D A U B   M E T
L I S T E N     K N I T
    S A L A     B A T H E
J I P H T H A H E L   S H E N
U L A I   A S I D E   T I M E
S A I D   S H A G E   E N A M
T I R E   H A N E S   D E N Y
```

**PUZZLE 64**

```
B A S A L   C U O M O   A L I
A G A P E   A R R A U   R I D
D A V I D S F I R S T W I F E
E P E E   H E M   E L O D E A
    C O E     T R A M
J E Z E B E L S H U S B A N D
A V I   S T A T E   T I M O R
R A P T   S N E R D   S I R E
I D I O M   D E M O N   S S A
B E N J A M I N S M O T H E R
    U R I S     I T O
A R E N A S   D A N   D A R K
J A C O B S S E C O N D S O N
A S H   O I L E R   O L I V E
R H O   U S A R E   R E N E W
```

**PUZZLE 65**

```
  N O B   N I N E   T H U S
G E R A   A Z A L   H A N A N
A B D A   A R O D   A L I K E
L A E L   S I M E O N I T E S
    T R E E S   I S A   E S T
      N O N   T R A P
A S S I G N E D   B A K E R
S I E G E   T I P   A L I V E
K N E A D   M U S T E R E D
      L I C K   A T E
A M I     O I L   A D D E D
C O M P E L L E S T   O N E S
T O L A D   L A K E   E S A U
S N A R E   E V I L   R U L E
  S H E N   D E N Y   S E T
```

**PUZZLE 66**

```
      S A L A   L A D E D
  R E T A I N   A M A Z E D
R E T I R E D   M O R E V E R
E P H R O N   R   S T R I V E
F U N   N   R O T   S   S E E
E T A M   R O M A N   S E L L
R E N E W E D   R O B E   O
  D   A H A     T E A   P
      R O P E   F E D
    M   A   E D E R   A D A H
R I C H   R O L E   N E B A I
A S A   A   M I S S   F I N D
H E R E S   I S H I   I D D O
A R E L I   T H E N   L A E L
M Y S I A   E A R S   E N D S
```

424

PUZZLE 67

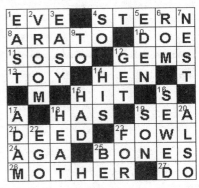

PUZZLE 68

PUZZLE 69

PUZZLE 70

PUZZLE 71

PUZZLE 72

**PUZZLE 73**

**PUZZLE 74**

**PUZZLE 75**

**PUZZLE 76**

**PUZZLE 77**

**PUZZLE 78**

**PUZZLE 79**

**PUZZLE 80**

**PUZZLE 81**

**PUZZLE 82**

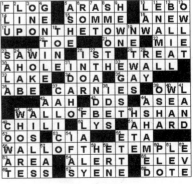

**PUZZLE 83**

**PUZZLE 84**

**PUZZLE 85**

**PUZZLE 86**

**PUZZLE 87**

**PUZZLE 88**

**PUZZLE 89**

**PUZZLE 90**

**Puzzle 91**

**Puzzle 92**

**Puzzle 93**

**Puzzle 94**

**Puzzle 95**

**Puzzle 96**

**PUZZLE 97**

**PUZZLE 98**

**PUZZLE 99**

**PUZZLE 100**

**PUZZLE 101**

# WORDSEARCH ANSWERS

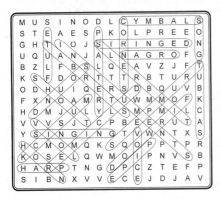

**PUZZLE 1**

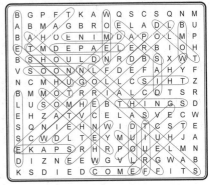

**PUZZLE 2**

**PUZZLE 3**

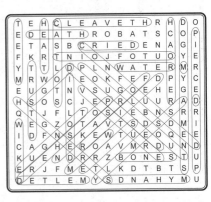

**PUZZLE 4**

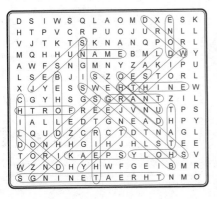

**PUZZLE 5**

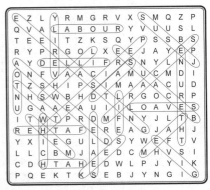

**PUZZLE 6**

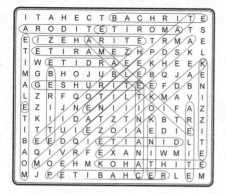

**PUZZLE 7**

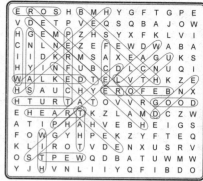

**PUZZLE 8**

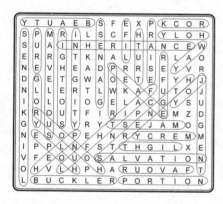

**PUZZLE 9**

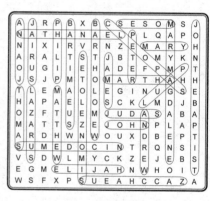

**PUZZLE 10**

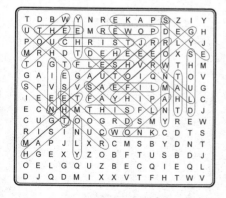

**PUZZLE 11**

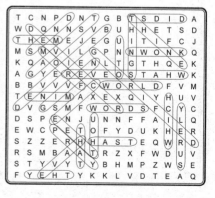

**PUZZLE 12**

432

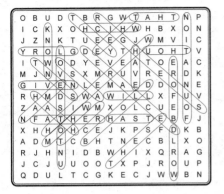

**PUZZLE 13**

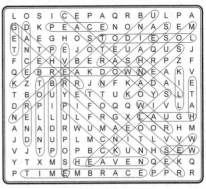

**PUZZLE 14**

**PUZZLE 15**

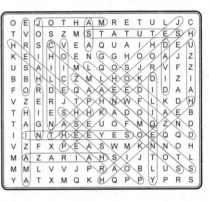

**PUZZLE 16**

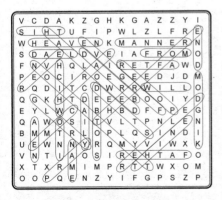

**PUZZLE 17**

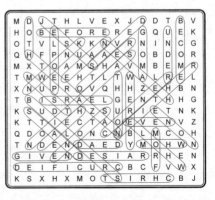

**PUZZLE 18**

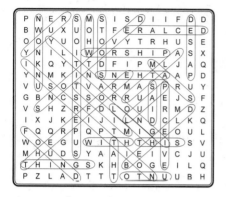

**PUZZLE 19**

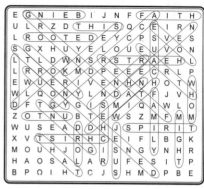

**PUZZLE 20**

**PUZZLE 22**

**PUZZLE 21**

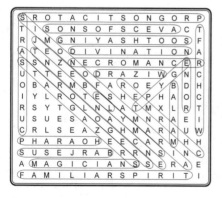

**PUZZLE 23**

**PUZZLE 24**

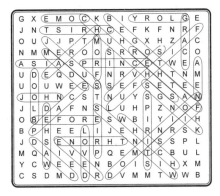

**PUZZLE 25**

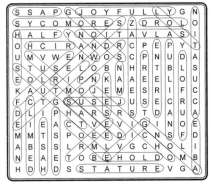

**PUZZLE 26**

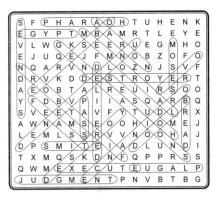

**PUZZLE 27**

**PUZZLE 28**

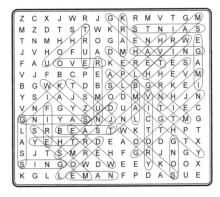

**PUZZLE 29**

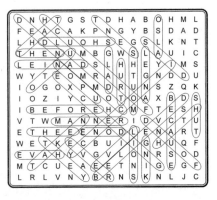

**PUZZLE 30**

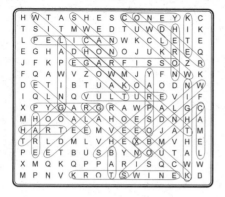

**PUZZLE 31**

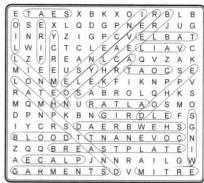

**PUZZLE 32**

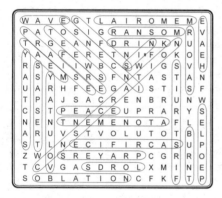

**PUZZLE 33**

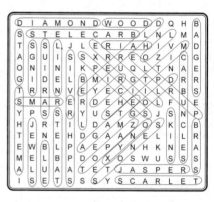

**PUZZLE 34**

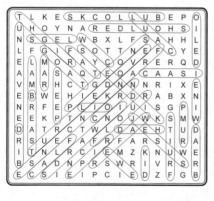

**PUZZLE 35**

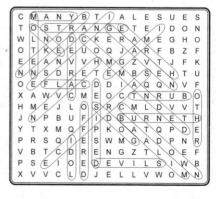

**PUZZLE 36**

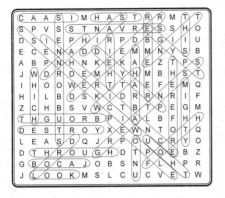

**PUZZLE 37**

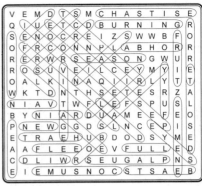

**PUZZLE 38**

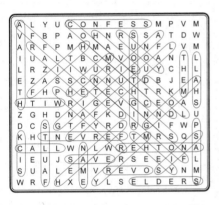

**PUZZLE 39**

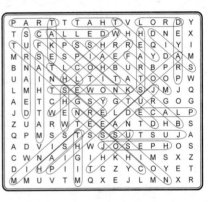

**PUZZLE 40**

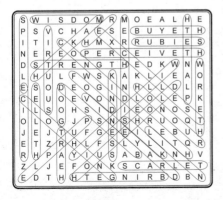

**PUZZLE 41**

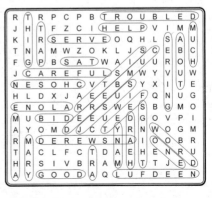

**PUZZLE 42**

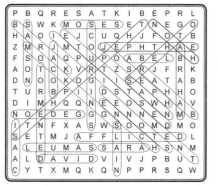

**PUZZLE 43**

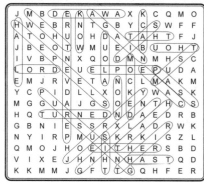

**PUZZLE 44**

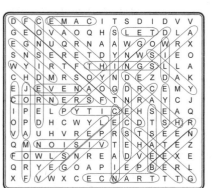

**PUZZLE 45**

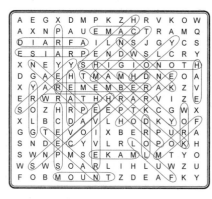

**PUZZLE 46**

**PUZZLE 47**

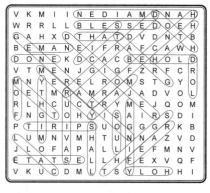

**PUZZLE 48**

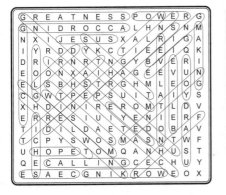

**PUZZLE 49**

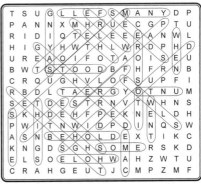

**PUZZLE 50**

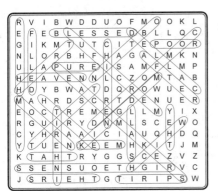

**PUZZLE 51**

**PUZZLE 52**

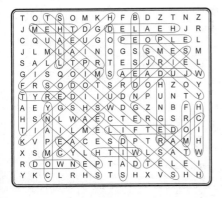

**PUZZLE 53**

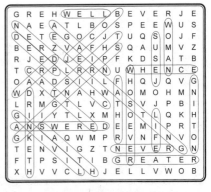

**PUZZLE 54**

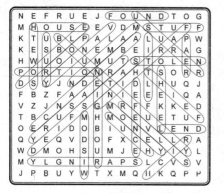

**PUZZLE 55**

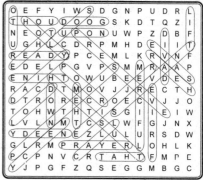

**PUZZLE 56**

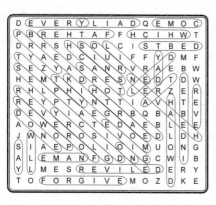

**PUZZLE 57**

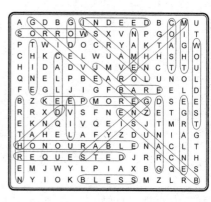

**PUZZLE 58**

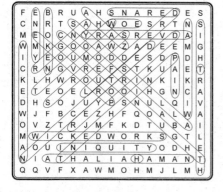

**PUZZLE 59**

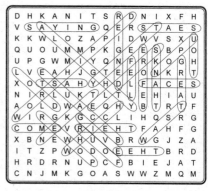

**PUZZLE 60**

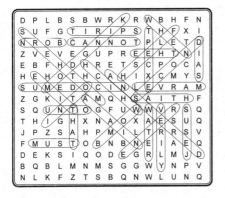

**PUZZLE 61**

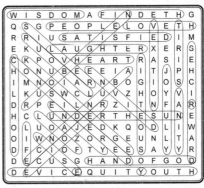

**PUZZLE 62**

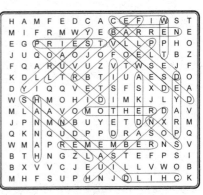

**PUZZLE 63**

**PUZZLE 64**

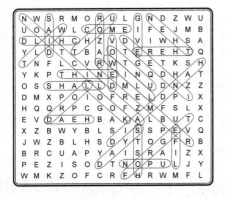

**PUZZLE 65**

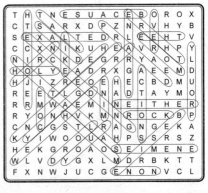

**PUZZLE 66**

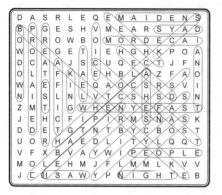

**PUZZLE 67**

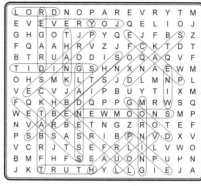

**PUZZLE 68**

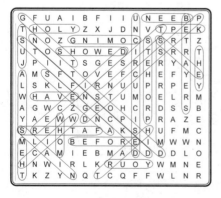

**PUZZLE 69**

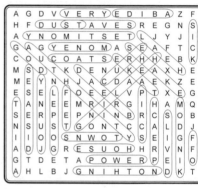

**PUZZLE 70**

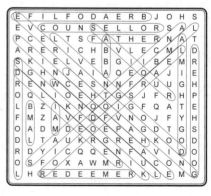

**PUZZLE 71**

**PUZZLE 72**

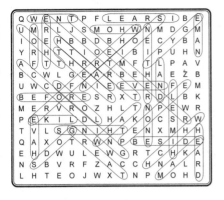

**PUZZLE 73**

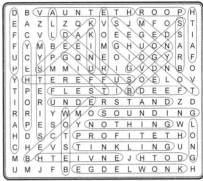

**PUZZLE 74**

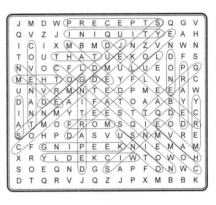

**PUZZLE 75**

**PUZZLE 76**

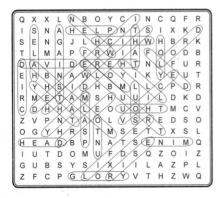

**PUZZLE 77**

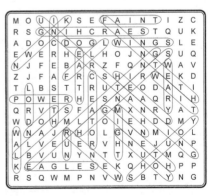

**PUZZLE 78**

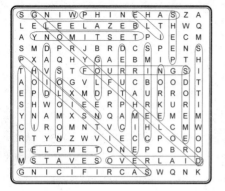

PUZZLE 79

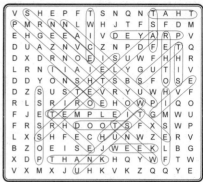

PUZZLE 80

PUZZLE 81

PUZZLE 82

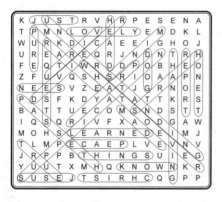

PUZZLE 83

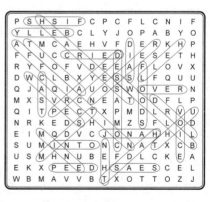

PUZZLE 84

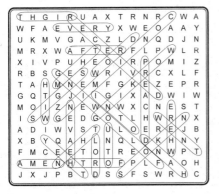

**PUZZLE 85**

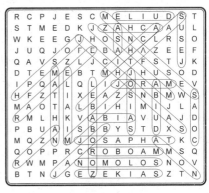

**PUZZLE 86**

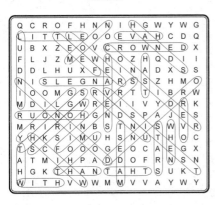

**PUZZLE 87**

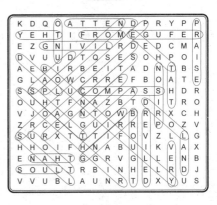

**PUZZLE 88**

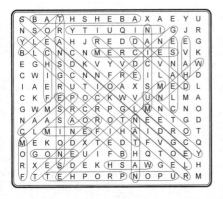

**PUZZLE 89**

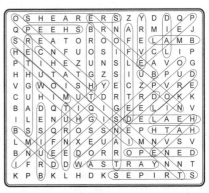

**PUZZLE 90**

**PUZZLE 91**

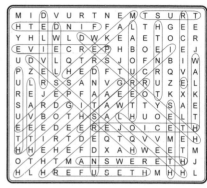

**PUZZLE 92**

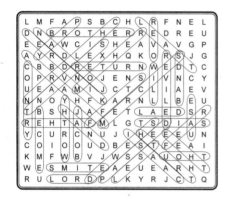

**PUZZLE 93**

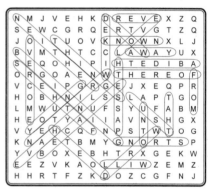

**PUZZLE 94**

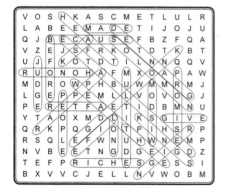

**PUZZLE 95**

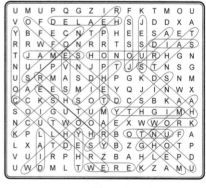

**PUZZLE 96**

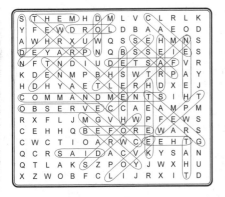

**PUZZLE 97**

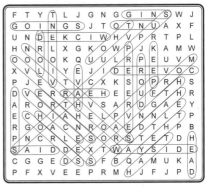

**PUZZLE 98**

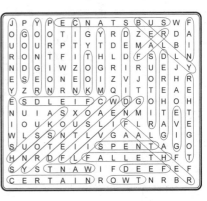

**PUZZLE 99**

**PUZZLE 100**

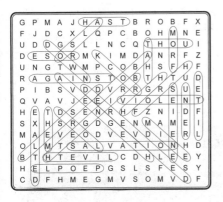

**PUZZLE 101**

# MORE GREAT BIBLE PUZZLES!

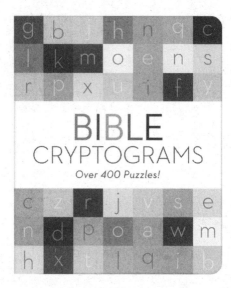

Drawn from the King James Version, these 404 cryptograms
each provide a brief passage featuring substituted letters that
you'll need to decode to solve the verse. Covering the people,
places, things, and ideas of scripture, *Bible Cryptograms*
will entertain and educate you, delivering important
Bible truths in an enjoyable puzzle package.

Paperback / 978-1-64352-733-8 / $12.99